COMPLIANCE IN
EUROPEA

C000139112

Compliance in the Enlarged European Union
Living Rights or Dead Letters?

GERDA FALKNER
Institute for European Integration Research of the Austrian Academy of Sciences, Vienna

OLIVER TREIB
Institute for Advanced Studies, Austria

ELISABETH HOLZLEITHNER
University of Vienna, Austria

with

EMMANUELLE CAUSSE, PETRA FURTLEHNER,
MARIANNE SCHULZE *and* CLEMENS WIEDERMANN

Routledge
Taylor & Francis Group

LONDON AND NEW YORK

First published 2008 by Ashgate Publishing

2 Park Square, Milton Park, Abingdon, Oxfordshire OX14 4RN
711 Third Avenue, New York, NY 10017

Routledge is an imprint of the Taylor & Francis Group, an informa business

First issued in paperback 2018

British Library Cataloguing in Publication Data
Compliance in the enlarged European Union : living rights
  or dead letters?
  1. Social legislation - European Union countries
  I. Falkner, Gerda II. Treib, Oliver III. Holzleithner,
  Elisabeth
  344.2'401

Library of Congress Cataloging-in-Publication Data
Falkner, Gerda.
  Compliance in the enlarged European Union : living rights or dead letters? / by Gerda
Falkner, Oliver Treib and Elisabeth Holzleithner.
     p. cm.
  Includes bibliographical references and index.
  ISBN 978-0-7546-7509-9
  1. Law--European Union countries. 2. International and municipal law--European
Union countries. 3. Effectiveness and validity of law--European Union countries. 4.
Compliance. 5. European Union countries--Social policy. I. Treib, Oliver. II.
Holzleithner, Elisabeth,
1970- III. Title.

  KJE5057.F35 2008
  341.242'2--dc22

                                                                            2008018466

ISBN 978-0-7546-7509-9 (hbk)
ISBN 978-1-138-37652-6 (pbk)

Contents

List of Figure and Tables

Figure

Tables

Preface

This book is the result of a perennial research project supported by the Austrian Ministry of Science under the TRAFO programme for transdisciplinary research (whose funding is gratefully acknowledged).

We trust that our dedication to teamwork and discourse across disciplinary boundaries has left its mark on the final publication: the chapters follow a stringent plan and the sections on each country are fully synchronised to allow for direct comparison. All parts were read and commented on multiple times by all co-authors, and several sections are based on joint work such as strategy reports and workshop protocols extensively discussed in the entire group.

After some uncertainty about how justice could best be done to the specifics of working in a collaborative empirical project with a group of researchers too large to co-author the project book (in the sense of truly co-writing as a group, in equal work shares, all parts of the text), we decided to follow the suggestion of the publisher to include the names of the project directors on the book cover, and then all names with details on the (main) responsibilities for individual parts of the text inside the book. This is meant to express, from the outset, that the book is a coherent text, much more similar to a co-authored book than to a loose edition collection. The project directors were indeed involved in the entire work: they answer for the overall design of the project, the day-to-day management of the research, the guidance of the group of co-researchers (then all employed for this project at the Political Science Department of the Institute for Advanced Studies in Vienna), and finally for framing and, to a varying extent, for (re-)drafting the chapters.

It is important to mention that, in addition to the authors represented in this book, Andreas Obermaier and Caroline Wörgötter also contributed to the empirical field work during the last phase of the project. We would also like to thank Miriam Hartlapp and the anonymous referees for valuable comments on an earlier version of the manuscript. Our special gratitude goes to the numerous experts and practitioners who participated in our focus groups and strategy workshops or dedicated time to the project in other ways. We are very much indebted to Caroline Wintersgill as the Senior Commissioning Editor of Ashgate, who did a very dedicated and efficient job, and finally to Elisabet Torggler at the Institute for Advanced Studies, who helped us with the layout of the manuscript and with assembling the index.

We would also like to thank the entire group of collaborators for a cooperative experience the results of which will hopefully also be fruitful for the readers of this book. Note that the practitioners not only shared their experience with us but also their hope that 'dead letters' can finally be turned into 'living rights'.

Gerda Falkner (Overall Project Director)
Elisabeth Holzleithner and Oliver Treib (Project Co-Directors)

Chapter 1

Introduction:
The Challenge of Implementation
Research in the New Member States

Gerda Falkner, Oliver Treib and Elisabeth Holzleithner

This chapter begins by outlining the theme of the book: the practice of European Union (EU) social legislation in Central and Eastern European countries (CEECs). We highlight the importance of studying policy implementation as a crucial phase of the policy cycle. We outline the empirical and methodological approach we chose to shed light on how accession countries attempt to translate EU social policies into domestic practice. We also give an overview of the state of the art in EU implementation research, and of the EU legislation pertaining to our study. The chapter closes with a brief description of the structure of the book.

The Theme of the Book: How Does EU Social Law Work in Practice in Central and Eastern Europe?

On 1 May 2004, ten new member states from Central and Eastern Europe and the Mediterranean joined the European Union. They had to align their policies and their administrative and legal systems with the requirements of the *acquis communautaire* (i.e., the approximately 80,000 pages of EU law representing the status quo of European integration) even before joining and although their policy legacies were in some areas far behind the EU standards. Further, their legal and administrative systems were in need of major reforms to allow the proper enforcement and application in practice of the huge body of EU law.

We aim to take stock of this process. If there are shortcomings in transposition, enforcement or practical application, what are the reasons and how could they eventually be mended? The EU directives on working time, employment equality, and the equal treatment of women and men in employment will serve as our practical examples.

Implementation as Crucial but Difficult Phase of the Policy Cycle

The aforementioned questions are of vital importance for the functioning of European integration: there is no use for the EU in adopting intricate rules for a unified market, if they remain dead letter in large parts of the Union.

A recent study revealed that non-respect of jointly adopted rules and policies has already been a significant problem in the 15 'old' member states of the EU (Falkner, Treib, Hartlapp and Leiber 2005, chs 14 and 15). Only 11 per cent out of 90 implementation cases studied represented correct and timely transposition into domestic law, and 69 per cent were delayed for at least two years or more. Based on these empirical data, implementation problems can certainly no longer be characterized as a 'statistical artefact' (Börzel 2001).

Already during the period preceding the 2004 enlargement, the European Commission made compliance with EU policies a priority (see official statements such as, for example, the Governance White Book 2001). Indeed, with Malta, Cyprus, and (most importantly, in this respect) eight Central and Eastern European countries now being part of 'the club', the issue of compliance with EU law is ever more pressing. The CEECs are transition states with a view to not only economics but also to their political and legal systems. Many of them had a long way to go to become full-fledged democratic systems with stable institutions. The early academic literature on the implementation performance of those CEECs that joined in 2004 indicated that transposition was rather dutiful during the pre-accession period. At the same time, scholars expected that 'the absence of these incentives should significantly slow down or even halt the implementation process' (Schimmelfennig and Sedelmeier 2005a, 226; see also Schimmelfennig, Engert and Heiko 2005, 29; 2005b, 28; Linden 2002, 371). Prospects appeared to be even worse: pre-accession studies on Europeanization in the CEECs highlighted failures during the phases that follow after the transposition of EU directives into domestic law. This suggests a need for post-enlargement studies on the practical effects of EU law.

The accession of Bulgaria and Romania, two countries with even graver problems in the field of court systems and the rule of law, yet again increased the exigency of compliance with EU rules. Despite vast preparatory work in the candidate countries, the European Commission had to express great concerns in its 2006 monitoring reports on Bulgaria and Romania: 'Bulgaria needs to demonstrate clear evidence of results in the fight against corruption, in terms of investigations and judicial proceedings. It also needs to further reform the judiciary' (European Commission 2006h, 1). The Commission also pressed for more efficient and systematic implementation of laws fighting fraud and corruption. Romania, too, was said to need to 'demonstrate further results in the fight against corruption. It also needs to consolidate the implementation of the ongoing justice reform and further enhance the transparency, efficiency and impartiality of the judiciary' (ibid., 3). Alarming assessments of similar nature may be found in the Commission's progress reports on Croatia and Macedonia – the two candidate countries that currently appear to be furthest advanced in their rapprochement with the EU (European Commission 2006c, 7–8; 2006f, 7–11).

Problems with the domestic fulfilment of EU legislation will thus remain a hot topic in the years to come.

To sum up, we aim to close a gap in existing literature by studying compliance in CEECs not only during the pre-membership phase but also following accession. Additionally, we look at the whole process of EU legislation implementation, hence including the difficult aspects of application and enforcement of laws. This is a demanding task (see below on our methods), but it is crucial to go beyond the analysis of available data on transposition rates or infringement proceedings, which prior research has all too often used as – rather poor – indicators for compliance. In the end, we believe, the analysis of different types of implementation problems and the identification of their causes can improve the situation in the new member states (in particular in Slovenia, Hungary, Slovakia and the Czech Republic) and avoid similar problems in forthcoming EU enlargements.

Policy Focus: Labour Law and Equality

For our complex study of practical implementation processes and adaptation results, it is indispensable to select a number of cases for in-depth qualitative analysis. Our *specific focus will be the implementation of EU social policy*, a policy area whose fate is of essential interest for the viability of the welfare state in Europe (for an overview of the EU's social dimension, see, for example, Leibfried and Pierson 1995; Shaw 2000; Falkner 2003). Eastern enlargement has revived debates about 'social dumping' within the Internal Market. Many of the new member states have low corporate tax rates, low wage levels, low non-wage labour costs due to low levels of welfare-state development, and relatively flexible labour markets with little employment regulation. With their accession to the European Union, other countries, where companies have to cope with higher production costs, are potentially exposed to competitive pressures leading them to lower their tax rates and social standards in order to remain attractive for investors. One of the remedies for this 'regime competition' is the creation of common social standards at EU level.[1] Properly implemented, these provisions could counter social dumping tendencies, and they could significantly improve the living and working conditions of many citizens in the accession countries.

It is to be expected that the EU's social policy directives should actually have a *substantial impact* in the new member states. A survey on the working conditions in the ten acceding countries plus Bulgaria and Romania, carried out by the European Foundation for the Improvement of Living and Working Conditions between 2000 and 2002, revealed that weekly working hours are on average much longer than in the EU15, with an average working week of 44.4 hours compared

---

1   We thus restrict our analysis to the realm of compulsory social legislation. Whether and to what extent the soft coordination techniques of the Open Method of Coordination (OMC) impact on the new member states is hence up to further research. For an overview of previous analyses on the OMC, see, for example, de la Porte and Pochet (2002); Zeitlin and Pochet (2005).

to 38.2 hours in the latter (Paoli and Parent-Thirion 2003, 45). Moreover, the share of workers who work very long hours is much higher than in the EU15; 38 per cent of the workers in the 12 acceding and candidate countries regularly work between 45 and 80 hours per week, whereas only 20 per cent of all workers do so in the EU15 (Paoli and Parent-Thirion 2003, 49). In addition, night and shift work are fairly widespread in the new member countries (Paoli and Parent-Thirion 2003, 52–7). This indicates that the implementation of the Working Time Directive, but probably also the other directives to be studied, will indeed make a noticeable difference there.

In addition to the Working Time Directive, a highly contested piece of EU social legislation (the Council of Ministers seemed unable to agree on its redrafting in 2006), we also study EU rules in the fields of equal treatment prohibiting discrimination between men and women, and a set of provisions fighting discrimination against individuals based on religion or belief, disability, age or sexual orientation. This is an important issue for the EU far beyond 2007, the European Year of Equal Opportunities for All. It should be added that there is, so far, hardly any reliable information at all on the fate of EU law in the fields of non-discrimination and labour law in the new member states.

Covering this *wide array of sub-fields within EU social policy*, we will be in a situation to draw some generalizations from our findings for the policy field as a whole. The conclusions will discuss in how far the results can be generalized across EU policies, at large. This choice of directives also allows us to link up to an existing qualitative study on compliance with EU standards. It should be mentioned that few analyses of this kind exist to date, as opposed to many recent studies of a quantitative character, based on official statistics and databases on transposition of EU directives. In any case, we can build on a study that has been praised as 'arguably the best available information on compliance' (Thomson 2007, abstract; von Falkner, Treib, Hartlapp and Leiber 2005) for the EU15. It included six labour law directives, most importantly also the Working Time Directive. What matters here is that choosing again cases from the social realm in its widest sense, and particularly also the working time issue, allows us to compare our new case studies from Central and Eastern Europe to the prior ones from the EU15. This was one of our concerns when choosing the policies and directives, in addition to the considerations of general policy interest and economic importance outlined above.

Our country selection includes *Slovenia, Hungary, Slovakia* and *the Czech Republic*. While it was not feasible to include all new EU members that joined the EU in 2004, these cases comprise one of the socio-economically least developed member states among the new entrants (Slovakia) as well as one that is comparatively advanced in economic terms (Slovenia). This assortment of empirical studies allows us to test whether the degree of economic development and, by implication, the expected adaptation costs for these countries, have an impact on the quality of implementation, as parts of the recent literature on the implementation of EU law suggest. Since qualitative research and, in particular, our approach aimed at evaluating implementation in its full sense demands a lot of travelling for interviews, contacts with practitioners and field research in the widest sense, it should be mentioned here that we also had to take into account the practicalities and budgetary capacities of our project.

This and considerations of the timing of membership explain why we could not include countries such as Bulgaria and Romania in our study. Part of our team is considering a follow-up project in these regions for the future.

Methods and Transdisciplinary Approach

Studying the domestic implementation of EU policies in an encompassing manner requires the accumulation of in-depth knowledge: firstly, about the conformity of national law with EU demands; secondly, about the effectiveness of domestic systems of law enforcement; and thirdly, about the quality of application of the law in practice. Therefore, complex and intricate empirical case studies were indispensable.

Our analysis proceeded in the following steps (for each country and directive studied, in turn):

1) *Semi-structured interviews* with the Ministry officials responsible, with experts from trade unions, employer's organizations and NGOs, and, at times, also with politicians in the member state on the reform requirements created by the directives and the state of implementation (including collection of domestic transposition laws and statistics).[2]
2) Analysis of the domestic *transposition law(s)*, statistics, and secondary literature (where available).
3) *Focus group sessions* involving representatives from a wide range of civil society representatives with in-depth knowledge about the cases studied. Such groups were held in each of the four countries. In order to foster conditions conducive to an atmosphere of trust and open discussion of potentially sensitive information, members were selected according to similarity of interests. In each country studied, three different focus groups engaged in a discussion, divided mainly according to the separation of interests between employers and employees but also other potential conflict lines where useful. Each focus group brought together between four and twelve local experts plus members of our research team for three to four hours. The themes discussed in the focus group sessions included the question of whether the participants considered the transposition laws satisfactory in light of the EU directive's goals and of their own ambitions and, most importantly, whether there were problems in the application and enforcement of the transposition law in practice, and why.

---

2   Since we guaranteed our interview partners anonymity, we refer to information garnered from our interviews with codes, which include a country abbreviation and a consecutive number. For example, the first interview conducted in the Czech Republic has the code Interview CZ1. Similarly, the focus groups held in the four countries have a code (e.g. Focus Group CZ1).

Focus group discussions allow for the gathering of high quality information that is indeed very reliable evidence compared to other sources. It is not just individual knowledge and related opinions that become evident in these facilitated sessions. Interaction within the group based on the input statements and questions also reveals shared experiences and potentially conflicting views, as much as joint understandings of everyday life and relevant background information that would be almost impossible to disclose in other ways (see the path-breaking article by Merton and Kendall 1946; see also Powell and Single 1996; Morgan 1997). We chose this method to gather information particularly about the state of affairs with regard to application and enforcement. At the same time, the group discussions also allowed the participants to learn more about the legal rights and opportunities offered to them and their clientele by EU law so that they could use this information to improve their situation. Hence, the flow of information in focus groups is two-way, and both the participants and the researchers can benefit.

4) *Strategy workshop*: a crucial event during our project was the final transnational workshop aimed at developing concepts for improving social rights in practice. Interest groups from the countries studied and Austria, representing those negatively affected by non-implementation (unions, works councils, feminist groups, etc.), and researchers discussed remedies for implementation gaps. The best target points for relevant lobbying were shared between countries; and strategies involving the European Commission and other – multi-lateral – actors, including NGOs, were discussed.

This workshop, which involved between four and five participants from each of the four countries, lasted for one day and was divided into three specialized working groups (on our three main issue areas) for a couple of hours.

The transnational character of this workshop allowed the participants to share insights and information with one another directly, across all countries studied in this project, and to jointly formulate strategies fighting potential discrimination and non-respect of social standards.

It should be mentioned here that this book targets a specific interface between disciplines – political science, law – and between theoretically informed research and practitioner knowledge. Our research questions underline that a large number of pressing social problems cannot be tackled by individual academic disciplines separately. Rather, a joining of forces and instruments in *transdisciplinary* research is of vital importance. Moreover, our object of study, implementation processes, especially the stages of application and enforcement, requires intense interaction between researchers and practitioners.

Clearly, the evaluation of implementation (or non-implementation) of EU law in the member states requires *legal expertise*. Hence, the first step involved the comparison of the standards set out by each directive with the provisions in each of the countries. However, the written word of legal texts transposing EU directives into national laws is but one facet of the wider process of 'implementation'. This process also includes the – potential shortcomings of – information on the part of those concerned; actions by public authorities needed to ensure proper application and enforcement; pre-existing and parallel national laws and routines that may not fit sufficiently well to allow for smooth adaptation; social and political conditions in particular areas or sectors that may depart from those expected in the context of law creation. All of these aspects, and others, can crucially impinge on the practical implementation of EU law.

Here, *political scientists* can add a number of decisive aspects to the traditional repertoire of lawyers. In addition to the aspects already mentioned above, explaining why a norm is applied in practice – or not – has been of great interest in this academic discipline. Attention to political structures in any country – such as federalism, parties or interest groups – is also one of its strengths. Another is moving beyond the study of formal rules and including in systematic studies the existence of unwritten joint understandings or social norms that may counteract positive law. Hence, co-operation of legal and political science scholars is the most promising approach if we want to find out how EU law is put into practice.

Among the different forms of disciplinarity as formulated by Sum and Jessop (2003), our approach is part of the area of transdisciplinarity. We support a far-reaching concept, namely addressee-oriented research with the aim of improving the action competencies of those individuals (and, more directly, their representatives) who in theory have been granted certain rights that may not always be respected in practice. In fact, scholarly analyses on implementation issues require the knowledge of practitioners and norm addressees if more than a legalistic comparison of legal texts is at stake. At the same time, however, citizens and their representatives in NGOs need detailed information about their rights in order to make full use of their potential. In transdisciplinary research, scientific knowledge should be 'contextualized so that it becomes part of the actors' problem resolution competencies and can be applied in their conflicts of interest and value' (Küffer 2001).

EU Implementation Research: State of the Art and Research Desiderata

As has already been outlined above, the implementation of policies enacted at the EU level is a particularly challenging task. The EU is marked by a highly decentralized implementation structure that leaves responsibility for policy execution to the member states. Like in some federal polities, the lower level of governance is in charge of administrative enforcement. If we focus on the implementation of EU directives, one of the major legal instruments of the EU, it also becomes apparent that even parts of the decision-making process are delegated to the domestic level. The standards laid down in directives have to be incorporated into national law by member states within a certain period of time. Only after this process of transposition is completed may the rules be applied by societal target groups and enforced by administrations and the legal system at the domestic level (see Figure 1.1).

Given the heterogeneity of interests among the actors involved in EU decision-making and the high consensus requirements, EU policies often contain fuzzy concepts and leave certain issues to the discretion of member states in order to facilitate agreement. What applies to implementation in general is thus particularly true for the domestic execution of EU policies: Crucial decisions that may be decisive for the success or failure of a given policy are regularly taken at the implementation stage.

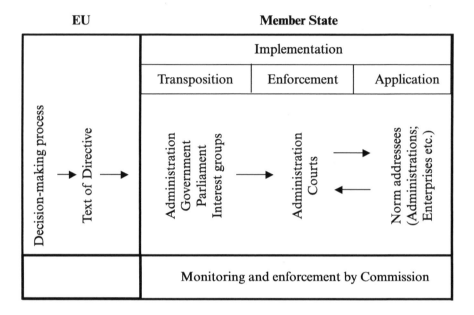

Figure 1.1   Stages and actors of the implementation process

It was not until the mid 1980s that EU scholars discovered compliance as an interesting issue, but since then the field has developed into one of the growth industries within EU research. The development of this area of research proceeded in three phases.

The Evolution of the Field: From Bureaucratic Problem-solving to the Worlds of Compliance[3]

The Single Market Programme acted as a stepping-stone to the *first phase of EU-related implementation research*. The programme involved a raft of legislative measures whose even implementation was seen as a precondition for the completion and smooth functioning of a Europe-wide market until 1992. In theoretical terms, the main inspiration came from domestic implementation studies, most importantly from the top-down school (Pressman and Wildavsky 1973; Van Meter and Van Horn 1975; Mazmanian and Sabatier 1983). Studies in the first phase thus portrayed the domestic implementation of European law as

---

3   For a more extended analysis, see Treib (2006).

a rather apolitical process whose success primarily depended on clearly worded provisions, effective administrative organization, and streamlined legislative procedures at the domestic level. At the same time, they also absorbed some of the insights of the bottom-up camp (Lipsky 1980; Hjern and Porter 1981; Elmore 1982), stressing the need for involving all relevant domestic actors (such as parliaments, important interest groups, or subnational entities) in the preparation of the countries' European negotiating position and for coordinating the negotiation and implementation tasks within domestic administrations, ideally by attaching responsibility for both phases of the policy cycle to one person (Ciavarini Azzi 1985; Krislov, Ehlermann and Weiler 1986; Siedentopf and Ziller 1988; Schwarze, Govaere, Helin and Bossche 1990; Schwarze, Becker and Pollack 1993; From and Stava 1993).

In the late 1990s, a *second phase* of research set off to analyse the 'Europeanization' of domestic political systems (Börzel 1999; Börzel and Risse 2000; Cowles, Caporaso and Risse 2001; Goetz and Hix 2001; Schmidt 2002a; 2002b; Featherstone and Radaelli 2003). In this context, scholars also returned to the narrower question of the domestic impact of European policies, as witnessed by the national implementation of European policy measures. Focusing mainly on environmental policy, many of the second-wave scholars pointed to the degree of fit or misfit between European rules and existing institutional and regulatory traditions as one of the central factors determining implementation performance (Duina 1997; 1999; Duina and Blithe 1999; Knill and Lenschow 1998; 2000a; Börzel 2000; 2003a). The emphasis thus moved from administrative and procedural efficiency to the degree of compatibility between EU policies and domestic structures.

The basic rationale behind the misfit argument was to reduce the complexity of analysing implementation processes by exploring how far the 'institutional filter' (Knill and Lenschow 1998, 610) provided by the compatibility between EU demands and domestic policy traditions *alone* could explain the implementation of particular pieces of EU legislation (Knill and Lenschow 1998, 610–11; 2001, 121–4). The main problem with this approach was that only few cases could actually be explained by an exclusive focus on the 'goodness of fit' (see the results of Knill and Lenschow 1998). Later studies confirmed its limited explanatory power (see, for instance, Haverland 2000; Héritier et al. 2001; Falkner, Treib, Hartlapp and Leiber 2005). In the end, therefore, it turned out that most cases required 'a lower level of abstraction, namely the independent analysis of the given interest constellations and the strategic interaction of domestic actors' (Knill and Lenschow 2001, 126).

Among the most important additional factors offered to explain successful implementation even in the face of high adaptation costs was the pressure of supportive interest groups, probably combined with outside pressure from the Commission (Börzel 2000; 2003a). This model assumed an unwilling state machinery that needed to be forced into compliance by societal or EU-level actors. An alternative view started from the implicit assumption that high degrees of misfit would spur resistance not primarily by governmental or administrative actors, but by negatively affected societal groups. Whether or not governments and administrations would be able to push through the required reforms thus it was seen to depend on institutional decision-making structures marked by low numbers of veto players or, alternatively, a consensual decision-making culture that facilitated compromises (Risse, Cowles and Caporaso 2001; Héritier 2001; Héritier and Knill 2001). These approaches still subscribed to the basic idea that the degree of misfit was an important determinant of implementation outcomes. In contrast, Haverland (2000) deemed the institutional reform capacities of domestic political systems to be even more important, arguing that the number of veto players in domestic political arenas *alone* could explain implementation outcomes *irrespective* of the 'goodness of fit'.

A growing uneasiness with the relatively narrow theoretical and empirical focus of earlier research gave rise to the *third phase* of EU implementation research. It is marked by a plurality of theoretical and methodological approaches. What ties the different contributions together is a desire to broaden the theoretical and empirical perspective in order to get a fuller picture of the conditions that drive domestic implementation processes. A first new development was that especially qualitative researchers began to discover the importance of domestic politics in determining the speed and correctness of legal adaptation to European directives. Along these lines, Treib (2003; 2004) showed that party political preferences of governments may have a decisive impact on transposition outcomes. In particular, he showed that party political preferences of governments may well override the 'misfit logic' according to which domestic governments should always try to defend their existing policy traditions. Similarly, Mastenbroek and van Keulen (2006, 38) argued that favourable government preferences 'may work wonders in overcoming misfit'.

The second remarkable development in the third wave was the growing popularity of quantitative studies. Thus, more and more scholars have come to use the easily available data on the Commission's infringement proceedings against member states to measure the amount of non-compliance with EU law (Mbaye 2001; Börzel 2001; 2003b; Börzel, Hofmann and Sprungk 2004; Tallberg 2002; Sverdrup 2004; Beach 2005). A second type of quantitative studies based their analyses on the transposition measures that member states officially notify the Commission of. One strand of this literature used transposition rates (Lampinen and Uusikylä 1998), sometimes also in combination with infringement data (Giuliani 2003). These rates, which represent the share of transposed directives against all applicable directives at a certain period of time, are regularly reported in the Commission's annual monitoring reports on the application of Community law. Another group of scholars used the transposition instruments reported in the Celex database (Borghetto, Franchino and Giannetti 2006), in domestic legal databases (Mastenbroek 2003), or in a combination of both (Berglund, Gange and van Waarden 2006), to determine when a particular directive was incorporated into national law.

In theoretical terms, most of these quantitative contributions are informed by compliance approaches developed in the international relations literature.[4] These approaches revolve around the dichotomy between voluntary and involuntary non-compliance. Scholars stressing problems of voluntary non-compliance argue that the willingness of states to comply with international commitments depends on the domestic costs and benefits of adaptation and on the costs of defiance. Where the costs outweigh the benefits, states will try to evade these burdens by non-compliance. Therefore, effective monitoring and sanctioning by international supervisory authorities is required to force unwilling states to comply. Therefore, this approach is known as the enforcement approach (see e.g. Downs, Rocke and Barsoom 1996). The management approach, in contrast, considers lacking administrative and financial capabilities at the domestic level or ambiguous norms to be the main sources of non-compliance. International organizations thus need to assist their members, by organising training programmes, by providing financial aid and the like (see e.g. Chayes and Handler Chayes 1993).

The theoretical insights of these statistical studies have hitherto been rather inconclusive. Some support the argument that structural properties of domestic polities, such as the number of veto players, have a significant impact on legal compliance (Lampinen and Uusikylä 1998; Giuliani 2003; Linos 2007), others do not (Mbaye 2001; Börzel, Hofmann and Sprungk 2004; Borghetto, Franchino and Giannetti 2006). Some conclude that support for European integration is an important factor that facilitates compliance (Mbaye 2001 with regard to public opinion; Linos 2007 with regard to government parties), others do not (Lampinen and Uusikylä 1998); while still others find a statistically significant *negative* correlation between these two variables (Börzel, Hofmann and Sprungk 2004). Some find a significant effect of indicators meant to measure the degree of changes required by the policies to be transposed (Borghetto, Franchino and Giannetti 2006; Linos 2007), others argue that misfit is a variable that cannot be operationalized adequately for the use in quantitative studies (Börzel, Hofmann and Sprungk 2004), and so on. The only factor that seems to be sustained in most quantitative analyses so far is various aspects of administrative capabilities (Mbaye 2001; Börzel, Hofmann and Sprungk 2004; Berglund, Gange and van Waarden 2006; Borghetto, Franchino and Giannetti 2006; Linos 2007).

This presents us with an interesting paradox: While qualitative studies in the third wave of research have increasingly come to embrace the political character of transposition, the results of quantitative research seem to point back to the arguments of the founders of EU implementation research, who had highlighted the importance of efficient and well-coordinated administrations.

As a first step towards solving this puzzle, Bernard Steunenberg has recently begun to develop an interesting formal model of the transposition process, which encompasses both a politicized and a more bureaucratic mode. He conceptualizes the process of incorporating a directive as a strategic game among several domestic players with distinct policy preferences (Steunenberg 2006; see also Dimitrova

---

4   It has to be noted, however, that there are also important qualitative studies that use this kind of framework (for example, see Zürn and Joerges 2004).

and Steunenberg 2000). Crucial factors in this game are the type of instrument that needs to be adopted to transpose a directive and the preferences of the actors whose agreement is required for the adoption of this instrument. The type of legal instrument (legislation, decree, etc.) decides on whether the actor constellation comprises the broad set of ministries, political parties and interest groups usually involved in enacting a piece of legislation ('horizontal coordination') or whether the process is determined by a smaller set of actors, or even by a single ministry, as is sometimes the case if a ministerial decree is sufficient to transpose a directive ('hierarchical coordination').

This model goes a long way towards a realistic conceptualization of the variegated political constellations to be found in individual cases of transposition. However, it does not allow for theoretical expectations as to how typical processes of transposition in a given country and in a given policy sector might look like. Are there country- or sector-specific patterns of the typical transposition instruments used? Does this result in typical patterns of rather politicized or rather bureaucratic transposition processes? And does a multi-actor constellation necessarily have to imply more problems than a single-actor constellation, or is it also possible that serious delays occur even if only one ministry is in charge of transposition?

An earlier study on the implementation of six EU social policy directives in the fifteen 'old' member states, which involved two of the authors of this book, offered an answer to these questions. The results of this inquiry demonstrated that simple causal arguments, such as the misfit or veto player hypotheses, or the first-wave focus on administrative and procedural factors, cannot explain the observed implementation processes. Instead, it is a complex web of administrative, institutional and actor-based factors that determines transposition outcomes (Falkner, Hartlapp, Leiber and Treib 2002; 2004; Falkner, Treib, Hartlapp and Leiber 2005, 277–316). Up to this point, the argument is not very different from Steunenberg's model or from the heterogeneous results of quantitative studies.

However, the empirical results of this comparative research suggested that there are huge inter-country disparities, but strong similarities among members of different groups of countries in the way they typically fulfil their EU-related duties.[5] This resulted in a typology of three 'worlds of compliance'. The three country clusters are characterized by ideal-typical procedural implementation styles. In the world of law observance, which comprises primarily of the Nordic countries, the presence of a culture of respect for the rule of law among political and administrative actors usually ensures fast and correct transposition (Falkner, Treib, Hartlapp and Leiber 2005, 317–41; see also Leiber 2005). In the world of transposition neglect,[6] the typical reaction to a EU-derived implementation duty is

---

5   This contrasts sharply with the findings of Dimitrakopoulos (2001), who identifies one single 'European style of transposition' across all the member states.

6   Originally, this country cluster was labelled the 'world of neglect'. Building on the empirical research presented in this book, we now suggest to slightly reformulate the label of this world in order to account for its crucial characteristic: neglect at the transposition stage. See Chapter 6 for a detailed discussion of the implications of our new empirical insights on Central and Eastern Europe for the worlds of compliance typology.

inactivity as the bureaucracies fail to initiate adequate responses. Characteristic are long phases of bureaucratic inertia and rather apolitical transposition processes. Greece, France or Portugal conform with this pattern (Falkner, Treib, Hartlapp and Leiber 2005, 317–41; see also Hartlapp 2005a). In the world of domestic politics, finally, administrations usually work dutifully, but successful transposition of EU law is typically a matter of conflict and compromise, and depends on the fit with the political preferences of government parties and other powerful players in the domestic arena. This is the largest cluster, involving countries like Austria, Germany, the Netherlands or the UK (Falkner, Treib, Hartlapp and Leiber 2005, 317–41; see also Treib 2003; 2004).

This typology contends that the controversial political interactions between political parties, powerful interest groups and other important political actors, which were described by scholars like Treib, or by Steunenberg's mode of 'horizontal coordination', are only typical for a certain group of countries. In other member states, transposition is usually a rather apolitical, bureaucratic process, as in Steunenberg's mode of 'hierarchical coordination' or as suggested by some of the quantitative findings. And in a third group of countries, the actor constellation may be similar to Steunenberg's multi-actor coordination, but it does not give rise to deadlocks and delays since all of these actors are culturally inclined to complying with the law no matter what the short-term disadvantages may be. This also suggests that many of the existing theoretical propositions are only 'sometimes-true theories' (Falkner, Hartlapp and Treib 2007), which are relevant in certain countries, but not in others. Political variables such as party political preferences, interest group pressure and veto players should have a major impact in the countries belonging to the world of domestic politics. Administrative factors should be particularly important in the member states forming the world of transposition neglect. And collectively shared cultural dispositions towards respecting the law should be able to explain the raft of transposition processes in the countries belonging to the world of law observance.

It remains to be established empirically whether and to what extent these country patterns can be confirmed beyond the specific areas studied by Falkner, Treib, Hartlapp and Leiber (2005). In particular, it will be interesting to find out how the new member states from Central and Eastern Europe will fit into this typology. The case studies presented in this book will shed light on this question.

Enforcement and Application: A Neglected Area of Research

Many of the previous studies have focused heavily on the process of incorporating EU provisions into domestic legislation. This is not to say that the stage of enforcement and application has been totally neglected. Yet, the specific logic of transforming the transposed EU provisions into practical policy has seldom been at the heart of EU implementation research. Moreover, especially recent quantitative research has ignored almost completely the practical side of implementation.

In the first phase of research, those who actually addressed issues of enforcement and application did not draw a sharp distinction between legal incorporation and the later stages of the implementation process. Instead, the main explanatory variables for all stages were clearly stated policy objectives and the availability of a well-organized state apparatus. With regard to enforcement and application, the main conclusion was that 'Community law, once it has been incorporated, is applied neither better nor worse than national law' (Ciavarini Azzi 1988, 199) because lower-level bureaucrats and target actors are often unaware of the European origins of a particular transposition law.

Contributions in the second phase of EU implementation research, to the extent that they analysed not only legal but also practical implementation (see, for example, Knill and Lenschow 1998; 2000b; Duina 1999; Börzel 2003a), did not systematically distinguish between factors that influence transposition and causal conditions that have an impact on enforcement and application, either. Typically, these contributions tended to treat the whole process of implementation as if it were following a single theoretical logic in which the 'goodness of fit' often played a crucial role. Therefore, little could be learned from this literature about the *specific* problems associated with transposition, enforcement and application, respectively.

Compared to earlier research, studies covering enforcement and application are a small minority in the third wave of research. One reason for this seems to be methodological: As more and more scholars have turned to quantitative approaches, enforcement and application issues have taken a back seat since there are simply no appropriate quantitative data for analysing the 'street-level' aspects of implementation.

Among the few exceptions is a study by Versluis (2003; 2004), whose explicit focus is on the enforcement of two directives from the field of chemical safety in four countries. She discovers major enforcement problems in some of her cases and argues that issue salience is crucial in determining whether domestic inspectors take a particular directive seriously or whether they ignore it (Versluis 2004). Also, the study of Falkner, Treib, Hartlapp and Leiber (2005; see also Hartlapp 2005a; 2005b) included not only transposition but also enforcement and application. Informed primarily by the insights of the top-down school in domestic implementation research, these studies present a set of institutional conditions that determine the effectiveness of domestic enforcement systems ('coordination and steering capacity', 'pressure capacity' and 'availability of information'), and they distinguish between different types of enforcement for different types of norms (Falkner, Treib, Hartlapp and Leiber 2005, 33–40). Applied to the fifteen member states included in their study, they find that the shortcomings of the domestic systems of enforcing labour law in four countries (Greece, Ireland, Italy and Portugal) 'are so significant in overall terms that we regard these countries as neglecting their duty to ensure not only legal transposition, but also a reasonable level of practical compliance' (Falkner, Treib, Hartlapp and Leiber 2005, 275).

One of the main goals of this book is to counterbalance the recent trend in EU implementation research towards neglecting what used to interest domestic implementation scholars from the early 1970s onwards: the process of 'translating policy into action' (Barrett 2004). We will thus study, in a detailed manner, the processes and problems of transforming EU legislation not only into domestic law but also into everyday practice on the ground. How will the new member states from Central and Eastern Europe perform in this respect? Did Eastern enlargement increase the group of countries with insufficient enforcement systems, and if so, what should be done about this?

Background and Contents of the EU Directives on Working Time and Equal Treatment

The empirical focus of this book is the implementation of three of the most significant pieces of EU legislation in the field of social policy and employment rights: the Working Time Directive, the Employment Equality Directive and the Equal Treatment Directive on discrimination between women and men in employment. These three directives cover a wide array of sub-fields within EU social policy. It should thus be possible to draw some generalizations from our findings for the policy field as a whole (see Table 1.1 for a summary of the three directives).

Table 1.1   The three sample directives

	Date of adoption	Transposition deadlines for CEECs	Main goals
Employment Equality Directive (2000/78/EC)	27.11.2000	01.05.2004 02.12.2006 (age and disability)	To prohibit discrimination based on religion or belief, disability, age or sexual orientation as regards access to employment, vocational training and promotion, and working conditions
Amended Equal Treatment Directive (2002/73/EC)	09.02.1976 (original v.) 23.09.2002 (cons. v.)	01.05.2004 (original v.) 05.10.2005 (cons. v.)	To prohibit direct or indirect gender discrimination as regards access to employment, vocational training and promotion, and working conditions
Amended Working Time Directive (2003/77/EC)	23.11.1993 (original v.) 04.11.2003 (cons. v.)	01.05.2004 (original v.) 02.08.2004 (cons. v.)	To improve the health and safety of workers by laying down maximum working time limits and minimum rest periods as well as annual leave entitlements

The three directives furthermore involve different types of law enforcement. The two equal treatment directives function primarily on the basis of individual enforcement: individuals who feel that their rights under the directives are violated are expected to take legal action. To this end, the court system must work in a reasonably effective way, individuals should have easy access to courts and they should have adequate information about their rights. In the field of working time, by contrast, administrative enforcement by labour inspectorates plays a more decisive role. These must be equipped with sufficient resources, must be well-organized and must have effective sanctions at their disposal to punish non-compliers.

The following sections will introduce the regulatory contents of these three directives.

Working Time

The Working Time Directive was originally adopted in 1993.[7] It was amended in 1999, 2000 and 2002 in order to cover the sectors and occupations that had been excluded in the 1993 directive.[8] Subsequently, it was re-introduced in a consolidated form in 2003.[9] The directive is certainly among the most controversial legislative projects within EU social policy. At the time of writing, a revision of the directives is in process at the European level. The negotiations have proven to be so controversial that the updated directive repeatedly failed to be adopted by the Council of Ministers (see below for more details).

The *general aim* of the directive is to improve the health and safety of workers by laying down minimum standards for the organization of working time (Article 1 of the 2003 consolidated version). To this end, it lays down maximum limits of daily and weekly working hours and defines minimum daily and weekly rest periods. The directive also regulates the protection of night workers and guarantees employees a minimum period of paid annual leave.

The Working Time Directive is thus based on a very wide interpretation of occupational health and safety, which assumes that working long hours is harmful to workers' health and therefore has to be limited. This framing gets to the core of the controversies surrounding the adoption of this directive. It was introduced in the pre-Maastricht era, when the only area in EU social policy where majority votes were achieved was the field of health and safety. In order to facilitate agreement among member state governments, the Commission thus strategically used its agenda-setting power and tabled the directive as a health and safety measure. This 'treaty-base game' (Rhodes 1995, 99) was criticized especially by the Conservative British government, which refuted this proposal not only because it confronted the UK with major reform requirements entailing considerable economic costs, but also on ideological grounds. After the adoption of the directive, the UK government even initiated action before the European

7   Council directive 93/104/EC, 1993 O.J. (L 307) 18.
8   Council directives 1999/63/EC, 1999 O.J. (L 167) 33; 1999/95/EC, 1999 O.J. (L 014), 29; 2000/34/EC, 2000 O.J. (L 195), 41; 2000/79/EC, 2000 O.J. (L 302), 57; 2002/15/EC, 2002 O.J. (L 080), 35.
9   Council directive 2003/88/EC, 2003 O.J. (L 299), 9.

Court of Justice, seeking to annul the directive on the grounds of its allegedly wrong legal basis. The Court, however, rejected all major claims of the UK.[10]

Underlying the debate on the directive was an even more fundamental controversy between the principles of worker protection on the one hand and flexibility for employers on the other. Not only the UK government had problems with the relatively rigid approach of the first draft directive. In many countries, working time debates at the time pointed towards increasing flexibility in order to allow for diverse work patterns, e.g. in the context of shift work or seasonal employment. Therefore, many governments sought the directive to allow for more flexibility instead of rigidly protecting the safety and health of workers.

Main standards and exemptions　As a result, the directive that was finally adopted in 1993 included a raft of individual exemptions and derogations. While the sectors and activities originally excluded from the scope of the directive, especially seafarers, transport workers, and doctors in training, were later covered by several amending directives (see above), these amendments even increased the range and diversity of the derogation options meant to account for the needs of individual sectors. In the end, therefore, the Working Time Directive certainly belongs to the most complex, some would even say arcane, pieces of legislation of EU social policy. The most important provisions are as follows:

As a general rule, workers may not work longer than 48 hours per week, including overtime (Article 6 of the 2003 consolidated version of the directive). However, the maximum weekly working time may be averaged out over a period of four, six or 12 months, depending on the type of occupation and, in the case of annual reference periods, on an agreement between both sides of the industry. Every worker has to be granted a consecutive daily rest period of 11 hours (Article 3), a consecutive weekly rest period of 35 hours (Article 5) and a break if the working day is longer than six hours (Article 4). However, these provisions may also be adapted to the needs of individual branches or activities. Night workers on average may not work more than eight hours per day. However, an absolute daily working time limit of eight hours applies to hazardous night work (Article 8). Again, derogations from night work limitations are available for specific branches. Furthermore, employers have to keep records on the regular use of night workers so that these may be monitored by labour inspector(ate)s (Article 11). Night workers are entitled to free health assessments (Article 9), and night workers suffering from health problems have to be transferred 'whenever possible' to suitable day work (Article 9). Finally, employees are entitled to at least four weeks paid annual leave, which may not be replaced by an allowance (Article 7).

Two general derogations have to be highlighted, as they represent core compromise solutions found in the course of the controversial negotiations. First, most of the basic provisions of the directive may be adjusted on the basis of an agreement between both sides of the industry. The question of the level at which

---

10　Judgement of the Court of 12 November 1996, Case C-84/94, *United Kingdom of Great Britain and Northern Ireland* v *Council of the European Union*.

these agreements may be concluded was a highly contested issue touching upon crucial features of domestic systems of industrial relations. Most trade unions and a number of governments pressed for centralized agreements involving trade union and employers' representatives. Employers' organizations and several governments, in contrast, wanted the directive to support the decentralization of collective bargaining by allowing for agreements at company level. In prolongation of its anti-union strategy, the Conservative UK government even insisted on workforce agreements that did not require union participation. In the end, the UK got its way: the directive allows for a wide array of adjustments of the basic provisions on the basis of an agreement between the management of an individual company and its workforce, without trade union involvement (Article 18).

Even more far-reaching is the individual opt-out from the 48-hour week (Article 22). In order to mitigate the expected costs arising from the directive, the UK government secured this opt-out possibility, which allows employees to work longer than an average of 48 hours per week if they voluntarily agree to do so.

ECJ case law on on-call duties   Finally, we need to highlight the ECJ's case law on on-call duties. In a preliminary ruling originating from a claim of a Spanish trade union of physicians, the ECJ decided that, contrary to practice in most European countries, on-call duties have to be treated as working time.[11] As a consequence of this doctrine, which the ECJ subsequently reaffirmed in a German case,[12] many member states had to fundamentally rearrange the shift systems in hospitals, emergency medical services and similar workplaces. Due to the considerable costs of these reforms, a process of revising the directive is currently underway at the European level to change the definition of working time to the effect that on-call duties would no longer be treated as working time. At the time of writing, however, the controversial debates among governments have precluded the revision from being adopted.

In sum, the Working Time Directive is a very complex piece of legislation, which regulates issues that are politically and ideologically highly salient and, in economic terms, may involve significant costs for employers.

Equal Treatment

The two further directives studied in this book form an important part of a broader anti-discrimination policy at the European level. The last decade has witnessed a significant proliferation of – prohibited – grounds of discrimination on different levels of EU law. Article 13 of the EC Treaty enumerates eight such grounds, empowering the Council to take suitable action to combat discrimination based thereon. The Charter of Fundamental Rights of the European Union lists even more grounds of discrimination as illegitimate (sex, race, colour, ethnic or

---

11   See Judgement of the Court of 3 October 2000, Case C-303/98, *SIMAP v. Conselleria de Sanidad y Consumo de la Generalidad Valenciana.*

12   See Judgement of the Court of 9 September 2003, Case C-151/02, *Landeshauptstadt Kiel v. Norbert Jaeger.*

social origin, genetic features, language, religion or belief, political or any other opinion, membership of a national minority, property, birth, disability, age, sexual orientation, nationality; see Article 21 (1, 2)).[13] The recent Racial Equality Directive,[14] the Employment Equality Directive,[15] and the Equal Treatment Directive fighting discrimination between women and men in employment,[16] which was amended in 2002[17] and re-enacted in a consolidated version in 2006,[18] now provide rather diverse levels of protection for people with the features covered by the respective grounds. In our project, we have focused on the implementation of the Equal Treatment Directive, and of the Employment Equality Directive with respect to *sexual orientation as well as religion and belief*.

Generally the idea of EU anti-discrimination law is to provide a basis for the development of 'a coherent and integrated approach towards the fight against discrimination' (European Commission 2004c, 5–6). It is supposed to allow 'for common legal and policy approaches covering the different grounds, including common definitions of discrimination. While recognizing the specific challenges faced by different groups, this integrated approach is based on the premise that equal treatment and respect for diversity are in the interests of society as a whole' (ibid.).

The Commission claims to have 'one of the most advanced legal frameworks to be found anywhere in the world' and stresses that innovations in national law must be implemented in all member states, requiring changes to national law in some and 'the introduction of an entirely new, rights-based approach to anti-discrimination legislation and policy' in others (ibid., 6). This chapter will provide a non-exhaustive overview of the two directives studied in order to lay the basis for an analysis of the extent to which the EU member states have indeed changed their legal systems in the manner envisaged by the Commission.

We will begin by highlighting a few commonalities and differences of the EU's provisions against discrimination, focusing on their aims, scope, exceptions, the role of positive action and of specialized bodies.

Purpose and concept   The purpose of the two directives is to 'put into effect' the 'principle of equality' (Article 1 Employment Equality Directive), respectively that of 'equal treatment for men and women'[19] and 'equality between men and women' (Article 1 (1)(a) Equal Treatment Directive). Article 2 Equal Treatment Directive rhetorically expands the purpose to mean 'full equality in practice', and

---

13   Charter of Fundamental Rights of the European Union, Dec. 7, 2000, 2000 O.J. (C 364) 1.

14   Council directive 2000/43/EC, 2000 O.J. (L 180) 22.

15   Council directive 2000/78/EC, 2000 O.J. (L 303) 16.

16   Council directive 76/207/EEC, 1976 O.J. (L 39) 40.

17   Council directive 2002/73/EC, 2002 O.J. (L 269) 15.

18   Council directive 2006/54/EC, 2006 O.J. (L 204) 23.

19   The terms 'man' and 'woman' also include transsexuals in their newly ascribed sexes after sex change surgeries; Judgement of the Court of 30 April 1996, Case C-13/94, *P* v. *S and Cornwall County Council*.

it further establishes an ambitious goal that distinguishes it from the Employment Equality Directive: According (only) to Article 1a Equal Treatment Directive, 'member states shall actively take into account the objective of equality between men and women' in all their political, administrative, and legislative activities within the scope of the Equal Treatment Directive. This can be regarded as an implementation of the principle of mainstreaming, which is also enshrined in Article 2, 3 (2) EC Treaty.

The EU has decided to use one *common definition* of equal treatment and discrimination, direct and indirect, in all directives covering discrimination. This is fortunate and will certainly be conducive to achieving coherence of anti-discrimination law in practice. Uniformly, *direct* discrimination is defined as the treatment of a person that is less favourable than the treatment of another person 'is, has been or would be' in a comparable situation. Clearly, the comparator need not 'exist'; establishment of the probability of 'his' or 'her' better treatment will be sufficient.[20] *Indirect discrimination* is when an apparently neutral provision, criterion, or practice would put persons with one property such as sex, race, ethnicity, etc., at a particular disadvantage compared with other persons, unless that provision, criterion, or practice is objectively justified by a legitimate aim, and the means of achieving that aim are appropriate and necessary. The directive's definition of *indirect discrimination* reflects ECJ case law on indirect discrimination on the basis of nationality. Whereas statistical evidence was previously necessary in order to prove a significantly disparate impact of an apparently neutral legal or policy measure when gender was involved, henceforth no proof is necessary 'that a "considerably smaller percentage" of one sex is affected' (Masselot 2004, 97). Such unfavourable treatment will not constitute discrimination if it can be justified objectively by a 'legitimate aim', if 'the means of achieving that aim are appropriate and necessary' (Article 2 (2)b Employment Equality Directive; Article 2 (2) Equal Treatment Directive). When it comes to direct discrimination, however, no objective justification is possible, though tendencies exist to justify even direct discrimination (Ellis 1998, 134–6). Either different treatment is justified, which means it is not discriminatory, or it constitutes direct discrimination, which is prohibited.

As a new legal development, the directives also outlaw *harassment*, an unwanted conduct related to the respective ground of discrimination (Article 2 (3) Employment Equality Directive; Article 2 (3) Equal Treatment Directive). Additionally, the Equal Treatment Directive contains a prohibition on *sexual harassment*, an unwanted conduct of a sexual nature. Sexual harassment is defined as any form of unwanted verbal, non-verbal, or physical conduct of a sexual nature with the purpose or effect of violating the dignity of a person, in particular when creating an intimidating, hostile, degrading, humiliating, or offensive environment (Article 2 (2) Equal Treatment Directive). *Instructing* anyone to discriminate on

---

20   Everything will then depend on the construction of the comparator, the person who is, was, or would be treated more favourably. An infamous case in point is the construction of the comparator by the European Court of Justice in its judgement of 17 February 1998, Case C-249/96, *Lisa Grant* v. *South West Trains Ltd.*

the basis of the prohibited grounds is also considered discrimination (Article 2 (4) Employment Equality Directive).

Article 2 (5) Employment Equality Directive contains a provision that renders it justifiable to qualify what constitutes discrimination on the grounds of religion or belief, disability, age, or sexual orientation in that the 'directive shall be without prejudice to measures laid down by national law which, in a democratic society, are necessary for public security, for the maintenance of public order and the prevention of criminal offences, for the protection of health and for the protection of the rights and freedoms of others' (Article 2 (5) Employment Equality Directive).

This reservation primarily, though not uniformly, refers to conduct on the basis of religious convictions. An issue such as proscribing the wearing of an Islamic veil at school and in public office will have to be considered in the light of this reservation as well as many other questions concerning the position of religion and belief in a democratic society (for an analysis from a liberal egalitarian perspective, see Barry 2001; for a pronounced multiculturalist standpoint, see Parekh 2000).

Scope and exceptions　The Equal Treatment Directive and the Employment Equality Directive are both confined to the sphere of work, generally speaking. This includes all dimensions of access to employment, working conditions, vocational training, and promotion in the private as well as public sectors and in public bodies (Article 1 Employment Equality Directive; Article 3 Equal Treatment Directive).

As an important limitation of its scope, the Employment Equality Directive is without prejudice to the national marriage and family laws of its member states (Recital 22, Preamble of the Employment Equality Directive), some of which make it possible for partners of the same sex to have their relationship legally recognized. The Employment Equality Directive contains one more limitation of scope concerning the armed forces. Member states may stipulate that the provisions concerning age and disability shall not apply to the military. This exception is remarkable for what it does not contain: namely an exception for sexual orientation. In contrast to the United States with its policy of 'don't ask, don't tell, don't pursue',[21] and in contrast to Great Britain's longstanding reservations,[22] homosexual orientation shall be no barrier to membership in the armed forces.

Both directives contain a reservation that justifies different treatment when occupational activities, their nature or the context in which they are carried out, demand a certain sex, sexual orientation, religion, or belief, if 'such a characteristic constitutes a genuine and determining occupational requirement, provided that the objective is legitimate and the requirement is proportionate' (Article 4 (1) Employment Equality Directive; Article 2 (6) Equal Treatment Directive).

21　See, e.g., US Department of Defense, Enclosure 2 of Department of Defense Directive 1304.26, available at http://dont.stanford.edu (accessed: 11 April 2007).

22　For a thorough examination of the policy and its consequences, see *Smith & Grady v. United Kingdom*, 29 European Court of Human Rights 493 (1999).

This general reservation will have to be interpreted narrowly, as the ECJ has stated repeatedly in cases where the sex of the applicant had been declared a requirement for occupation. However, the possibility of anti-subordination measures for members of disadvantaged groups has to be left open, such as hiring only women for battered-women's shelters.

Significantly, both Equal Treatment Directive and Employment Equality Directive contain a range of other justifications for different treatment. Turning to the Equal Treatment Directive first, it starts out with a general reservation for provisions that aim at the 'protection of women, particularly as regards pregnancy and maternity' (Article 2 (3)). 'Maternity' itself is a term that can be interpreted from very narrowly to rather broadly. The ECJ's case law has time and again opted for the broad version, thereby also strongly privileging maternity over paternity. It was also observed how a shift in language from maternity to motherhood can serve to rhetorically prepare a preference for maternal parenting in the case law of the EJC (Ellis 1998, 242), notably in the case *Hofmann* v. *Barmer Ersatzkasse*.[23] This has in some cases led to a deterioration of women's situation by giving member states the discretion to provide only for maternal but not for paternal leave. In the 1980s cases[24] the ideological framework was laid in a way that invoked a traditionalist 'ideology of motherhood' (McGlynn 2000, 29). Only since the middle of the 1990s have EU member states been required to provide for parental leave as an individual right of both men and women workers for at least three months.[25] However, it turned out that, where men can take paternal leave, their inclination to do so is regularly low (European Commission 2003d, 9). The member states' respective provisions usually grant women longer times of leave, an arrangement which ultimately serves the status quo of gendered societies.

The Employment Equality Directive contains an elaborate provision concerning 'occupational activities within churches and other public or private organizations the ethos of which is based on religion or belief' (Article 4 (2) Employment Equality Directive). Here people's religion or belief may constitute an occupational requirement. The exact formulation is of special interest: 'This difference of treatment *shall* be implemented taking account of member states' constitutional provisions and principles, as well as the general principles of Community law, and *should* not justify discrimination on another ground' (emphasis added). It seems that 'should' leaves more room for discrimination on another ground than 'shall' does. The next sentence makes obvious the complexity of the issue that this part of the provision deals with: 'Provided that its provisions are otherwise complied with, this directive shall thus not prejudice the right of churches and other public

---

23   Judgement of the Court of 12 July 1984, Case C-184/83, *Hofmann* v. *Barmer Ersatzkasse*.

24   Judgement of the Court of 26 October 1983, Case C-163/82, *Commission v. Italy* and Judgement of the Court of 12 July 1984, Case C-184/83, *Hofmann* v. *Barmer Ersatzkasse*.

25   Council directive 96/34/EC on the framework agreement on parental leave concluded by UNICE, CEEP and the ETUC, 1996 O.J. (L 145), *amended by* 1998 O.J. (L 10) 24, clause 2 (1).

or private organizations, the ethos of which is based on religion or belief, acting in conformity with national constitutions and laws, to require individuals working for them to act in good faith and with loyalty to the organization's ethos' (ibid.).

In the process of negotiating the directive, the intersection of rights to religious freedom and equal treatment on the grounds of sex or sexual orientation formed one of the most contested areas. The compromise enshrined in the delicate formulations found in the directive is 'complex and cumbersome' (Bell 2002, 118). It contains three dimensions. First and foremost, even though sexual orientation may be taken into account, the directive obviously does not permit the overt and direct exclusion of lesbians and gay men from access to employment in religious organizations (ibid., 117). Second, religion and belief may, where national law or practice permit, only be taken into account if and insofar as the ethos of the organization needs to be maintained. Context, especially the vicinity to core doctrines of the respective faith, will play a decisive role here. Finally, and turning to existing employees, it will have to be established with diligence what it means that a religious institution may 'require individuals working for them to act in good faith and with loyalty to the organization's ethos' (Article 4 (2) Employment Equality Directive). For example, can somebody who *is* not only homosexual but also *acts* according to this 'status' behave in good faith and with loyalty to the Catholic Church? Or can he or she be required to keep his or her sexual orientation a secret (ibid., 118)?

While these issues are hardly new, the careful and cautious formulations of the directive add a new dimension to their consideration. Any privileging of religion or belief over other grounds was to be avoided while still giving religious communities their due. It remains to be seen whether and how the interests of churches and other organizations based on belief will be balanced with the interests of those who depart from their ethos in any way but nevertheless want to work in such organizations. Inter-group conflict seems rather logical here and was carried out vigorously during the negotiations for the Employment Equality Directive (ibid., 117).

A highly contested field is that of *'positive action'*. According to the Equal Treatment Directive, member states are allowed to 'maintain or adopt measures within the meaning of Article 141 (4) EC Treaty with a view to ensuring full equality in practice between men and women' (Article 1 (8)). Such measures may provide for 'specific advantages' for the under-represented sex, aimed at making it easier 'to pursue a vocational activity or to prevent or compensate for disadvantages in professional careers' (Article 141 (4) EC Treaty).

The wording of the positive action provisions of the Employment Equality Directive is a bit more guarded and less inclusive. Member states are not required to refrain 'from maintaining or adopting *specific measures* to prevent or compensate for disadvantages' (Article 7 (emphasis added)) that are linked with any of the grounds referred to in the directive. The Employment Equality Directive does not specifically cite the pursuance of a vocational activity, and being guaranteed a 'specific advantage' may in some cases contain more than a package of 'specific measures'. We suspect that the demarcation line will be drawn when it comes to quota regulations. Quotas may, according to established case law of the ECJ, be implemented in favour of the under-represented sex under certain conditions, among them the provision of a 'saving clause' for equally qualified and socially disadvantaged men.[26] It is doubtful that quota regulations would be regarded as legitimate when it comes to the 'other' grounds.[27]

Procedures, bodies and remedies   Turning to the question of implementation and its monitoring, we find one of the most important differences between the directives. Of course, the directives hold that the member states are obliged to make their judicial and/or administrative procedures accessible to 'all persons who consider themselves wronged by failure to apply the principle of equal treatment to them, even after the relationship in which the discrimination is alleged to have occurred has ended' (Article 9 (1) Employment Equality Directive; Article 6 (1) Equal Treatment Directive). The directives also commit the member states to ensuring the participation of NGOs in the process of application of anti-discrimination law (Article 9 (2) Employment Equality Directive; Article 6 (3) Equal Treatment Directive).

The directives depart at two points. First, only the Equal Treatment Directive foresees that the member states are obliged to secure 'such measures as are necessary to ensure real and effective compensation or reparation' in relation to the damage suffered (Article 6 (2)). Second, yet again only the Equal Treatment Directive commits the member states to establishing 'a body or bodies for the promotion, analysis, monitoring and support of equal treatment of all persons without discrimination on the grounds of sex' (Article 8a (1)). Their tasks shall be to assist victims of discrimination in their seeking for recognition and redress and to monitor the situation concerning discrimination by conducting surveys and publishing reports with respective recommendations. The Directive specifies that in relation to all these tasks the body has to act *independently*.

Outlook

The EU stresses that the two equality directives, but also the Working Time Directive and many further acts of EU social regulation, provide only minimum requirements. Accordingly, the member states can choose to implement the framework proposed by the EU or go far beyond this in their domestic reforms. In what follows, we are going to establish whether more, or rather less, profound changes to pre-existing policies have indeed taken place in the countries we have studied.

---

26   The paradigm-setting decision by the ECJ is: Judgement of the Court of 11 November 1997, Case C-409/95, *Hellmut Marschall v. Land Nordrhein-Westfalen*.

27   An indication in favour of this interpretation is the special provision concerning Northern Ireland in Article 15 of the Employment Equality Directive.

Structure of the Book

The following four chapters will report our findings from the Czech Republic, Hungary, Slovakia and Slovenia in the fields of equal treatment and working time. Each of our country chapters begins by presenting some crucial background information on the respective political, legal and socio-economic systems. All of these are of crucial importance as potential explanatory factors that shape the way EU directives are implemented. These passages are also designed to offer an easy-to-grasp overview of recent developments for readers of the book who may be interested more in the region than the details of the policy development. The chapters can thus be used to learn about the four countries on their path from communist systems to EU member states. The chapters then move on to the core subject of the book: the discussion of how our three directives were transposed, enforced and applied in each country. They conclude with a summary of the most promising improvement strategies encountered in each country.

The concluding chapter summarizes the main country findings, offers a theoretical discussion that relates these findings to the previous literature on implementing EU legislation, and suggests strategies for overall improvement of the state of affairs.

Chapter 2

Czech Republic

Clemens Wiedermann

Background Information

Political System

The new Constitution of the Czech Republic, which was adopted on 16 December 1992 (Act No. 1/1993) and came into force on 1 January 1993, was influenced by the second constitution of the first Czechoslovak Republic and the Basic Law of the Federal Republic of Germany (Vodièka 2002, 240–341).

Earlier, the 'Velvet Divorce' in 1992, which was mainly the result of the second post-communist parliamentary elections, resulted in the split of Czechoslovakia. According to public opinion polls of May 1992, 6 per cent of Czechs favoured separate states and in Slovakia less than 11 per cent supported independence. The clear majority of the population in both territories would have favoured the continued existence of Czechoslovakia as a confederation, as a federal system or as a unitary state (Wightman 1995, 59).

However, the June 1992 elections were won by parties whose views on the nature of the state were incompatible and whose leaders were unable and unwilling to reach a compromise that would have secured the survival of Czechoslovakia. Coalition negotiations following the elections for the Federal Assembly between the two strongest parties, Václav Klaus' Civic Democratic Party and Vladimír Mečiar's Movement for a Democratic Slovakia, were doomed to fail from the beginning. Soon it turned out that the only solution, which both party leaders could accept, was two independent states. Popular approval for this fundamental decision was not sought. A referendum was never planned in the Czech provinces and also in Slovakia, where Vladimír Mečiar first had promised to hold one, it never took place (Wightman 1995, 69).

The Czech Constitution establishes a parliamentary republic and a unitary state. The President, who is the formal Head of State, is elected at a joint meeting of both chambers of Parliament (Article 54 of the Constitution of the Czech Republic). The President's most important competences are laid down in Articles 62 and 63: *inter alia* the President appoints and recalls the Prime Minister and the other members of the government; appoints Justices of the Constitutional Court, the Supreme Court and all other judges; is entitled to return an enacted law to Parliament with the exception of constitutional acts ('right of suspensive veto', see Article 50); is the supreme commander of the armed forces and appoints and promotes generals. Expressly mentioned was the President's competence to call a referendum on the accession of the Czech Republic to the European Union (EU) and to announce the results (Article 62 lit. 1).

The Parliament has two chambers – the Chamber of Deputies and the Senate. The Chamber of Deputies is made up of 200 representatives, who are elected for a four year term. It is the supreme legislative authority and has the final say on budgetary and legislative matters. The Senate is made up of 81 Senators, who are elected for a term of six years. One third of the Senators is elected every two years ('partial renewal' – Article 16). The elections to the Chamber of Deputies are based on the principles of proportional representation, while the elections to the Senate are based on the first-past-the-post-system (Articles 17, 18). Section 49 of the Parliamentary Elections Act (No. 247/1995 Coll.) stipulates a 5 per cent threshold for individual parties, while it is higher for coalitions (varying from 10 to 20 per cent).[1] The Senate may return bills to the Chamber of Deputies ('suspensive veto'). The Chamber of Deputies then has to take a second vote on that bill and can approve it by a majority of all deputies (Article 47). In conclusion, the Senate usually can only delay legislation but does not have veto power.

The government is the supreme executive power (Article 67). It is led by the Prime Minister and government members are appointed by the President, on the proposal of the Prime Minister. Within 30 days following its appointment the government must win a vote of confidence in the House of Deputies to be instated (Article 68).

While it is still debated whether a stable party system has become established or not, further fundamental changes seem to be unlikely. The most successful and dominant party in the first free elections in 1990, the Civic Forum, was a mixture of many different ideological movements that were held together by their rejection of the Communist past. Explicit cleavages, along which the parties could recruit voters, were hardly developed at that time. In 1991, a process of differentiation started. It had an impact on the Civic Forum – which claimed not to be a political party, but rather a movement – and finally led to its disintegration. Especially the disputes on how the goal of political and economic transformation should be reached led to the formation of three new parties: the liberal-oriented Civic Movement (OH), the liberal, market economy-oriented Civic Democratic Party (ODS) and the conservative-liberal Civic Democratic Alliance (ODA) (Mansfeldová 2004, 226–7).

Over time, parties with a more or less stable electorate became established. In the first period the ODS was the dominant party, winning the elections to the Chamber of Deputies in 1992 and 1996 and leading the governments under Prime Minister Václav Klaus. After struggling with problems in the first elections, the Czech Social Democratic Party (CSSD) was able to win the general elections in 1998 and formed a minority government under Prime Minister Miloš Zeman. The CSSD repeated its election victory in 2002 and formed a coalition government under Prime Minister Vladímir Špidla. As a result of the 2002 elections, three further parties continued to be represented in the Lower House of Parliament: the

---

1   For an overview of the electoral system see (Mansfeldová 2004, 250).

Czech People's Party (KDU-CSL) which is a conservative Christian-democratic party; the Freedom Union-Democratic Union (US-DEU), which is a right wing party with a strong emphasis on liberal ideas. These two parties formed an election-coalition and together with the CSSD governed between 2002 and 2006. Finally, the Communist Party of Bohemia and Moravia (KSCM) had a very stable electorate throughout all elections in the post-communist era. It gains most support from the older generations of the population and from groups of younger voters, most of whom are confronted with unemployment. So far, KSCM has been confined to opposition as it has failed to find a coalition partner (Kostelecký 1995; Mansfeldová 2004).

Table 2.1   Governments of the Czech Republic (1993–2006)

Period	Government	Parties	Political orientation
Jan.1993– July 1996	Klaus I	OF/KDU-CSL/ODA/ KDS	Anti-communist, Christian Democratic, Right Liberals, Conservatives
July 1996– Jan. 1998	Klaus II	ODS/KDU-CSL/ODA	Right Liberals, Christian Democrats, Conservatives
Jan. 1998– July 1998	Tošovský	Different parties, several ministers that were not affiliated to parties	–
July 1998– July 2002	Zeman	CSSD (minority government)	Social Democrats
July 2002– Sept. 2006	Špidla (followed by Gross and Paroubek)	CSSD/KDU-CSL/US-DEU	Social Democrats, Christian Democrats, Liberals

Source: Own compilation from multiple sources.

Václav Klaus succeeded Václav Havel as the President of the Czech Republic in 2003. Klaus is the only Head of State in Europe who overtly opposes the deepening of the European integration process. In April 2005, he initiated a campaign against the Treaty establishing a Constitution for Europe, which led to conflicts especially with the European Parliament. At the same time, there were serious discrepancies with the government about his foreign policy competencies, since in his capacity as Head of State he made EU critical remarks abroad (Lazarova 2005).

Another important fact is the political apathy of a portion of the population and the rising discontent with politics among voters ('*Politikverdrossenheit*'). The election turnout rate was 96.8 per cent in the first free elections in 1990. It has fallen steadily since and reached 58 per cent in the 2002 elections. The turnout rate at the referendum on accession to the European Union held in June 2003 was 55.21 per cent.

Euroscepticism within the Czech Republic, as mentioned above, is highlighted by the remarks of the Head of State. According to the classification of Taggart and Szczerbiak (2002, 7), two important parties – the ODS and the KSCM – are 'soft eurosceptical' parties (Linden and Pohlman 2003). While during the 1990s the KSCM could even have been described as 'hard eurosceptical' (Taggart and Szczerbiak 2002, 14), its position toward European integration softened somewhat as the accession date drew closer. This noteworthy euroscepticism among the elites is also a sign of the widespread euroscepticism within the population (Linden and Pohlman 2003, 319). However, during the phase of implementation of the *acquis communautaire* only pro-European parties were in the government: the CSSD from 1998 on, the KDU-CSL and the US-DEU from 2002 on. Furthermore, in the referendum on EU accession in June 2003, more than 77 per cent of all voters supported EU membership.

Legal System

The reform of the legal system seems to be one of the most difficult projects of the transition period. The main problems are of direct relevance for the implemention problems discussed in later sections of this chapter: a lack of well-trained judges, especially shortly after the regime change; shortcomings in the education of lawyers in general; limited capacities in many areas of the legal system, which results in lengthy proceedings; and parts of the population are uninformed about their rights and about the possibilities of access to courts. In this context corruption has to be mentioned, which doubtlessly exists to a certain extent and sometimes poses a serious threat to the functioning of the courts and the administrative bodies (Anderson and Gray 2007; Transparency International 2005, 144–7). The Commission welcomed the progress made during the transition period, but also asserted that further reforms were needed (European Commission 2002c; 2003b).

The Supreme Court is located in Brno, the traditional centre of Czech jurisprudence. There are two high courts, one in Prague and the other in Olomouc. Furthermore, there are regional courts and district courts. All in all, the Czech judicial system has four levels. Since no special labour courts exist, individual labour conflicts are subject to civil proceedings before a court on the same footing as other civil court proceedings. There are no special labour tribunals, also within the courts of appeal (the regional courts), though often separate departments dealing with labour cases exist. The courts of general jurisdiction are also responsible for the surveillance of the administrative bodies. The Supreme Administrative Court, which is foreseen in Article 91 of the constitution of 1993, was not created until 2002 (Vodièka 2002, 266). Established on 1 January 2003, it is located in Brno. So, finally, a system of administrative justice with two instances was created: specialized chambers in regional courts and cassation before the Supreme Administrative Court.

The Constitutional Court, also located in Brno, has gained an important role in the legal system. Its adjudication gave the impression of being 'Europe- and integration-friendly', even before the Czech Republic's accession to the EU. In several judgements (*Škoda Auto case* in 1997, *Milk quota regulation case* in 2001,

Pension Insurance case in 2002)[2] it made reference to and based its reasoning on the principles of European law. The mentioned cases were seen as promising examples of application of European law by courts of the 'new' member states (Kühn 2005, 3).

Socio-economic Background

Most analysts assessed the economic development of the Czech Republic after 1989 positively. Until 1996, the country was even perceived as the most successful transition economy in Central and Eastern Europe. The term 'The Czech miracle' was created, which described an economic transformation with minimum unemployment and no hyperinflation (World Bank 1999, 1). This miracle came to a halt in 1997, when the situation began to deteriorate and a three year recession set in.

Table 2.2   Basic economic developments in the Czech Republic (1993–2004)

	1993	1994	1995	1996	1997	1998	1999	2000	2001	2002	2003	2004
Real GDP growth (%)	0.06	2.22	5.94	4.16	-0.73	-1.15	1.21	3.89	2.64	1.49	3.21	4.69
Unemployment rate (%)	4.40	4.30	4.10	3.90	4.80	6.40	8.60	8.70	8.00	7.30	7.80	8.30
Inflation rate	21.01	13.41	10.22	8.70	8.28	11.21	2.78	1.38	4.91	2.76	2.05	2.83
General government balance (% of GDP)	-	-	-13.39	-3.08	-2.44	-5.02	-3.65	-3.65	-5.92	-6.75	-12.45	-2.97

Source: OECD.

The downturn was attributed to incomplete reforms of the financial sector and a lack of determination in combating economic crime. The latter was also a serious problem in the privatization process. The term 'tunnelling' (*tunelování*) was created, which stands for a specific form of insider's trading rooted in privatization and post-communist economic reforms. These practices and shortcomings during the mass privatization of state owned enterprises by the so-called 'voucher privatization' during 1992 and 1995 contributed to the economic problems of the country at the end of the decade (Nellis 1999, 10–12; Ellerman 1998).

The social democratic government that came to power in 1998 took measures to improve the economic climate, resulting in a remarkable increase of foreign direct investment and economic growth. A problem that persists is the rising public deficit, which is one of the largest of any EU member state. During the accession process, the Commission already criticized the high government expenditures

2   These cases are available in English at: http://www.concourt.cz (accessed: 30 March 2007).

and several times asked for reforms in the area of pensions and health care (European Commission 2002c, 48, 134; see also Council of the European Union 2004a, 61–6).

The constant rise of structural unemployment as well as regional differences in unemployment rates constitute serious problems. In the capital Prague and in other large cities the unemployment rate is low, while high rates can be found in North Bohemia or North Moravia (more than 20 per cent), regions that traditionally were characterized by heavy industry, coal mining and steelwork (Vidovic 2002, 40; Tscherteu 2002). Long-term unemployment, which was not a serious problem until the mid 1990's, rose sharply from 1998 onwards. The general decline in employment after 1989 has disproportionately hit women. Consequently the female unemployment rates today are 3 to 4 percentage points higher than those of men. The sharp decline in employment during the transition period has created a difficult employment situation for young people. Youth unemployment is about twice as high as the total unemployment rate, around 17 per cent (Vidovic 2002, 40–43).

The Charter of Fundamental Rights and Freedoms, which is an integral part of the constitutional system of the Czech Republic (see Article 3 of the Constitution), establishes freedom of assembly in Article 27. It lays down the right to associate freely and mentions in particular trade unions, which are established independently by the state and which are not subject to any restrictions whatsoever.

In 1990, first efforts were made in the Czech and Slovak parts of then Czechoslovakia to institutionalize social dialogue. The government, cooperating with trade unions and newly established associations of employers and entrepreneurs, created a tripartite forum, which was first called 'Council of Social Agreement', but then changed its name to 'Council of Economic and Social Agreement' (RHSD) (Hála et al. 2002, 6). The government supported this nationwide tripartite dialogue until 1992. The then elected conservative and liberal government downgraded the forms of collective bargaining. Social dialogue was reinforced when a social democratic government took office in 1998. This government's policies showed comparatively stronger willingness to support the high-level tripartite body and other forms of social dialogue (Casale, Kubinkova and Rychly 2001; Hála et al. 2002).

This supreme tripartite body deals with areas such as economic policy, labour law relations, social issues, wages, labour safety and the integration of the Czech Republic to the European Union. The Plenary Session – the RHSD's top negotiating body – consists of the Prime Minister, seven other government members, seven representatives of trade union confederations and seven representatives of employers' associations (see Articles 2 and 4 of the Statutes of the Council of Economic and Social Agreement). The RHSD has no statutory right to intervene in the law-making process, and its conclusions and general agreements are not of a binding nature; therefore the RHSD plays a more advisory and consulting role. During the 1990's, trade unions tried to increase the level of obligation of the general agreements of the RHSD, but employers and the government heavily opposed these efforts (Hála et al. 2002,

6). In general there is only a rather narrow framework for binding agreements of the social partners because the Czech labour law lays down many comprehensive and universally binding provisions. There is a clear predominance of statutory rules over descriptive guidelines and over the delegation of regulatory power to collective agreements. This undermines the overall scope of collective agreements (Hála and Kroupa 2005; Hála et al. 2002, 34–6).

Nevertheless, on lower levels trade unions have some potential to act on behalf of their members' interests. Under Czech law, trade unions and their bodies are the legitimate representatives of employees in labour relations. Thus only the trade unions have the right of collective bargaining, where they represent all employees – also non-members. Collective agreements, both at industry and enterprise level, which regulate wages and a wide range of other issues concerning labour conditions, have become an important part of industrial relations. Furthermore, the Labour Code contains provisions that entitle trade union bodies to monitor compliance with labour law by the employer and the right to carry out checks on health and safety issues (see Section 22 and 136 of the Labour Code) (Casale, Kubinkova and Rychly 2001, 3). These provisions award trade union bodies effective instruments to force employers to comply with labour law regulations, especially in the field of occupational health and safety. In reality, however, trade union representatives hardly ever use these powers. Since they are 'normal' employees – besides their activity as trade unionists – they are in the same way affected by the tense situation on the labour market. They often try to avoid extensive conflicts with their employer and, therefore, do not apply the control mechanisms the law provides them with (Interview CZ13).

A total of 1.3 million employees, which is about one quarter of all employees, are organized in trade unions. The largest trade union confederation is the Czech-Moravian Trade Union Confederation (CMKOS), which associates 33 unions that have around one million members altogether.[3] The largest union within the CMKOS is the Czech Metalworker's Federation (KOVO) with approximately 300,000 members. The CMKOS sends six of the seven employees' representatives to the Plenary Session of the RHSD. Other noteworthy trade union confederations are the Confederation of Arts and Culture (KUK) with close to 100,000 members, and the Association of Independent Trade Unions (ASO) with approximately 200,000 members (Hála et al. 2002, 23–5). As other European countries, the Czech Republic has also experienced a long-term decline of union membership. In 1990, 84 per cent of all employees were members of a trade union. The share of union members among employees has constantly dropped since and reached 22 per cent in 2003. Despite the decline, confidence in the unions remains stable, and they are still seen as necessary to safeguard employees' interests (Kroupa, Vasková and Hála 2004; see also European Commission 2006g, 25).

The two most important employers' organizations are the Confederation of Employers and Entrepreneurs (KZPS) and the Confederation of Industry and Transport (SPCR). Both of them participate in the RHSD. Approximately a

---

3   For a list of affiliated unions, see http://www.cmkos.cz/affiliated-unions (accessed: 28 February 2007).

total of 10,000 to 12,000 enterprises and self-employed workers are affiliated with employers' organizations. This is only a small part of the 2,063,883 enterprises and self-employed people that were registered in 2000; 31,000 of them employing more than 20 people. Employers in the Czech Republic have hardly felt the necessity to affiliate in the past. Membership contributions are not tax deductible so far, which might be a disincentive for affiliation (Mormont 2004, 38).

After the Communist period of 'paternalistic state provision', a 'ubiquitous system of social protection' and 'false egalitarianism' (Castle-Kanerova 1997), modified concepts for social policy were created. These concepts are rooted in the First Republic (1918–1939). Hence, social policy legislation was conceptualized with a reference to the social democratic past of the 1920s (Castle-Kanerova 1997, 224). The current Czech welfare state has great similarities with the German or Austrian welfare state, which means that it also has a certain resistance to change (Potucek 2004, 265). Unlike most of the other CEECs, neoliberal public policy concepts of the World Bank and the International Monetary Fund did not gain decisive influence on the restructuring of social policy (Potucek 2004, 263; Manning 2004).

The Czech welfare state has great similarities to the *Bismarckian* type of welfare state and the conservative welfare regime (Esping-Andersen 1990). It is basically financed by contributions of employers and employees, and in some areas the state assists with the tax financing of some social security benefits. The system of social security has four main components:

1) a compulsory social insurance that is financed by contributions of employees and employers. It includes a sickness insurance scheme, an old-age pension scheme and an unemployment insurance scheme;
2) a health insurance that is separated from the sickness insurance. It provides benefits in kind and is financed partly by insurance contributions and partly by the state;
3) a tax-financed social support scheme that focuses on means-tested benefits especially for families with children;
4) a social assistance scheme (residual scheme /'last safety net') that is supported by public funds and government grants to local authorities (Tröster 2000, 205; Filipic 1998).

The Czech welfare state expanded during the transition phase instead of being affected by retrenchment like most of the other welfare systems during that period. All in all, the expenditures to the social and health protection system increased from 17.9 per cent of the GDP in 1990 to 21.8 per cent in 2002 (Potucek 2004, 255).

Relevant Aspects of Societal Order

Particularly with a view to EU standards in the field of minority protection, it should be mentioned that the Czech Republic has a dominant ethnic and national majority of Czechs who constitute about 95 per cent of the population. Further ethnic groups are Germans, Roma, Poles, Moravians, Silesians and Hungarians, who form part of the overall population of about 10 million people. In the 2001 census only 11.716 people defined themselves as Roma, while informal estimates suggest that the actual number of Roma is between 15 and 30 times as high. Many prefer not to declare a Romany nationality or identity because of fear of negative consequences. Discrimination of Roma doubtlessly exists in areas like education, employment, access to medical care and housing. In the course of the 'Velvet Divorce' a new law on citizenship was enacted which in fact made it difficult for some groups of Roma to obtain Czech citizenship. Due to an amendment of the respective law in 1999 the situation improved considerably and there are now only a few stateless Roma left (European Commission 2004e). More and more often, Roma successfully take legal measures against discrimination (European Network of Legal Experts in the Non-discrimination Field 2005b, 50). However, there are also cases where especially lower courts did not consider minority rights adequately.[4] Though the lower courts are legally bound by the Supreme Court's decisions, they sometimes try to contravene them by delaying procedures or by not fully applying the Supreme Court's reasoning. In the transition period, law enforcement and application often does not function properly, as these examples suggest. One of the reasons for that is probably a Communist heritage: There exists a certain negligence towards the law in general, and a basic commitment to legality is not always definitive.

In addition to Roma, homosexuals are a frequent target of discrimination. Homosexuals are confronted with physical violence, verbal abuse and other forms of harassment. They sometimes experience discrimination in areas like health services, housing and other public services. On the other hand, public opinion concerning legislation for homosexuals has been rather open-minded. In 2000 and 2001, surveys revealed that the majority of Czechs supported the adoption of a new Registered Partnership Bill (Procházka, Janík and Hromada 2003, 12). This Act was also adopted by the Parliament on 15 March 2006, which had to override a veto of president Vaclav Klaus. It received exactly the necessary majority of 101 out of the 200 votes in the Chamber of Deputies. The Czech Republic now has one of the more progressive and liberal legislations in the field of same-sex partnerships in Europe (BBC 2006).

Discrimination based on religion appears to be a marginal problem in the Czech Republic. In its self-perception it is the most atheistic country in Europe, and Czechs refer regularly to the irreligious aspects of their society. Religion is banned from the public sphere to a large extent and is regarded as a purely private matter (Interview CZ9). If religion plays a role in the public debate, it is

---

4   A statue holding a baseball bat in the premises of a restaurant with the inscription *'Go and get the gypsies'* was not regarded as harassment or insult by either the regional and the high courts. A wall, which was built in Usti nad Labem to divide houses inhabited by Roma from the rest of the settlement, was regarded as lawful by regional and high courts. In both cases the Supreme Court in Brno annulled the judgements (European Network of Legal Experts in the Non-discrimination Field 2006, 57).

mostly linked to the unsettled property disputes between the Catholic Church and the state.

Another form of discrimination is experienced by women, who are not only discriminated against in the field of employment (as will be shown below in more detail). Domestic violence appeared to be a serious problem during the transition period and its abatement therefore was one of the government's priorities in the field of equal treatment policy (Ministry of Labour and Social Affairs of the Czech Republic 2005, 100). Women are clearly underrepresented in elected bodies. Between 1994 and 2002, the women's ratio in the Chamber of Deputies was around 16 per cent; in the Senate between 11 and 12 per cent; in regional boards of representatives between 13 and 23 per cent (Pavlík 2004, 47). Privatization made childcare more expensive and less accessible, which is a further barrier for the equal participation of women in the labour market (Pollert 2003, 337). The Gender Sensitive Human Development Index (HDI) of the UNDP confirms a deterioration during the post-transition phase: In 1990 the Czech Republic was ranked at eighth place; by 1998 it had dropped to 33rd (Pollert 2003, 335).

The post-Socialist phase brought many changes for the Czech Republic but not a complete overhaul of the former system. Traces of the Communist period, but also from the First Republic and the Bohemian kingdom under Habsburg rule can be detected. One can follow the thoughts of Ralf Dahrendorf that the transition of the institutions from an authoritarian regime to a democratic society can take place in six months, that the transformation from a centrally planned economy to a market economy takes six years, but the change of peoples' habits, attitudes, behaviour and values needs around 60 years to be transformed (Potucek 1999, 172).

On the one hand, the repressive character of the Communist regime is out of the question. On the other hand, it is also not appropriate to regard this era as exclusively disastrous and to think that afterward everything changed for the better at once. Parts of the population were able to lead a reposeful life, including a moderate standard of living. The Communist system was not only oppressive and already in the short term an economically untenable system but also a functioning and, to a certain degree, particularly during the first stages of its existence, a socially legitimate system (Illner 1998, 143). Especially in the perception of the people, who by and large supported the transition process, there are problematic aspects in the phase following Communism. Improvements are appreciated in societal areas like democracy and civil rights, the quality of consumption, the economic situation in general, environmental protection and health. Nevertheless, some negative developments are perceived in areas like crime, housing and the distribution of income (Illner 1998). Particularly crime became a severe problem after the regime change as crime rates rose dramatically (e.g. in 1989/90 an increase of 52 per cent in the whole country and 181 per cent in Prague) (Hagan and Radeova 1998, 207). Regarding all this, it comes as no surprise that parts of the population retain positive memories of the Communist era, and these facts can explain the success of the KSCM.

One should bear in mind that transition – especially in the course of privatization – itself produced a great deal of crime and corruption. The partly random circumstances of transition made it easy for members of the 'old' managerial elites to divert and convert economic resources into quick and illegal profits (Hagan and Radeova 1998, 202). This general disrespect for the rule of law of the pre- but also the post-transition elites entrenched a widespread cynicism about law, its function and its binding nature. Also 'normal' citizens became convinced that a basic commitment to legality is not a moral and civil value of high importance for the functioning of society and state. The opinion diffused more and more that crime can be accepted and that one can get away with it. All this is connected to the low trust in and little respect for the judiciary. The following statement shows the relevance of these problems for one of the main topics of our research, namely law enforcement and application: '… individuals who have lived for a generation or more in a police state are unlikely to immediately turn to the judiciary to resolve their grievances. This would be so even if such a legal bureaucracy was given the power and resources to fully enforce the law, neither of which has been the case in the Czech Republic' (Hagan and Radeova 1998, 203).

Transposition of EU Directives

Membership negotiations with the Czech Republic started officially in March 1998 and were concluded in December 2002. The most important steps concerning the compliance of national law with EU requirements were taken within that period. The harmonization in the field of labour law and social policy was an ongoing process, which was accomplished in several steps. The most important of these steps was the so-called 'European' or 'Harmonization Amendment' (No. 155/2000 Coll.), which substantially amended the Labour Code (No. 65/1965 Coll.) and came into effect on 1 January 2001. It has not only intended to transpose the Working Time Directive, the Equal Treatment Directive and the Employment Equality Directive but also several other EU directives in the field of social affairs. Besides the 'Harmonization Amendment', further acts were necessary to comply with our three directives, especially in the field of equality in the workplace. Interestingly – as will be shown below – further legislation with the aim to harmonize was enacted even after the closure of negotiations in December 2002 and after the accession to the EU in May 2004. The assumption that the transposition of EU directives would slow down or even come to a halt after the accession does not hold true for the Czech Republic. On the contrary: some adaptation steps were taken before the accession, some after that date, and in some areas adaptation has not been completed yet (Falkner, Causse and Wiedermann 2006).

The transposition of EU law was in some areas an uncontroversial process, while in others sparked political debates emerged. On the one side, the relevant actors often alluded to the superiority of European law and the need to transpose it in a certain period of time. Characteristic are the comments of Vladimír Špidla (then Minister of Labour and Social Affairs) in a legislative committee of the Czech Parliament. He argued that the amendments that harmonize Czech law with European guidelines have to be accepted by the parliament the way they are, since the provisions stem from EU directives (Interview CZ6). On the other hand, many political forces wanted their interests to be considered, also when it came to the transposition of European legislation. Though the harmonization of domestic law was sometimes regarded as a somewhat technical procedure ('copy and paste'), political conflicts still characterized the transposition of crucial aspects of EU labour law.

Working Time

Working time regulations stem from the era when the Czech Lands were part of the Austro-Hungarian Empire. The current Labour Code, including the principles of the working time regime, was enshrined in 1965. Apart from that act there were two decrees that dealt with working time. The working time regime of the Czech Republic always had one interesting peculiarity: rest periods were part of working time. Therefore, the statutory maximum working time was 42 hours 30 minutes, including five rest periods of 30 minutes. This abnormality did not cause serious problems during the transposition of the Working Time Directive. It was simply abolished, and now rest periods are not included in the working time, like in all other European countries.

The main actor in the transposition process was the Ministry of Labour and Social Affairs, where the bill was also drafted before it was forwarded to the Parliament. The generally open nature of the legislative drafting process allowed for intensive participation of the two sides of industry. The working time issue was just one among others, since Act No. 155/2000 transposed many directives in the field of labour and social law. The RHSD (The Council of Economic and Social Agreement), the supreme tripartite body, had a certain influence (Interview CZ5). The trade unions supported the Working Time Directive and its transposition from the very beginning, while the employer's side opposed large parts of it. They wanted all possible derogations to be considered and demanded 'more flexibility', which in their eyes was not realized by the transposition of the Working Time Directive (Interview CZ3).

Within Parliament the conservative-liberal ODS – the main opposition party – tried to oppose large parts of the 'Harmonization Amendment' and especially the new working time provisions. It tried to obstruct the legislation by proposing 200 amendments to the government's bill. Some of these amendments may have been constructive, but in a fast-track legislative process, which tried to transpose large parts of the *acquis* in the field of social policy at once, the government decided not to review them. So none of the ODS's proposals was taken into consideration (Interview CZ5).

The Parliament adopted the 'Harmonization Amendment' (No. 155/2000 Coll.) despite the partly strong opposition. It can be described as a 'big reform' in the field of working time because several provisions regulating working time affairs were changed. The two decrees with specific working time provisions were abolished. Several relevant provisions can now be found in Sections 83 ff. of the Labour Code (Chapter III: Working Time and Rest Periods). This reform was comparatively drastic, and the results were interpreted as creating a 'new system' (Interview CZ5). The most important changes concerned the formal structure and the overall system and not material provisions (e.g. 40 hours of effective weekly working time before and after the change, but with the above mentioned peculiarities). Apart from two specific topics (that will be discussed below) Act No. 155/2000 transposed the Working Time Directive correctly.

Derogations were hardly used by the social democratic government because it was against its 'philosophy' when transposing the directive. Only in areas where it was regarded as absolutely necessary were some derogations as provided for in Article 17 of the Working Time Directive even considered. Examples for derogations transposed are: the reduction of daily rest periods, the possibility to work on public holidays, the length of a shift for 'security forces',[5] and derogations in the field of public transport. In particular, the 'Art. 22-opt-out' was not used, though the employers' side vigorously demanded the consideration of this individual opt-out possibility.

A closer look at the working time provisions shows that Czech law was, and still is after transposition, more generous than the Working Time Directive in some areas. Basically there is a daily rest period of 12 hours per 24 successive hours in Czech law, while Article 3 of the Working Time Directive demands eleven hours. Czech law stipulates a break after four-and-a-half hours of continuous work, while Article 4 of the Working Time Directive stipulates a break when the working day is longer than six hours.

Nevertheless, two topics are still a matter of debate, both of which are however well known also in many other EU countries. The first is the fact that the government was not willing to consider the ECJ's case law when transposing the Working Time Directive. That means that the *SIMAP*[6] and the *Jaeger*[7] case have not been incorporated into Czech legislation. These two judgements state that time spent on-call at the workplace must be regarded as working time. The government regarded itself only obliged to transpose the Working Time Directive 'as such' without taking account of ECJ jurisprudence, while the trade unions favoured legislation that implemented these rulings. Therefore, the current definition of working time in the Czech law is as follows: 'Working time shall mean any period in which an employee is engaged in work for his employer.' (Section 83.1 Labour Code) The interpretation of this legal definition does not include on-call and standby times, which can be regarded as a breach of the Working Time Directive (Interview CZ11).

Currently, discussions in the European Parliament, the Commission and the Council about a revision of the Working Time Directive revolve around this problem (Röpke 2005). Therefore, Czech experts regard it as a 'European

---

5   In the Czech Republic also police forces, customs, wardens and fire brigades are considered 'security forces'.

6   Judgement of the Court of 3 October 2000, Case C-303/98, *SIMAP v. Conselleria de Sanidad y Consumo de la Generalidad Valenciana.*

7   Judgement of the Court of 9 September 2003, Case C-151/02, *Landeshauptstadt Kiel v. Norbert Jaeger.*

problem' and not as a Czech national problem. The Czech government supports a solution at the European level that does not define on-call and standby-times as 'pure' working time. In case of another solution in the Council and the European Parliament, it considers making use of the individual opt-out possibility. Initially, this provision – which runs counter to the basic principles underlying the Working Time Directive – was created on demand of the UK government to retain a deregulatory working time regime. In the beginning, the UK was the only member state to apply this provision (Kenner 2004). Apparently, it is becoming more and more relevant for further member states – like the Czech Republic – to sidestep the impact of the ECJ's decisions.

The second 'legal problem' is the fact that under the current Czech law every single employment contract is interpreted separately. Section 69 of the Labour Code stipulates: 'If an employee has agreed to more than one employment relationship, the rights and duties (obligations) ensuing from each shall be considered independently, unless this Code or other statutory provisions stipulate otherwise.' The current interpretation of this provision is that an employee can have a second employment contract. The working time of the second employment contract only needs to be shorter than the first one, which is regarded as the 'main contract'. 'Shorter' means that just 15 minutes are enough to fulfil this requirement (Interview CZ11; Focus Group CZ2). Though the concerned employee effectively works much longer than 40 (48) hours, this is not perceived as a breach of working time regulations. The Working Time Directive itself is silent on this issue. As long as European working time regulations do not explicitly prohibit the exceeding of the maximum weekly working time because of 'double contracts', Czech experts do not see any need for adaptation. While such double contracts occur in practice, no reliable data is available (Focus Group CZ2).

Equality in the Workplace

The transposition of the Equal Treatment Directive and the Employment Equality Directive is currently characterized by disarrangement and diffusion. A bill for a unified anti-discrimination act was drafted. Though strong endeavours have been made, this new Anti-discrimination Act was finally not adopted by the Parliament, and in the current political situation it is rather uncertain that new anti-discrimination legislation will be enacted. Therefore, there are now dozens of equal treatment and anti-discrimination provisions scattered over many different laws. These provisions are not always consistent and sometimes they are deficient. Besides these shortcomings, the newly established equal treatment body (Governmental Council for Equal Opportunities for Women and Men) does not have much in common with the body envisioned by the Equal Treatment Directive (Article 8a).

Equal treatment and anti-discrimination policies are new to the Czech Republic (Interview CZ1). Before, there were only universal provisions, for example in the Civil Code (No. 40/1964 Coll.). Section 11 et seq. contains general provisions on the right to the protection of human dignity. On the constitutional level, the Charter of Fundamental Rights and Freedoms in its Article 3 prohibits discrimination on the ground of 'sex, race, colour of skin, language, faith, religion, political or other conviction, ethnic or social origin, membership in a national or ethnic minority, property, birth, or other status'. It does not provide specific protection in the field of e.g. sexual orientation or disability. Nevertheless, it is argued that grounds not explicitly mentioned are contained implicitly in the saving clause 'other status' (Boucková 2005). However, these constitutional provisions are very general and often not directly applicable.

Also, the criminal law contains provisions that aim at the elimination of discrimination. The Criminal Code (No. 140/1961 Coll.) contains several provisions that prohibit blatant forms of discrimination. These are crimes of violence against a group or individuals, crimes of defamation of an ethnic group, belief or faith, race and instigation of hatred against a group of persons. This group of crimes, which gravely affect community relations, cover only the most serious incidents (Boucková 2005). Therefore, they are only applicable in severe cases and do not guarantee specific protection against discrimination of women, homosexuals and religious groups in the labour market.

It is a challenging task to describe the legal transposition of the Equal Treatment Directive and the Employment Equality Directive. Contrary to other member states, the Czech Republic did not enact one uniform anti-discrimination act, which fulfils the requirements of all European directives dealing with discrimination.[8] Instead of such an 'umbrella act' a 'diffusive legal arrangement' was chosen. This means that the right to equal treatment was addressed in non-discrimination provisions in all the laws that regulate any employer-employee relation (Pavlík 2004). The reasoned statement in the bill of the new Anti-discrimination Act includes a non-exhaustive list of all national laws that are concerned by the EU's equal treatment and non-discrimination policy. It contains 57 laws that already had to be amended and will have to be changed in the future, should European legislation so require. This 'diffusive model' has serious disadvantages. The legislation easily becomes inconsistent in that it uses different legal terms and varying definitions.

The two most important laws concerning the Equal Treatment Directive and the Employment Equality Directive are the Labour Code (No. 65/1965 Coll.) and the new Employment Act (No. 435/2004 Coll.). Basically, the Labour Code governs a labour relation after the conclusion of a labour contract, while the Act on Employment covers relations before the conclusion of a contract, i.e. the access to employment (Interview CZ4. Further laws that now contain equal treatment and anti-discrimination provisions are: Act on Service by Members of the Security Forces (No. 361/2003 Coll.); Act on Service in the State Administration (No. 218/2002 Coll.); Act on Service by Members of the Armed Forces (No. 221/1999 Coll.); School Law (No. 561/2004 Coll.); Law on Pay in the Private Sector (No.

---

8   Related directives are e.g.: Council directive 2000/43/EC of 29 June 2000 implementing the principle of equal treatment between persons irrespective of racial or ethnic origin; Council directive 79/7/EEC of 19 December 1978 on the progressive implementation of the principle of equal treatment for men and women in matters of social security.

143/1992 Coll.); Law on Pay in the Public Sector (No. 1/1992 Coll.). The coming into effect of some of the laws (No. 361/2003 Coll.; No. 218/2002 Coll.) that contain relevant anti-discrimination provisions has been postponed repeatedly, and was not yet completed at the time of writing.

Three of the numerous adaptation-steps so far in the field of equality at the workplace are important. Firstly, the 'Harmonization Amendment' of 2000 included the first significant adoption of equal treatment and anti-discrimination provisions in the Labour Code. Secondly, an amendment to the Labour Code of 2004 (No. 46/2004 Coll.) brought more detailed and improved provisions for the definitions of direct and indirect discrimination, of harassment and sexual harassment, and of the scope of exemptions. Thirdly, the new Employment Act of 2004 contains many equal treatment provisions, which are particularly applicable in the field of access to employment.

The procedures concerning these acts were not particularly controversial. The main reason is that especially in the beginning, equality in the workplace was not regarded as a topic of importance. Consequently, during the debate relating to the 'Harmonization Amendment' in 2000 other topics evoked more controversies, like e.g. the working time issue. Equality was regarded as 'just one topic among all the others' (Interviews CZ1; CZ6).

As already mentioned, due to the inconsistency of equal treatment laws in the Czech Republic, the current legal framework is insufficient. Besides, further shortcomings impede the proper transposition of the Equal Treatment Directive and the Employment Equality Directive. Section 150 of the Labour Code prohibits certain types of work for women. Based on that provision, the Ministry of Health enacted an ordinance (No. 261 of 1997) which *inter alia* prohibited several types of work for women generally, contrary to EU law. Section 150 of the Labour Code was changed in 2004 (No. 436/2004 Coll.). It now only prohibits the employment of women endangering motherhood. The above-mentioned ordinance was abolished and replaced by a new one (No. 288 of 2003), which only prohibits certain work for pregnant and breastfeeding women, for mothers until the end of the ninth month after giving birth and for juveniles. The new legal framework is by and large in accordance with European requirements and implements directive 92/85/EEC.[9] Nonetheless, Section 150 (1) still prohibits certain types of work for women in the mining industry, which is a breach of the Equal Treatment Directive. On the other hand, Section 150 is based on the International Labour Organization (ILO) Convention on Underground Work (Women) of 1935.[10] Article 2 states that 'No female, whatever her age, shall be employed on underground work in any mine.' Article 3 allows a few exemptions from that basic rule. The Czech Republic inherited its ratification in 1993 and therefore had the international obligation to insert Section 150 in its current form

---

9   Council directive 92/85/EEC of 19 October 1992 on the introduction of measures to encourage improvements in the safety and health at work of pregnant workers and workers who have recently given birth or are breastfeeding.

10   ILO Convention C045, Convention concerning the Employment of Women on Underground Work in Mines of all Kinds.

into the Labour Code. The ILO Underground Work (Women) Convention gives its signatory states the possibility to denounce the treaty every ten years. It is likely that the Czech Republic will do so after the next term (Interview CZ7).

A specific topic regarding the transposition of the Equal Treatment Directive is the composition of the new equal treatment body as provided for in Article 8a. The Government Council for Equal Opportunities for Women and Men ('The Council') was established by Government Resolution No. 1033 of 10 October 2001. Such a resolution does not have the status of generally binding legislation approved by the parliament. Therefore, it is doubtful whether the resolution meets the requirements of Art. 8a Equal Treatment Directive. 'The Council' has a narrow mandate in the field of equal treatment between men and women; further areas (e.g. discrimination based on sexual orientation or religion) are not covered by its work. Moreover, the competencies of the Council are limited, since it does not have much more than an advisory function vis-à-vis the government. It cannot provide any independent assistance to victims of discrimination in pursuing their complaints and it cannot conduct independent surveys in cases of discrimination.

Faced with this rather unsatisfactory state of affairs, the *failure of a draft Anti-discrimination Act* should be mentioned here as a kind of *excursus*: first ideas concerning a new law against discrimination, which would have fulfilled the 'umbrella model', came up in 2000. The government's draft refers explicitly to the European dimension. Section 1 (1) clarifies: 'Pursuant to the law of the European Communities, this Act regulates the right to equal treatment in the following matters: ....' In a footnote to this first Section several relevant EU directives are enumerated, *inter alia* the Equal Treatment Directive and the Employment Equality Directive.

Section 1 defines the scope of application. Sections 2 and 3 contain definitions of all the relevant terms. They are in accordance with European legislation and with the ECJ's case law. Furthermore, 'quasi-definitions' of religion, belief, sexual orientation and sexual identity are included. Section 5 contains exemptions from the principle of equal treatment; paragraph 5 specifies employment in a church or religious society. Part Two of the draft contains measures of protection against discrimination, primarily legal action in civil courts. Section 7 (2) provides for access to financial compensation for non-proprietary loss. The whole draft would have fulfilled the requirements of European law much better than the current legal situation.

However, the political climate in the Czech Republic in general was not supportive of new anti-discrimination legislation. The bill was drafted in the Office of the Government by human rights lawyers and also by experts from NGOs working in that field. The government dealt with the bill for the first time in 2004 when it only had a very narrow majority of just one vote in the Chamber of Deputies. As a consequence, it regularly encountered difficulties in getting parliamentary approval of its bills. Furthermore, one of the coalition partners of the Social Democrats, the KDU-CSL, partly opposed the bill, arguing that all the relevant EU directives had already been transposed correctly (Interview CZ6). Also, large parts of the 'Thatcherist' ODS opposed the new act, arguing that it interfered too much in the private employer-employee relationships and that all the provisions to secure equality in the workplace were already enshrined in Czech legislation. In general, the party discipline within the Czech Parliament is relatively low. Parties only set forth rules on voting behaviour in a few areas of legislation. Equal treatment and anti-discrimination do not belong to these policy areas. Therefore, objectors of the Anti-discrimination Act can be found across party lines in the Chamber of Deputies (Interview CZ12).

Finally in 2005, the government adopted the draft and sent it to Parliament in early 2006. The bill passed all three readings in the Chamber of Deputies and was forwarded to the Senate. The Senate rejected the bill, returning it to the Chamber of Deputies for a second vote. This time it failed to gain the necessary absolute majority of all delegates (see Article 47 of the Constitution of the Czech Republic).[11] As a consequence, the new Anti-discrimination Act was finally rejected.

The odds are against an encompassing reform of anti-discrimination legislation in the near future. Conservative political forces generally dominate the Senate and will therefore probably obstruct new attempts for reform. Equally, the current President does not favour such legislation. Moreover, the new government, which came to power in January 2007, and is dominated by conservative parties (ODS/KDU-CSL), is likely to stall plans for new anti-discrimination legislation (Focus Group CZ1).

To sum up: the adoption of the new Anti-discrimination Act would have been crucial for the transposition of the *acquis* concerning equality in the workplace (Boucková 2005). The Czech Republic will continue to breach especially the Equal Treatment Directive but also the Employment Equality Directive in case of further inactivity in that area.

Application and Enforcement

The legal adaptations in the areas researched were numerous. Nevertheless, as demonstrated above, the Czech legal framework is not yet in full compliance with the three EU directives researched. However, these problems in the realm of transposition appear less serious compared to the severe shortcomings in the field of application and enforcement.

Application Problems

General problems   There are serious difficulties concerning the application of the Equal Treatment Directive, the Employment Equality Directive and the Working Time Directive. They affect EU-derived legislation as much as to 'purely' national legislation (Interviews CZ12; CZ5). Generally, these problems are rooted in the shortcomings of the court system, the inadequate supervision by the state, and

---

11   In this second vote in the Chamber of Deputies, only 84 instead of the necessary 101 Deputies voted for the bill: 45 Deputies voted against.

the relatively high unemployment rates in large parts of the Czech Republic. Another reason is the complexity of the whole subject (in the case of the Working Time Directive) and the fact that the issue is entirely new and therefore persons concerned sometimes do not know how to deal with or how to 'use' these rights (in the case of the Equal Treatment Directive and the Employment Equality Directive) (Interviews CZ5; CZ11; CZ1).

This is linked to a general problem: application of EU law in the Czech Republic is often hindered by a lack of information and specialized knowledge. Therefore, also two years after accession to the EU, sometimes 'old' Czech legislation is applied instead of 'new' legislation transforming EU law. Cases are referred to the higher Courts of the Czech Republic rather than to the ECJ. In some respect, the 'strange', 'complicated' and 'external' procedure of the preliminary ruling is avoided (Mucha et al. 2005). There are hardly any preliminary rulings requested by Czech courts. Remarkably, one of the very first preliminary ruling procedures linked to the Czech Republic[12] deals with the Working Time Directive. Again, this procedure deals with the question of the definition of working time and whether a doctor's work on-call at the hospital forms part of work. The request for a preliminary ruling mentions the *Jäger* case where these questions were already decided.

Probably the most serious hurdle for a proper application of labour law provisions is the high unemployment rate as employees fear losing their jobs (Interviews CZ2; CZ7; CZ12). Employers will rather dismiss a 'trouble maker' than employees who acquiesce to bad working conditions. In this context, provisions from European legislation that tend to protect employees who try to enforce a claim by legal action against their employer (e.g. Article 7 Equal Treatment Directive) have little practical impact. By and large, they are transposed correctly and the provisions can be found in national legislation, but they have little effect in reality. Furthermore, the pressure on employees increases because the labour market is small. This means that employees who insist on their rights and entitlements will sooner or later be known within a branch and could face blacklisting (Interview CZ12).

Moreover, a vivid 'civil legal culture' hardly exists in the Czech Republic. In the Communist past, civil procedures for the individual enforcement of rights were not foreseen. Solutions concerning problems in labour relations had to be found in a different way. Even in cases where employees know their rights and entitlements very well, they are not willing to go to court (Interviews CZ2; CZ7). They prefer negotiations with the employer or maybe no action at all. Sometimes even the trade unions discourage employees from going to court, since they do not have much hope for a positive outcome and expect to achieve better results by informal negotiations with the employer. For example, around two thirds of women do not believe that they could have any success with a court proceeding following discrimination in the workplace (Putnová 2003). This can all be seen in connection with the overall low confidence in and the little satisfaction with

---

12   Reference for a preliminary ruling of 11 February 2006, Case C-437/05, *Jan Vorel v. Ceský Krumlov Hospital.*

the performance of courts in the Czech Republic in general (Interview CZ8; see also Anderson, Bernstein and Gray 2005).

Working time   Working time provisions are not applied properly in the Czech Republic. Overtime seems to be a serious problem and in many sectors a 'normal' phenomenon. The average working time in the Czech Republic is traditionally high and is considerably longer than in the EU15 (Government of the Czech Republic 2005, 9). Overtime should be paid or compensated with time off. However, there are many cases of malpractice and employers sometimes do not award extra free time or extra payment for overtime worked. Regularly, overtime on Saturdays or Sundays – times that should be factored higher – is not compensated adequately, if compensated at all. Another problem relates to the granting of breaks in so-called 'one-person enterprises'. For example, salespersons in small stores or night nurses are affected by this problem. These employees simply cannot take breaks due to the organization of their workplace. Habitually, employers do not shorten the shift and at the same time do not grant a higher salary for exceeding working time. In general, shifts are often too long (Interview CZ11).

Working time affairs 'traditionally' cause particular problems in the health care sector. It is characteristic that one of the first referrals for a preliminary ruling from the Czech Republic involves a hospital (see above). Another sector where overtime work occurs regularly is the food industry. Commonly, employers try to reduce their staff as much as possible, which automatically raises the overall working hours for those remaining. Workers have to perform up to 50 hours of overtime per month. Overtime is also reported as frequent in trade chains and in the telecommunication sector, where the overall personnel recently was reduced from 27,000 to 8,000 (Interview CZ13; Focus Group CZ2).

Because of the tense labour market situation and the relatively low wage levels, employees hardly ever protest against these abuses. The trade unions admit that it is often difficult for them to act in cases when employees work excessive overtime. It is often the employees themselves who want to work overtime, since they hope to earn more money (Focus Group CZ2).

In the field of working time, Czech employees appear to be a little better informed about their rights and entitlements. Contrary to the field of equality in the workplace it is a rather 'old' subject employees and their representatives have always dealt with. The topic of working time is much more in the focus of trade union work than equality in the workplace. In general, Czech employees hesitate to use courts as a way of conflict settlement. If an employee risks a court trial against his/her employer, it is very unlikely that the matter in dispute will be working time. Around 90 per cent of the cases pending have to do with unjustified dismissal. This again has something to do with the high unemployment rate: somebody who was already laid off then tries to get 'as much as possible out of it'. Somebody who has an employment contract would not risk court proceedings because of 'some little breaches of working time regulations' (Interview CZ5).

Another serious problem is the recording of the employees' working time. The Working Time Directive itself does not contain an obligation to record working time. Such an obligation only existed when the 'Article 22-opt-out' was considered

(Article 22c Working Time Directive), which is not the case in the Czech Republic. Nevertheless, there is a general obligation for employers 'to keep records of individual employees' working time, overtime work, stand-by and night work' (Section 94 Labour Code); but many employers keep incomplete records or none at all. This makes it difficult for labour inspectorates to conduct their inspections and for the individuals to enforce their rights (Interview CZ11).

Often employees are, more or less overtly, forced to agree to some specific equivocal clauses. One of these clauses is that the general salary, agreed upon in the labour contract, includes overtime. Therefore, the employee cannot demand any additional payment for overtime. The labour authorities and labour inspectorates receive a lot of complaints about this practice. However, it is not against the law, and there are no legal means for the persons concerned (Interview CZ13).

Equality in the workplace   Many of the provisions on equal treatment in the workplace are violated in everyday practice. For example, job advertisements are often discriminatory and gender-neutral terms are rarely used (Interview CZ4). References to the female gender are reserved only for traditional female occupations like office assistant, nurse or cleaning personnel (Pavlík 2004).

In the course of application procedures, young women are regularly requested to answer discriminatory questions about their family life, future plans and about possible pregnancies. The new Employment Act prohibits any form of discrimination in the access to employment (see Sections 2 and 4).[13] Because the knowledge on that new legislation prohibiting such practices is slowly disseminating among employers and staff managers, it is estimated that discriminatory questions during job interviews will be asked less frequently in the future. Nevertheless, this will not improve the situation for young women in the labour market. Some employers overtly express the opinion: 'What should you ask all these questions for? You can see it anyway when somebody is a woman and young.' (Focus Group CZ3).

The discrimination of young women is fostered by counterproductive labour law provisions in the field of leave in the case of the sickness of family members – in particular children. Sections 127 and 128 of the Labour Code and the Government Decree No. 108/1994 create a generous framework in this area.[14] Though both women and men are entitled to this type of leave, it is usually women

---

13   This Act describes itself as 'in accordance with law of the European Union' (Section 1) and therefore has to be interpreted in accordance with the case law of the ECJ. It is also accepted among Czech lawyers that posing discriminatory questions during a job interview is unlawful. However, a 2005 survey revealed that half of all women are asked discriminatory questions during job interviews. In the 30–39 age group, 73.9 per cent and in the 20–29 age group 61.3 per cent reported such experience. Women with university education (67.9 per cent), women living in Prague (71.9 per cent), and women with higher net income (71.4 per cent) are more affected (Kadavá 2005).

14   The sickness of a child is regarded as an impediment to work on the side of the employee. S/he may take leave during that time and must not be dismissed. The leave is generally unpaid, but in some specific cases also paid.

who care for ill family members. Employers therefore sometimes complain about the non-productive times of women and the substitutes they have to employ; the employment of young women is viewed as a risk (Interview CZ7; Focus Group CZ3).

Considering this, it is no surprise that unemployment among women is considerably higher than among men. Overall, in 2002 the unemployment rate among women was 9 per cent and 5.9 among men. The number of unemployed women also rises faster and women face higher rates of long-term unemployment (Pavlík 2004).

The most pressing and in fact most obvious problem for women in the labour market is unequal pay, which is not covered by our sample directives but by the Equal Pay Directive.[15] The gender pay gap remained rather constant during the 1990s and the first years of the following decade. Women have been earning around 75 per cent of men's wages. Female university graduates earn 65.1 per cent of their male colleagues' salary. In the group of senior management – where salaries are highest – women only earn 58.7 per cent of their male counterparts' salaries (Havelkova 2005, 35). It can be observed that the higher up the educational ladder women reach, the more likely they are to suffer pay inequalities. Generally, female university graduates have about the same earnings as men with a secondary school certificate – that is one level of education lower (Pollert 2003, 343).

Due to discrimination in the field of promotion, there is no area where women are adequately represented in decision-making positions. European legislation (see Articles 1 and 3 Equal Treatment Directive) and the Czech legal framework (e.g. Section 1 (3) Labour Code) both prohibit any form of discrimination concerning promotion. Some figures illustrate the current situation: regional presidents and the mayor of Prague: no women; top managers: 8 per cent; senators: 12 per cent; Board of the Czech National Bank: 12 per cent; Constitutional Court judges: 14 per cent; regional authority directors: 23 per cent; Supreme Court judges: 26 per cent (Havelkova 2005, 38). In the private sector the situation tends to be slightly worse. Women in top positions (boards of directors and supervisory boards) in the different branches are rare: In a few branches (e.g. the telecommunications and postal services) there are no women at all in such positions. In most of the positions women hold a share of 3 to 10 per cent (e.g. mining, electrical engineering and electronics, commerce, finance and insurance, services, construction). Only in some branches is the women's ratio higher than ten per cent (e.g. transport, metallurgy and metal processing, information technologies and systems, agriculture and wood exploitation) (Putnová 2003).

Although no reliable data exists, there is no doubt among experts that sexual harassment in the workplace is a widespread phenomenon. Estimates conclude that 30 per cent to up to two-thirds of Czech women have experienced or have encountered sexual harassment in the workplace. Further estimates assume that the vast majority of these cases are never reported and therefore do not have any

---

15   Council directive 75/117/EEC of 10 February 1975 on the approximation of the laws of the member states relating to the application of the principle of equal pay for men and women. See also Article 141 (1) EC Treaty.

legal consequences (Pavlík 2004; Havelkova 2005, 40). This is in line with the fact that there are no court cases dealing with sexual harassment. The few cases that came up were discussed publicly, but usually they were regarded as a kind of 'oddity' and not as the expression of a widespread practice. Sometime these cases were 'turned upside down', with the woman being blamed for wrongful complaining or irresponsible handling of the topic (Interview CZ12).

Homosexuals and their representatives in the Czech Republic currently are by and large satisfied with the legal situation in the area of equality in the workplace (Interviews CZ8; CZ10). Two other legal issues were more pressing in the past: firstly, the inclusion of sexual orientation in the anti-discrimination clause of the Constitution (Article 3 of the Charter of Fundamental Rights and Freedoms); secondly, the enactment of a law on registered partnerships that would, to a certain extent, give registered partnerships of same-sex couples the same status as heterosexual marriages (Procházka, Janík and Hromada 2003). Such a law ('Registered Partnership Bill') was recently adopted (see above).

The fight against discriminatory provisions in criminal law was finalized in 1990. Already prior thereto, Czechoslovakia was one of the first countries to decriminalize consensual sexual conduct among adults of the same sex in 1961. After the fall of the Communist regime, homosexual activity was still considered to be a crime if the partner was 17 or younger. The criticized Section 244 of the Criminal Code was abolished as early as 1990 (No. 175/1990 Coll.) when homosexuality was put on equal basis with heterosexuality in this field. Since then, the legal minimum age for heterosexual and homosexual relations is 15 years (Procházka, Janík and Hromada 2003, 10).

Experts regard discrimination or harassment of homosexuals in the workplace as rather infrequent (Interviews CZ8; CZ10). One of the few surveys among gays and lesbians that deal with this topic nonetheless reveals the following figures: 12 per cent out of a group of 267 respondents stated they were seriously discriminated against in some of their jobs because of their sexual orientation, or they at least considered it probable. Twenty-five per cent declared that they were confronted with some form of harassment in the workplace. Another interesting aspect in this context is to what extent homosexuals are open about their identity in their employment. Overall, 32 per cent are never open, 33 per cent are partly open and 35 per cent are open (Procházka, Janík and Hromada 2003, 23). Those who hide their sexual orientation do so typically because they fear negative consequences from their employer or their colleagues.

One reason why there is a relatively more tolerant attitude towards homosexuality in the Czech Republic compared to other countries is the fact that religion in general and specifically Catholicism have a weak influence on public discourse. This is sometimes stated as a reason for the progressive legislation and a less-strained public atmosphere (Interview CZ8, see also Procházka, Janík and Hromada 2003).

Discussing discrimination in the workplace based on religion in the Czech Republic is a difficult undertaking. The Czech Republic regards itself – and is often regarded – as the most atheistic country in Europe. The Czech identity is more linked to a pride on the 'brave heretics' (Hus) from the past and the country's historical opposition against the Catholic centres ('away from Rome and Vienna'). Forty years of Communist rule contributed to the marginalization of religion in the public sphere. Most of the parties – except the KDU-CSL – give no priority to religious topics or overtly oppose any demands from the side of the religious communities. All in all, religion plays a secondary role in the public and the private sphere. In the Czech Republic, it is not exceptional that a Catholic hospital hires employees that are not baptized. There are cases of Catholic schools where teachers are not Catholic and some are even 'more or less' openly practicing homosexuals (Interview CZ9).

There is no real religious majority that could be regarded as the 'dominating norm' that would be patronized by the state and its bodies. As an opinion poll in 2004 showed, only 32 per cent of respondents claimed to believe in God, while 49 per cent identified themselves as atheists (US Departement of State 2006, 1). They can therefore be regarded as the largest 'belief' group, followed by Catholics who officially represent around 39 per cent of the population. Of these 39 per cent only a very small part regularly attends church and declares their religious affiliation publicly. It is the Catholic community, which regards itself as discriminated in some respects. The government largely rejects property restitution claims by the Catholic Church. When it came to power, the Social Democratic Party stopped a procedure that should have restored large estates and around 700 buildings to the Catholic Church. The most prominent restitution conflict involves the St Vitus Cathedral, the centrepiece of the Hradcany Castle in Prague; the conflict has been ongoing for more than 13 years now, and it is heatedly discussed by the public (Asiedu and Horakova 2005). Other topics that play a certain role in public life are the funding of the churches, the possibility of religion as a school subject or clerks in hospitals and the army. Discrimination in the workplace based on religion does not come up as a public topic.

Courts

A further crucial condition for ensuring compliance with labour law is that the court system works reasonably well to ensure that individuals can claim their rights in court. In principle, anybody who was discriminated against can bring an action in court in the Czech Republic. This is guaranteed by the Constitution (Article 81), by the Charter of Fundamental Rights and Freedoms (see Chapter Five, Articles 36 et seq.) and by the specific provisions stemming from the Employment Equality Directive and the Equal Treatment Directive (e.g. Section 7 (4-6) Labour Code, Section 4 (10) Employment Act). There are no formal legal barriers that would deter the persons concerned from going to court.

However, the Czech court system does not provide a good possibility for individuals to enforce their rights. It is expensive and risky. Due to partly inconsistent adjudication there is legal uncertainty. The proceedings often last too long, sometimes more than three years. For several reasons the trade unions, the labour authorities and the labour inspectorates from time to time openly dissuade persons from seeking redress in the courts.

Because there are no labour courts, the civil courts deal with labour law affairs. Occasionally, 'labour senates' within a civil court are set up at the discretion of the president of the respective court. However, the experience is that these 'labour senates' do not improve the quality of the court trial significantly. As an alternative, trade unions want conflicts to be settled out of court. The employers are also quite dissatisfied with the court system. All in all, they do not regard courts as a strong possibility to sue their debts or to enforce their rights (Focus Groups CZ2; CZ3).

Overall, the most serious problem concerning the effectiveness of civil courts is the length of procedures: five years duration are no exception. The violations found by the European Court of Human Rights may act as an illustration for this problem.[16] Often the Czech Republic does not meet the requirements of Article 6 (1) of the European Convention for the Protection of Human Rights and Fundamental Freedoms, which demands that '... everyone is entitled to a fair and public hearing within a reasonable time ...'.

In general, it seems that the population does not trust the courts as institutions of conflict settlement. Once an employee has taken legal action, there is no real chance that the conflict will be settled in a conciliatory manner and, consequently, the employer is assumed to try to get rid of the recalcitrant employee as soon as possible (Interviews CZ7).

Another serious problem that seems to be specific for the Czech Republic is the partial lack of uniform adjudication. This is sometimes justified by a strong emphasis on the constitutionally enshrined independence of judges (see Articles 81, 82). Regularly different courts decide the same or a similar case differently. Thus, there is often no predictability and legal security for the people concerned. Experts even go so far as to suggest that there is one common Czech law, but because of the different jurisdiction there is in fact a North-Bohemian law, a South-Moravian law etc. Some judges are stubborn when it comes to implementing decisions of the higher courts. Another reason is a lack of information; judges of lower courts often do not know about recent judgements of higher courts. A former minister of justice stated that this is the main problem of the legal system (Interview CZ7; CZ14).

Sometimes the 'legal culture' in general is harshly criticized and even regarded as one of the main reasons for deficiencies in the future application of EU law. There is no case-law tradition, and judges orientate themselves more towards continental European law traditions, which are much closer to legal positivism than to the systematic of modern European law (Kühn 2005). There are examples of sound application of European law, especially by the higher courts of the

---

16   See *inter alia*: Judgement of the ECHR of 26 October 2004, no. 73578/01, *Pistorová v. the Czech Republic;* Judgement of the ECHR of 26 October 2004, nos. 47269/99 64656/01 and 65002/01, *Konecný vs. the Czech Republic*; Judgement of the ECHR of 2 November 2004, no. 76343/01, *Havelka v. the Czech Republic*; Judgement of the ECHR of 14 December 2004, no. 58358, *Becvár and Becvárová v. the Czech Republic*; Judgement of the ECHR of 21 December 2004, no 71551/01, *Skodáková v. the Czech Republic*; Judgement of the ECHR of 13 December 2005, no. 14044/04, *Thon v. the Czech Republic.*

Czech Republic. On the other hand, the practice of Czech ordinary courts was even described as 'anti-European' or 'isolationist'. There are serious doubts that many ordinary judges are fully aware of the fact that they have to deal with the bulk of European law and that it is up to them to ensure the priority of EU law over national law (Kühn 2005, 3–5).

Only few court cases have dealt with the relatively new topic of anti-discrimination law. Most cases reported have to do with discrimination on the ground of racial and ethnic origin (European Network of Legal Experts in the Non-discrimination Field 2005a; 2005b; 2006). Cases concerning sexual orientation or religion and belief cannot be found in the published reports. Also, the interviewees could not recall such a case. As for equal treatment between men and women in the workplace, there were hardly any cases at all (Interviews CZ4; CZ14). Consequently, there are no leading cases that could build up a deterrence effect. This again does not raise the pressure on employers to comply with equal treatment or anti-discrimination provisions. Experts also cannot specify to what extent the concept of the shift of burden of proof assists the victims to institute legal proceedings and to win discrimination cases, since there is a lack of experience in this domain.

The Ministry of Labour and Social Affairs prepared information booklets for judges to raise their general knowledge about the 'new' anti-discrimination legislation and especially the ECJ case law, but it is not certain if the distribution of these booklets has had any significant impact (Interview CZ7).

In public discourse, including the Czech parliament, the general threat of several anti-discrimination provisions possibly being misused in the court was stated. Misuse in the sense that an employee goes to court and seeks redress for an alleged violation though there was no discrimination at all and s/he wants to take revenge for another reason. The small number of cases suggests, however, that there is no such abuse, at least not on a larger scale.

As regards working time issues, it can be added that court procedures are in general not an ideal way to settle conflicts in this area, as they typically occur during employment. A lawsuit may trigger victimization and the employee might risk his/her dismissal. Also, an employee cannot win much in such a procedure about the breach of working time provisions. 'The employer always finds ways to get rid of such a trouble-maker.' This fact – seen in conjunction with the high unemployment rate – keeps many employees from going to the courts to enforce their rights (Interview CZ5).

Labour Inspectorate

There are a couple of statutory sources for the work of the labour inspectorates. The new Employment Act (No. 435/2004 Coll.) contains provisions that regulate administrative sanctions in the field of discrimination (Sections 139 and 140). The prescribed fines for natural persons and legal entities in case of violation can go up to 1 million CZK (approximately €35,714). However, basically the Employment Act is applicable before a contract of employment is concluded. Its main objective is to adjust 'state employment policy, the goal of which is attainment of full employment and protection against unemployment' (Section 1). Among other things, the Act regulates active employment policy, employment service, the employment of foreign nationals and unemployment benefits. It is not a specific Act for the enforcement of existing labour law and for the work of the labour inspectorates. For this purpose a new law was enacted, which established a new system of labour inspection.

Until 1 July 2005, mainly the labour authorities were simultaneously responsible for the supervision of the adherence of the labour law and the creation of jobs for the unemployed. This caused a structural conflict that prevented the labour authorities to fulfil their supervision task properly. They could hardly impose fines on employers for breaching working time regulations on one day and then ask them to cooperate in the creation of new jobs on the next (Interview CZ5). Therefore, a new law was enacted that established separate labour inspectorates that now fulfil the monitoring function (Act on Labour Inspections; No. 251/2005 Coll.). These new labour inspectorates are organized regionally. The labour inspectorate's office seat is in Opava (Section 2 Act on Labour Inspections) and there are eight further offices that are responsible for their respective districts. The Ministry of Labour and Social Affairs is the labour inspectorate's superior administrative body. It supervises them and coordinates their work (Section 2 (3) Act on Labour Inspections), but it does not conduct any inspection task on the ground.

Section 3 Act on Labour Inspections defines the scope and competencies of the labour inspectorates. The supervision of labour law provisions concerning working time is mentioned in Section 3 ('Inspectorates inspect the observance of obligations stemming from ... legal provisions determining working hours and periods of rest'). The task of supervising equal treatment and anti-discrimination provisions is not mentioned explicitly in this basic provision, which suggests that these topics do not have high priority in the work of the labour inspectorates.[17] The possible penalties for breaches of provisions in areas like 'working time' (Section 15) or 'occupational safety at work' (Section 17) are also much higher than those in the area of 'equal treatment' (Section 11).

The labour inspectorates can undertake unheralded investigations in the companies. The fines were raised considerably by the new Act (up to 2 million CZK = 71,430 Euro). There are misdemeanours for the different areas of labour law. The fines in the area of equal treatment (Section 11 of the Act on Labour Inspections) go up to 400,000 CZK. Fines in the area of working time (Section 15 of the Act on Labour Inspections) can go up to a maximum of 2 million CZK. The possibility of such high fines was the main reason why some MPs opposed the new act, because they are seen as a serious threat to the existence of many companies. In reality such high penalties are rarely imposed; the average penalty

---

17   The terms 'equal treatment between men and women', 'religion' and 'sexual orientation' are not mentioned in the new Act. Nevertheless, there is an 'indirect' competence for the labour inspectorates to supervise the observance of equal treatment and anti-discrimination law. In the Sections on misdemeanours and administrative offences, reference is made to the relevant basic anti-discrimination provisions in the Labour Code (Section 1 (4)).

is around 15,000 CZK (€536). Generally, the labour inspectorate's strategy is not to impose fines immediately. The guidelines of the Ministry of Labour and Social Affairs also suggest that the efforts to reach consensus with the employers should have priority. The employers first should be requested to discontinue overt shortcomings. In case an employer does not follow this request a fine will be threatened (Interview CZ13).

The latest data available on the Czech Republic show that in 2004 (when the labour authorities were still in charge of inspection tasks) the overall staff assigned to tasks in the authority consisted of 437 employees. The number of inspectors directly involved in the performance of supervision tasks was 232. They conducted 15,256 visits during 2004. On 235 occasions it came to a cessation of work activities, and the overall number of administrative fines imposed was 829 (European Commission 2004d). These figures hardly permit a conclusion on the efficiency of the current inspection system. Since the newly established labour inspectorate had not been in existence for too long when we conducted our interviews, it is even more unclear if it can fulfil its monitoring function successfully. It appears that the supervision is effective in some areas, while it is not in others (Interview CZ5). Occupational health and safety as well as working time affairs belong to those that have higher priority than e.g. equal treatment affairs. The labour inspectors themselves state that they do not have a lot of experience with this issue (Interview CZ13).

The efficiency of the state supervision in the field of equal treatment and anti-discrimination was evaluated in an NGO-report in 2004. Official statistics from 2002 showed that the labour authorities performed 10,583 audits in which 1,610 breaches of employment regulations were revealed. 228 cases had to do with discrimination, but the statistics do not further distinguish between the different grounds of discrimination and they do not disclose information about penalties or sanctions (Pavlík 2004, 27). Probably, most of the cases that have something to do with discrimination are linked to Roma. Furthermore, there are also some cases that have to do with unequal pay for equal work or work of equal value. Concerning the topics of discrimination on the ground of sexual orientation or religion no cases were reported (Bouckova 2005). The interviewed experts mentioned that in general only few penalties are imposed as a reaction to breaches of anti-discrimination provisions. If so, the penalties are usually not higher than 15,000 CZK (€536). The fact that discrimination is often hard to prove is a serious problem for the labour inspectors. In case of obviously disadvantageous treatment of an employee, employers give various reasons that are hard to verify. Such difficulties of evidence also occur in civil procedures, but there the principle of shifted burden of proof (§ 133a Civil Procedure Code) facilitates the situation of the party concerned. The shift of burden of proof basically does not exist in administrative procedures, as it is not provided for in the EU directives as well as in Czech legislation.

High unemployment and the tense situation on the labour market also hamper the work of the labour inspectors. To a certain extent they have to rely on the cooperation of the employees and their representatives since they can provide information in a fast and straightforward way. The new law on labour inspections also stipulates the participation of employees and trade unionists in the inspection process. Repeatedly, employees hide relevant information because they want to avoid conflicts with their employer. Finally, inspection protocols are signed which do not reflect the real situation of an enterprise. And it can happen that 'employees sign a protocol which says they have worked eight hours a day while it was ten or 12 in fact' (Interview CZ13).

The overall assessment of the effectiveness of the labour inspections is varied. The labour inspectorates themselves describe their inspection system as all in all effective and important for employees to be protected against illegal behaviour of their employers. Nevertheless, they confess that further resources would make it much easier for them to fulfil their tasks properly. Employers' organizations regard the existing system as adequate and do not see any need for a further strengthening of the labour inspectorates. Trade unions, in contrast, are pushing for a further expansion of the powers and resources of the labour inspectorates. NGOs are particularly dissatisfied with their work. According to them they are inactive and very sceptical concerning equal treatment issues (Interview CZ2).

Equal Treatment Body

There is no proper equal treatment body in the Czech Republic, as foreseen in Article 8a of the Equal Treatment Directive. A framework of different institutions, which can be described as 'three-body-system', deals with equal treatment or anti-discrimination affairs. These three bodies are: The Government Council for Equal Opportunities for Women and Men ('The Council'), The Unit for Equality of Women and Men ('The Unit') and The Committee for Elimination of All Forms of Discrimination against Women ('The Committee'). A general problem all these institutions share is a high fluctuation of staff. Consequently, there is a lack of 'institutional memory' within the framework of the 'equal treatment bodies' of the Czech Republic (Interview CZ15).

'The Unit' is simply an administrative department within the Ministry of Labour and Social Affairs and does not have any direct contact with the people concerned. In addition, it is not adequately staffed and has a weak position within the Ministry. One of its most important tasks is preparing the annual report about the fulfilment of the government's priorities and procedures in the promotion of equality for men and women (for example, see Ministry of Labour and Social Affairs of the Czech Republic 2005). Although it has competent and motivated leadership, it is quite understaffed, short of resources and therefore could not gain a decisive position in the equal treatment policy.

'The Committee' is a sub-unit of the 'The Government Council for Human Rights', which deals with the specific topic of equality in the workplace only as a sub-issue. Its agenda is linked to the UN Convention on the Elimination of All Forms of Discrimination Against Women (CEDAW) and not primarily to the equal treatment policy of the EU. In general, 'The Committee' has a considerable impact on the equal treatment policy within the Czech Republic (Pavlík 2004).

Only 'The Council' was created especially to promote equality between women and men and in fulfilment of Article 8a of the Equal Treatment Directive.

However, the 'The Council' is not a real body or institution (Interview CZ12). It is a council without any supervisory or enforcement functions that is subordinated to the government, installed by a governmental decree (Government Resolution No. 1033 of 10 October 2001). Its main function is an advisory one in the area of creating equal opportunities between women and men. It makes recommendations to the government, coordinates activities of the different ministries, identifies current problems in the equal treatment policy and evaluates the effectiveness of the implementation of the principle of equality of women and men. It has 23 members, who are delegated from several ministries, the two sides of industry and some NGOs.

The overall assessment of 'The Council' is that it has not gained an important role so far and does not have any significant effect on the equal treatment framework in the Czech Republic. It does not have any executive or controlling powers. The members – especially those from the ministries – do not attend the meetings regularly. It is short of resources (or rather hardly has any resources at all), and some of its members are not experts in the field of gender equality (Pavlík 2004, 23; Havelkova 2005, 18).

Apparently, the 'Government Council for Equal Opportunities for Women and Men' was installed for 'European reasons', to satisfy the Commission's demand for a fostering of the equal treatment policy during the negotiation process. In the 'Regular Report on Czech Republic's Progress Towards Accession' the Commission mentions the establishment of that body as an improvement in the equal treatment policy (European Commission 2002c, 82). The question is whether the Commission did not know about the inefficiency of that body or if it did not give much priority to that topic.

Other Aspects of Application and Enforcement

The Ministry of Labour and Social Affairs altogether plays an important role in the application and enforcement of social and labour law. It does not, however, conduct any supervision and enforcement tasks in enterprises. Nevertheless, it is the labour inspectorates' superior body and determines the guidelines of their work (Interview CZ13). Moreover, it provides all the relevant information and it is a central contact point for works councils, trade union organizations and other societal groups. Some of the most competent experts in the different areas of social and labour law work within the ministry and they are in regular contact with representatives of civil society. There is an ongoing exchange of information, which on the one hand supports the work of NGOs and trade unions and on the other hand is an important input to the legislative work of the ministry. For example, representatives of NGOs were involved in the drafting of the new Anti-discrimination Act. The trade unions had an important say in several amendments of the labour code and intensively collaborated in the drafting of new bills.

There are further institutions that have to do with the enforcement and the application of the Employment Equality Directive and the Equal Treatment Directive. There is the Government's Council for Human Rights, which is headed by the Deputy for Human Rights and has eight sub-committees. Some of these committees deal with discrimination based on sex, sexual orientation or religion and belief. This Council was commissioned by the government to prepare the legal transposition of the EU anti-discrimination directives, therefore the decisive preparatory work on the bill of the new Anti-discrimination Act was conducted there.

Moreover, there are so-called 'Gender Focal Points' in every ministry. Due to Government Resolution no. 456 of May 2001, every ministry had to install one part-time position (four hours per day) as of 1 January 2002 for an employee who is to be assigned the agenda of equal opportunities for women and men. Though the basic idea of such 'Gender Focal Points' is positive, there does not seem to be a specific strategy or concept behind their creation. In fact, they do not have sufficient resources, nor do they not have any competencies or powers, and they have little support from their superior administrative posts. All in all, the contribution of these 'Gender Focal Points' to the equal treatment policy in the Czech Republic is very small.

Conclusions and Improvement Strategies

As demonstrated in this chapter, the Czech Republic's problems and shortcomings in the overall implementation performance are manifold. Already the transposition phase was not completed successfully, since only the Working Time Directive was transposed essentially correct and in time. The two equality directives were not effectively incorporated in Czech legislation. The new Anti-discrimination Act, which would have fulfilled the European requirements comprehensively, was in discussion for several years, but finally failed due to lack of political support in parliament.

However, even if the shortcomings in transposition are serious, those in the field of application and enforcement are much more grave. Civil procedures are all in all not an effective way to enforce individual rights. The labour inspectorates cannot guarantee a continuous supervision of equal treatment and working time provisions. Further factors that hinder the proper application of labour law are the high unemployment rate, a weakly developed civil society as well as the novelty and complexity of the respective subjects. It is crucial to develop certain strategies with the aim to improve the overall situation.

First of all, it is of vital importance that the Czech Republic finally aligns its domestic law with the European requirements. The proposed Anti-discrimination Act, which would have been a promising reform in the field of equal treatment and anti-discrimination, finally failed in Parliament. At present, substantive legislative changes appear unrealistic, therefore, Czech legislation is now far from being in accordance with European law in this area. An equal treatment body – as demanded by the Equal Treatment Directive – needs to be installed soon. Currently, there is no institutional setting that supports the equal treatment and anti-discrimination policy adequately.

Improving the enforcement of social and labour law is of course also a question of resources, which would give way to a better supervision of the enterprises and their compliance with labour law provisions. The training of labour inspectors could be improved and new and complex topics like equal treatment and anti-discrimination affairs could receive more attention. More resources to civil courts would mean shorter proceedings, training of judges and a higher quality of the judgements generally.

The installation of labour courts could be a decisive improvement, allowing judges to specialize on labour law disputes. Furthermore, lay judges who are usually part of an industrial tribunal could bring experience and understanding for labour disputes to the task. Such a labour court system may enhance confidence among employees and employers as well and therefore increase the motivation to go to court if necessary. Stronger NGOs with enough resources could assist people in such endeavours. They are in direct contact with the people concerned. If they could provide legal aid to victims, more cases would be filed, thus creating a settled case law. A tax deduction system, as it exists in Slovakia and Slovenia, where employees can donate one or two per cent of their income tax to a NGO, could improve the financial situation of NGOs. However, such a system runs the risk of lopsidedness as enterprises may establish their own 'NGOs' and then request their employees to donate their tax deduction thereto.

The institutional setting needs to be improved. As already mentioned, an equal treatment body with adequate resources and competencies should be installed. Sub-units of such an equal treatment body within the regions would be very helpful to promote the equal treatment policy in rural areas as well. There is also the idea to establish an independent 'gender ministry' which focuses exclusively on gender relevant topics like equal treatment in the labour market and social security schemes, equal pay, education programmes in schools, domestic violence, etc.

Media campaigns that target the Czech society at large and that promote equal treatment and anti-discrimination as positive values would be very useful. Current governmental efforts in the media are only very cautious. Equal treatment and anti-discrimination affairs should also have their place in the curricula of schools to increase awareness among young people.

Provisions in the social security schemes that foster the unequal treatment of women and men should be abolished and a viable alternative encouraging men to involve themselves in childcare should be created. Another focus should be the realization of the principle of equal pay, neglect of which is the source of further problems.

Finally, groups that have similar interests in these areas can improve their cooperation. In the Czech Republic, trade unions and NGOs did not build up a closer cooperation in recent years. Together they could have a much stronger voice in public and when dealing with the government, thus having more impact in the decision-making processes and other policy areas.

In conlusion, the Czech implementation of the three selected EU directives was characterized by high degrees of political contestation at the transposition stage, which, in the case of the two equality directives, gave rise to a political deadlock that has so far prevented the successful completion of the process. What is even worse, the analysis has revealed serious shortcomings in the practical implementation of the law in terms of enforcement and application.

The next Chapters will show whether the other three countries display similar implementation styles. Finally, it will be up to the concluding Chapter to discuss how these patterns might be integrated into the 'worlds of compliance' typology developed for the EU15.

Chapter 3

Hungary

Emmanuelle Causse

Background Information

Political System

After the Turkish occupation in the sixteenth and seventeenth centuries and the Austrian Habsburg rule until 1918, the Hungarian state experienced only a short period of independence before the installation of the Communist regime in 1948 and the integration of the country into the Soviet block.

During the past 20 years, Hungary has changed tremendously. Even within the Communist block, the Hungarian state had been more liberal in the 1980s than the majority of Eastern Communist regimes. Private economic activity at a low scale, rudimentary forms of private enterprises, as well as a relative religious freedom were progressively allowed (Örkény and Csepeli 1994, 259; Phillips, Jefferey, Laslo and Hulme 2006, 594). The transition from a Communist system to a liberal democracy was a 'soft transition' without popular uprising. Already in 1988, before the fall of the Communist leader Kádár, who had been in power since 1956, political pluralism gained momentum (Örkény and Csepeli 1994, 260; Kontler 2002, 465). Hence, the transition was comparatively smooth. The political system was reformed and a democratic legal system respecting the rule of law was established. Economic liberalization brought new development perspectives as well as new difficulties. Still, Hungary managed to remain among the economic frontrunners of the new EU member states.

Hungary is nowadays a unitary state and a parliamentarian Republic, which constitutionally protects the separation of powers. Formally, the Soviet-style constitution of 1949 is still in force. However, important reforms amended most of the constitutional text (e.g. Act XXXI of 1989 and Act XL of 1990). The President of the Republic (*Köztársasági Elnök*) is a weak institution elected every five years by the parliament (Article 29/A of the Constitution). Presidential powers are largely ceremonial, but his/her political role depends, in practice, on the political party composition of the government and the parliament. The Hungarian Government's (*Kormány*) main functions are to defend and guarantee constitutional and public order, the rights of citizens and the implementation of the law. The government also ensures the formulation and implementation of social and economic policies, defines the state system of social welfare, health care services and their funding, and is involved in the development of foreign policy (Article 35 of the Constitution). The Prime Minister is elected by the parliament following a simple-majority vote, while Ministers are appointed by the President on the proposition of the Prime Minister (Article 33 of the Constitution). Governmental power is heavily concentrated in the hands of the Prime Minister.

The Hungarian National Assembly (*Országgyűlés*) is the supreme body of the state power and popular representation (Article 19 (1) of the Constitution). The parliament is a unicameral chamber consisting of 386 members elected for four years on the basis of two different representative principles: 176 members are elected in individual constituency elections on the basis of the principle of territorial individual representation, while 210 members are elected through party (national or county) lists and party-political representation. In parliament, legislative supervision is exercised during plenary sessions through questions and interpellations as well as in parliamentary committees – including a Committee on European Integration Affairs (*Európai Integrációs Bizottság*). In addition, some parliamentary control bodies have been created such as the State Audit Office and the institution of the Parliamentary Commissioners (Ombudspersons), which deal with civil rights, the rights of national and ethnic minorities and with data protection and freedom of information (Article 32/B of the Constitution). The independence of the parliament is guaranteed by the absence of an executive dissolution power. The Hungarian National Assembly's main role is to debate, amend and pass the bills that are prepared by the government and by the administration (Körösényi 1999, 260).

The Hungarian political system is a multi-party system in which parties play an important role (Kéri 1995, 134; Szoboszlai 1992, 327). In comparison with other Central and Eastern European countries, the different governments have been quite stable and came into power in regular elections. During the summer of 2004, due to poor opinion poll results, the socialist Prime Minister Péter Medgyessy was forced by his party to resign. He was replaced by another socialist: Ferenc Gyurcsány. This episode did not prevent the socialist-liberal coalition to enter the Hungarian electoral history in April 2006 when it became the first government to win consecutive terms since the regime change in 1989.

The newly established democracy and the pluralist political landscape were not sufficient to prevent the so-called 'transition blues', i.e. the growing disappointment after the transition (Csepeli 2000; Örkény and Csepeli 1994, 261). High at the beginning of the 1990s, the level of citizens' satisfaction and trust in the performance of democracy, the value of political participation and in the institutions themselves deteriorated quickly (Kontler 2002, 475); it remains at a low level. A recent study shows, for example, that only 25 per cent of Hungarians trust their government and only 19 per cent trust their parliament (Österreichische Gesellschaft für Europapolitik 2006, 8). Therefore, the stability of the Hungarian democracy has not been secured via 'high legitimacy', but rather via 'stable apathy' (Körösényi 2002, 334).

The perspective of EU membership prompted a second revival of citizens' political interest. Hungarian public opinion has consistently backed the political elite's aspirations to lead the country into the EU (Batory 2002, 6). The referendum

Table 3.1   Governments of Hungary (1990–2006)

Period	Main party	Coalition parties	Political orientation
May 1990– July 1994	Hungarian Democratic Forum (MDF) Prime Ministers: Antall and Boross (from December 1993)	Independent Smallholders' Party (FKGP), Christian Democratic People's Party (KDNP)	Christian-national government, anti-communist, conservative and pro-European
July 1994– July 1998	Hungarian Socialist Party (MSZP) Prime Minister: Horn	Alliance of Free Democrats (SZDSZ)	Social liberal and social democratic government, pro-European, and partisan of modernization
July 1998– May 2002	Federation of Young Democrats-Hungarian Civic Party (Fidesz-MPP) Prime Minister: Orbán	Independent Smallholders' Party (FKGP), Hungarian Democratic Forum (MDF)	Centre-right government, anti-communist and partisan of hard bargaining with the EU
May 2002–	Hungarian Socialist Party (MSZP) Prime Ministers: Medgyessy and Gyurcsány (since October 2004)	Alliance of Free Democrats (SZDSZ)	Social-liberal and social-democratic government, pro-European

Source: Körösényi (1999); Tóka (2004); own internet research.

on EU accession on 12 April 2003 showed large support (83.9 per cent), although participation was low (45.6 per cent). EU enthusiasm has, however, undergone significant changes since the end of the 1990s. According to survey results, the level of support increased continually until autumn 2002. At that time, 67 per cent of the respondents professed that EU membership would be a good thing. In spring 2003, just prior to the accession referendum, this support was still at 63 per cent (European Commission 2004a, 4). Since then, the number of EU membership supporters has decreased to such a point that Hungary is today one of the most euro-sceptic member states. The last Eurobarometer results show that only 39 per cent of the persons interviewed consider Hungarian EU membership a good thing, only 41 per cent perceive the benefits of EU membership as positive and only 39 per cent have a positive image of the EU conjecture – as opposed to 50, 52 and 44 per cent, respectively, in the European Union as a whole. Hungarian public opinion seems to be the most sceptical towards the EU among the new member states studied in this project (European Commission 2005b). The growing dissatisfaction towards the EU and national political structures also extends to the legal system.

Legal System

Separation of powers and basic guarantees of independence are established in the constitution and in constitutional jurisprudence (Open Society Institute 2001, 197). Article 50 (3) of the Constitution states that '*judges are independent and responsible only to the law'*. The Constitutional Court has ruled that there must be no political connection between the judiciary, the legislative and the executive power and everyone has to obey the judgements of the courts and no one may change, annul or supervise them (Decision 51/1992 [X. 23.] AB). The National Council of Justice (*Országos Igazságszolgáltatási Tanács*), created by the 1997 reform of the judicial system, is responsible for the management of the judiciary – previously exercised by the Minister of Justice (Article 50 (4) of the Constitution). It ensures the separation of the judiciary from the executive and the self-regulation of the judiciary.

According to the Constitution and following the 1997 reform, the judicial power is exercised at four-levels: the Supreme Court of Justice, the Appeal Courts (regional courts), the Metropolitan Courts or County Courts and the Local and Labour Courts (Hungarian Office of the National Council of Justice 2006; Kádár, Pardavi and Zádori 2003, 3). The 111 local courts are the first instance for minor crimes and small claims. The 20 labour courts (*Munkaügyi Bíróság*) act as first instance courts in legal disputes arising from employment and social security related issues. Since their creation in 1973, the number of cases resolved per annum in labour courts has increased progressively. Around 29,000 cases were filed in 2003 and their processing is considered to be slow – taking one to two years in first instance – but meticulous (Tóth, Nacsa and Neumann 2004, 2). The 20 county courts (*Megyei Bíróság*) constitute the second level of the judicial system. They hear appeals from local and labour court decisions. In cases specified by law, they have first instance jurisdiction – e.g. in civil cases with a minimum value of HUF 5 million (about €19,000) and criminal cases with a sentence up to life imprisonment. The Regional Appeal Courts (*Ítélőtábla*) were created in 2003 and 2005 to reduce the workload of the Supreme Court. Their establishment followed an important ruling from the Constitutional Court declaring that the failure to establish courts of appeal violated an express reference to an Appeal Court as part of the administration of justice in Article 45 (1) of the Constitution (Decision 49/2001 [XI. 22.] AB). These courts have no first instance jurisdiction and they adjudicate appeals to county courts' decisions. Finally, the Supreme Court of Justice (*Legfelsőbb Bíróság*) is both a trial court and the highest judicial authority, which plays an important role in interpreting doctrine. It is the final court of appeal of general jurisdiction and it may review cases on merits as well as on facts (Lichtenstein 2001, 4).

The Constitutional Court (*Alkotmánybíróság*) is charged with reviewing the constitutionality of laws and statutes brought before it, as well as the compliance of these laws with the international treaties that the government has ratified. Interestingly, the power to initiate constitutional review is not limited to institutions but also includes individual citizens affected by them. The Constitutional Court is comparatively powerful and constitutional judges have adopted quite an activist role (Boulanger 2003, 7).

In general, politicians and the public believe in the importance of recognizing and respecting judicial independence as a matter of principle. Still, public criticisms of the judiciary by government officials, in particular under the centre-right government between 1998 and 2002, have threatened the necessary social and political consensus to protect judicial independence (Open Society Institute 2001, 191–2). Moreover, the executive retains strong influence over the financing of the judiciary. Despite the formal right of the National Council of Justice to draft its own budget proposal, the government routinely submits a parallel proposal, which in practice is the one that is accepted by the parliament. This has led to the consistent under-funding of the judiciary and thereby limited the possibility to increase the number of judges and court staff in proportion to the growing caseload (Open Society Institute 2002b, 115–17). Since 2000, an attempt has been made to reduce judges' workload by expanding the authority of judicial clerks.

These remaining problems partly explain Hungarian citizens' scepticism towards their legal system. After the euphoria and strong expectations in the first years of transition, disappointment gained momentum again and trust in judicial institutions subsequently dropped. For example, in 1991, 73 per cent of the public trusted the courts as an institution. This rate dropped to 51 per cent in 1996 (Körösényi 2002, 334; 1999, 21). The lack of confidence in the court system was also mentioned in several interviews (Interview HU4, Focus Group HU1). Hungarian citizens' mistrust in the judiciary is not only inherited from the Communist era, but also due to suspicion of incapacity and sometimes corruption.

Adjustment to EU law has also brought a fundamental change to the Hungarian legal system (Kühn 2005, 1). After the elimination of the Communist legal principles and the adoption of a new set of rules, a second set of reforms came soon thereafter, already anticipating EU membership. Since EU accession, Hungarian courts fulfil a twofold role of applying both national and European law (Kühn 2005, 1). In order to ensure this principle, the familiarization of Hungarian judges with EU law – through for example training courses and exchange programmes – was necessary. Moreover, in 2003, in preparation of EU accession, the Hungarian parliament adopted an act on initiating preliminary rulings (Lomnici 2005, 7; Tünde 2003).

Socio-economic Background

By the time of EU accession, Hungary was considered to be one of the economic frontrunners of the new member states with a structure promoting social dialogue and a developed welfare state system.

The first transition years were characterized by two major economic phenomena: privatization and recession. As a result of the rapid privatization, as well as of the growth of small and medium-sized businesses and of the inflow of foreign capital, more than 80 per cent of the GDP was already produced by the private sector in 2001 (Galgóczi 2001, 51). The very sharp and deep recession experienced in Hungary in the early years of transition was a common phenomenon among the Central and Eastern European countries. Between 1989 and 1993, the GDP fell by 18 per cent. Investments, output and consumption also dropped. The inflation reached 35 per cent in 1991 resulting in a large external deficit. In 1995, in order to cope with this deficit, a rigorous stabilization package, the so-called 'Bokros package', named after the then-Minister of Finance, was introduced. Since 1997, the economic situation has improved. Output, investment and consumption augmented. The inflation slowed down and in 1999 the GDP again reached its 1989 level (Oblath and Richter 2002, 2) and continued to decrease since then (European Commission 2006e, 92). However, public deficit remains high and in July 2004 the European Council considered the Hungarian government deficit to be excessive (Council of the European Union 2004b). In 2005, it slightly increased to 6.1 per cent of the GDP (European Commission 2006i, 249).

Table 3.2   Basic economic developments in Hungary (1993–2004)

	1993	1994	1995	1996	1997	1998	1999	2000	2001	2002	2003	2004
Real GDP growth (%)	-0.58	2.95	1.49	1.32	4.57	4.86	4.15	5.20	3.85	3.50	3.39	4.65
Unemployment rate (%)	12.10	11.00	10.40	9.60	9.00	8.40	6.90	6.30	5.60	5.60	5.80	6.00
Inflation rate (%)	21.28	19.49	25.55	21.20	18.48	12.64	8.44	9.89	8.56	8.92	6.82	6.00
General government balance (% of GDP)	-6.62	-11.13	-7.56	-5.87	-7.24	-8.04	-5.62	-3.01	-3.55	-8.41	-6.37	-5.36

Source: OECD.

The employment situation has changed profoundly after 1989. Unemployment became one of the main curses of the transition period. Officially almost non-existent under Communism (0.2 per cent in 1989), unemployment peaked in 1993, at around 12 per cent (Employment Office 2004). This rate steadily declined afterwards, and further stagnated in the past few years, reaching 7.2 per cent in 2005 – a situation more favourable than the EU average (Organization for Economic Co-operation and Development 2006). However, disparities in terms of employment exist between social groups and regions (Hungarian Ministry of Employment and Labour 2004; Köllô and Nacsa 2005).

The Hungarian Constitution does not only state that 'the economy of Hungary is a market economy' (Article 9 (1)), but also that 'labour unions and other representative bodies shall protect the interests of employees, members of co-operatives and entrepreneurs' (Article 4).

With the collapse of the state-socialist system, new trade unions were formed and the Communist union underwent a fundamental reform. Six trade union confederations are presently active in Hungary; they are involved at the European level and associated with the European Trade Unions Confederation (ETUC). One of their major achievements is that they have not only survived the first decade of the transition and adapted successfully to the new conditions, but have also had an impact on the development of the new socio-economic system (Héthy 1999, 8). However, the liberalization of the economy, the privatization of state companies, the division of large enterprises or the downscaling of sectors with a traditionally high level of unionization weakened their influence in some parts of the industry.

Union membership has declined considerably and the prestige of unions among the population is nowadays comparatively low (Körösényi 1999, 133–5). A high percentage of Hungarians are sceptical about the unions' capacity to improve working conditions (Frege and Tóth 1999; Wierink 2006, 20). According to the Labour Force Survey, union membership among employees dropped to 16.9 per cent in 2004, that is 2.8 percentage points less than in 2001. This decline is also made obvious by the data of the Tax and Financial Control Administration, which recorded about 3.9 million union members before the transition in 1990 and only 600,000 in 2003 (Balogh and Neumann 2005).[1]

In order to defend the interests of their members, trade unions exploit two major avenues, which opened in the 1990s: the participation in public policy formation and implementation on the national level, including pre-legislative consultation via the Interest Reconciliation Council, and the cooperation with employers at company, sectoral and regional level (Héthy 1999, 11). They also use traditional means of action and protest such as demonstrations, strikes and road blockage. However, such measures have only rarely been employed (Körösényi 1999, 137–8).

The business and employers' organizations, by contrast, prefer to use lobbying and informal political consultation to promote their interests. They are organized in eight employers' confederations, which until recently formed an umbrella organization associated with the Union of Industrial and Employers' Confederations of Europe (UNICE) (Sissenich 2005, 176).[2] These organizations are frequently the successors of old organizations representing state enterprises. However, the newly instituted 'freedom of membership' led to a decline in members during the transition period (Wierink 2006, 26). The lack of representativeness of employers' organizations is partly due to the high sectoral and regional fragmentation – comparable to that of trade unions. Such developments reduce their capacity to negotiate (ibid.).

Social dialogue has been promoted in Hungary via the tripartite Interest Reconciliation Council (*Érdekegyeztető Tanács, OÉT*), composed of representatives from the union confederations, the employers' organizations and the government. Created in 1988 and restructured in 1990, the OÉT contributed to the preparation of new labour legislation (Héthy 2001, 21–6). Orbán's centre-right government abolished the OÉT, thereby weakening Hungary's structures of socio-economic

---

1   There are two official sources that supply data on trade union membership in Hungary: the Labour Force Survey of the Central Statistical Office, which includes a separate section on unionization every third year since 2001, and the Tax and Financial Control Administration, publishing annually information on union membership, since membership fees are tax deductible. The outcomes of these two statistical studies for 2003 and 2004 are quite similar and have been summarized by Eszter Balogh and László Neumann (2005). A report by the European Commission provides very similar data (European Commission 2006g, 25).

2   Since then, the umbrella organization was dissolved and the Confederation of Hungarian Employers and Industrialists (MGYOSZ - *Munkaadók és Gyáriparosok Országos Szövetsége*) is now the only Hungarian member of UNICE (Tóth and Neumann 2005).

consultation. Two newly established bodies, the National Labour Council and the Economic Council, which lacked a horizontal coordinating structure, replaced it. The socialist-liberal government in power after 2002 re-established the Interest Reconciliation Council and sought to negotiate with the social partners in this and more specialized fora (Sissenich 2005, 172; Taschowsky 2004).

Currently, the Interest Reconciliation Council acts as a consultative and – to a limited extent – decision-making forum as well as a channel of information for both sides of industry. Its competences cover primarily wage and employment issues but can also be extended to general economic policy. The government is expected to discuss issues of employment policy with the Interest Reconciliation Council and to ensure that agreements reached there are enacted in government policy and in legislation (Körösényi 1999, 138–9). However, despite participating parties' trust in tripartite cooperation, the Interest Reconciliation Council faced difficulties, 'of which representation and legitimacy problems as well as the weakness of the social partners could be regarded as the most important ones' (European Foundation for the Improvement of Living and Working Conditions 2003, 140). To cope with such problems, a law on national social dialogue regulating the OÉT was drafted and submitted to parliament in February 2006. The innovation of this proposal in comparison with former practice is that it identifies the circle of participants in the forum. Participation of trade unions and employers' associations will depend on a certain number of strict criteria stated in the law (Berki and Neumann 2006). At the time of writing the draft has not been passed by parliament.

The Hungarian Constitution also guarantees a developed welfare system (Articles 70/D to 70/F of the Constitution), the origins of which can be found between 1880 and 1910 in the creation of the social security system (Szikra 2002, 1; Phillips, Jefferey, Laslo and Hulme 2006, 587). Later, the so-called Communist welfare state ensured security – although at a relatively low level – to virtually the whole population in the areas of labour, pensions, health care, education, family benefits and housing (Ferge and Juhász 2004, 234). After 1989, the government tried to maintain the social benefits of the Communist regime. In 1995, the 'Bokros package' led, to a certain extent, to the dismantling of the former welfare system. All in all, social expenditure as a percentage of the GDP has been shrinking since 1990 (Ferge and Juhász 2004, 241). Between 1991 and 1998, state expenditures on education, health, culture and social provisions were cut by over 26 per cent in real terms, dropping from 38.2 per cent of GDP to 28.1 per cent (Phillips, Jefferey, Laslo and Hulme 2006, 588; Hoós 2002). Since then, they have stagnated with few improvements after the 2002 parliamentary elections (Ferge and Juhász 2004, 241).

The 1991 Employment Act institutes an unemployment insurance scheme in line with European standards (Ferge and Juhász 2004, 241–2). The public pension system was reformed in 1997 into a four-pillar system, including provisions for those who are unable to fulfil the eligibility criteria, an earnings-related scheme, a privately funded scheme and a voluntary private pension enacted in 1993 (Ferge 2003, 143). The legal pension age is quite similar to general European standards: 62 years for both men and women who have worked for at least 20 years. An independent Health Insurance Fund was established and three main sources of funding were developed: social insurance contributions paid by employers and employees, general revenues financed by the state budget and direct payments (Orosz, Klára and Czibere 1999, 3, 4; Gaál 2004, 113). Family benefits, quite developed in Hungary under the Communist regime, remained mostly the same. Parents with children are eligible for different benefits, the payment of which depends on the age of the children, their number, and the income of the family (Ferge and Juhász 2004, 242–3; Gál, Mogyorósy, Szende and Szivós 2003, 24). However, they encourage childcare at home rather than parents to work and are therefore not fully in line with the EU emphasis on the reconciliation of work and family life (Ferge and Juhász 2004, 242–3).

Relevant Aspects of Societal Order

Particularly with a view to EU standards in the field of minority protection, it should be mentioned that the Hungarian society is multicultural. Act LXXVII of 1993 on the Rights of National and Ethnic Minorities recognizes 13 national minorities, i.e. ethnic groups: Armenian, Bulgarian, Croatian, German, Greek, Polish, Roma, Romanian, Ruthenian, Serbian, Slovakian, Slovenian and Ukrainian. The Minorities Act provides them with a degree of cultural autonomy, educational and linguistic rights as well as a system of local and national minority self-government (Kádár, Farkas and Pardavi 2001, 5).

The Roma are the largest minority and constitute the most disadvantaged group in Hungarian society. The situation of the Roma is problematic, as in many other Central and Eastern European countries (European Commission 2003a, 36). They face significant difficulties in terms of educational attainment, access to public service and health care, and their unemployment rate is three times higher than in the non-Roma population (European Commission against Racism and Intolerance 2004, 18–21).

Persons with disabilities, although protected against discrimination and subject to positive measures to facilitate their inclusion, still face barriers in access to services (Halmai 2005b, 67–8). Their labour market participation is low, the majority receive passive benefits and many of them are threatened by the risk of social exclusion (Hungarian Ministry of Employment and Labour 2004, 6). Under the Communist regime, the Hungarian Constitution affirmed the equality of men and women. However, the de jure equality was far from the de facto equality. It was assumed that gender equality had been achieved through the law and that so-called 'women's problems' had been resolved through a well-developed state subsidized childcare system, paid pregnancy leave, infant care and so on. The initial Communist project to radically change the traditional representations and expectations for femininity and masculinity was rapidly abandoned and the private sphere remained the space for traditional and hierarchical gender ideologies (Szabó 2003, 32).

After the regime change, the situation of women did not really improve. 'Resurgent gender discrimination, a withdrawal of state support for childcare and parental leave, weak feminist movements, and the low level of women's participation in parliament all suggest the decline in women's position' (UNIFEM 2006, 19).

Women's employment characteristics compared to men show a varied picture. Unlike most member states, their unemployment rate is lower than that of men (5 and 6.3 per cent respectively). However, one should not forget that women's inactivity rate is exceptionally high: almost 47 per cent of women in the active age group were inactive in 2002 (Hungarian Ministry of Employment and Labour 2004; UNICEF 1999, 26).

The availability of services for childcare and care for family members, one of the basic requirements for the participation of women in the labour market and the reconciliation of family life and employment, has been weakened since the introduction of the liberal economic approach in Hungary. The number of places in day nurseries for children up to three years decreased dramatically in the beginning of the transition period and then at a smoother pace from 1990 onwards. However, no adequate replacement was provided. As regards care services for sick or elderly family members, the situation is characterized by weakness in support structures and low levels of access (Halmai 2005a, 72–3; UNIFEM 2006, 35–9; Hungarian Ministry of Employment and Labour 2004, 4).

Women's participation in national politics is below the EU average. As of October 2006, the rate of women in the national government with senior minister position was only 14 per cent – 10 percentage points below the EU average – while the rate of junior ministers was 25 per cent – close to the EU average. The rate of women in the National Assembly was only 10 per cent, compared to 23 per cent in the EU as a whole (European Commission 2006d).

The situation of homosexuals has improved progressively. Homosexuality was decriminalized in 1961, but it was only in the 1990s that sexual minorities were granted more rights. On 8 March 1995, the Constitutional Court struck down a law barring homosexuals from common-law marriage. In Hungary, common-law and formally married couples have the same rights. Any couple that lives together permanently is considered married under common law. The court stated that if 'defining [formal] marriage as a union between man and woman is not an unconstitutional discrimination', the previous law limiting partnerships – i.e. the so-called 'common-law marriage' – to 'those formed between adult men and women' was unconstitutional and ordered the parliament to take the necessary steps to recognize same-sex partnerships by 1 March 1996 (Decision 14/1995 [III.13.] AB). On 21 May 1996, the parliament opened common-law marriage to same-sex couples, giving them access to most marriage-related rights except adoption. Thereby, Hungary, without allowing formal marriage between gay couples, was the first Eastern European country to extend most of traditional partner rights to same-sex couples.

Also, in 2002, after several petitions to the Constitutional Court and a recommendation from the European Parliament Committee for Foreign Affairs, the Constitutional Court ruled that Articles 199 and 200 of the Hungarian Penal Code were unconstitutional and had to be abolished (Decision 37/2002 [IX. 4.] AB). These articles were discriminatory in the sense that they not only stated a different age of consent for sexual contacts between same-sex partners

(18 instead of 14 normally), but also qualified such acts as 'fornication against nature' (Takács 2005).

Although legal protection of gays and lesbians and their social opportunities have increased in recent years, public opinion towards them is still rather negative. Surveys state that in 2003, around one-third of Hungarian respondents viewed homosexuality as an illness and about every seventh respondent considered it to be a form of deviant behaviour. On the other hand, almost one third considered homosexuality as a private matter of the individual, but only one tenth regarded the right to choose a same-sex partner as a basic right (Takács 2005, 4).[3]

This is also confirmed by the limited visibility of gays and lesbians in the public sphere. They often do not disclose their sexual orientation and their participation in NGOs is limited. However, a few specific gay, lesbian and bisexual organizations have been set up in recent years in order to enhance the visibility of their interests; to lobby for legal protection against sexual orientation discrimination and for the recognition of legal rights for homosexual individuals and couples; and to assist them in the defence of their rights.

Hungary has a long tradition of religious tolerance. In 1895, Law XLIII proclaimed religious freedom for all and opened the possibility to set up 'recognized' denominations. During the Communist regime, religious freedom existed only according to the Constitution. Persecutions were frequent at the beginning of the regime. Then, in the 1970s and 1980s, worship within religious buildings was tolerated, but strict state control remained. This resulted in a strong secularization of the Hungarian society, even if churches turned out to be the largest surviving forces of civil society after the fall of Communism (Schanda 1999, 298–301). There is no state religion in Hungary. 'Freedom of thought, freedom of conscience and freedom of religion' are guaranteed by the Constitution and 'the church and the State shall operate in separation' (Articles 60 (1) and 60 (3) of the Constitution respectively). Religion is regarded as a private matter and Hungarians keep their religious belief and practice confidential.

'Religiosity' is also lower than in most countries of Western Europe. Although religious identity is considered to be in one way or another part of the personal identity for more than 95 per cent of the population, church attendance is less than 15 per cent (Schanda 1999, 298). According to a 2001 census conducted by the Statistical Office, Hungarians claimed affiliation to 260 different religious communities (Hungarian Central Statistical Office 2006). Catholicism remains the main religion representing more than half of the population, followed by the Calvinist and the Lutheran churches, while about 15 per cent of the population do not declare a religious affiliation (Hungarian Central Statistical Office 2006).

However, anti-Semitism remains a serious problem in Hungary. It reportedly manifests itself through anti-Semitic acts and expressions such as slogans voiced by hooligans during football matches or as public denial of the Holocaust (European Commission against Racism and Intolerance 2004, 21).

---

3   Surveys conducted by the Medián Opinion and Market Research, Omnibus Research Project 1997, 2002, 2003, Sample size N=1200.

Transposition of EU Directives

Having developed stable institutions guaranteeing democracy, the rule of law and human rights as well as a market economy, Hungary was considered to comply with the Copenhagen political criteria, which are 'a prerequisite for the opening of any accession negotiations', and was then included in the 'first wave' of six countries with which the Luxembourg European Council of December 1997 agreed to open EU accession negotiations (European Council 1997). During the negotiation phase, Hungary was subject to intensive screening by the European Commission on the transposition into national legislation of 31 chapters of the *acquis communautaire*.

The successive Hungarian governments were willing to comply with the Copenhagen criteria and, even if social policy was not considered to be the most relevant chapter of the *acquis communautaire*, efforts were made to meet EU requirements in that field under the close inspection of the European Commission. Therefore, in its final report on Hungary's preparation for membership, the European Commission stressed that 'Hungary is essentially meeting the commitments and requirements arising from accession negotiations in the areas of labour law, equal treatment of women and men, health and safety at work, social dialogue, public health, employment policy, social inclusion and social protection and is expected to be in a position to implement this *acquis* as from accession'. However, it also stipulated that 'some legal adjustments are needed [notably] in the fields of labour law, equal treatment of women and men at work' (European Commission 2003a, 36). Three years after this report and two years after accession, it is therefore interesting to analyse whether the Working Time Directive, the Employment Equality Directive and the Equal Treatment Directive have been transposed correctly into national legislation.

Working Time

Before 2001, Hungarian labour legislation was already quite developed and strongly inspired by EU regulations, the German social model, and influenced by advice from international agencies such as the International Labour Organization. Therefore, only relatively minor legal changes were required to comply with the Working Time Directive. The 2001 amendment was an effort to transpose nine EU directives and thereby to complete the harmonization of Hungarian labour law with the *acquis communautaire*. However, while opposition parties and trade unions accepted the adoption of the other eight directives, they strongly opposed the new regulation on working time (Act XVI of 2001), which became a highly controversial political issue.

The then centre-right government was accused of proposing overly flexible legislation that was disadvantageous for employees. Trade unions tried to organize a mass demonstration and the largest opposition party made a motion of referendum to prohibit Sunday work. While the opposition and trade unions accused the government of being unwilling to compromise and avoiding the use of social dialogue institutions, the government accused them of still being anchored in their Communist past (Neumann 2004, 14–15). No agreement was reached with the social partners on the amendment of the Labour Code and the rather complicated draft law remained largely incomprehensible for the public (Interview HU2, HU9B). Ironically, even if the 2001 amendment introduced greater flexibility allowing employers to decrease the cost of employment (Köllô and Nacsa 2005, 32), most of the contested provisions had existed previously (Interview HU2, Interview HU9B), hence some perceived the controversy as a pretext for political opposition on doctrinal questions (Interview HU9B).

In 2002, the new socialist-liberal government adopted Act XIX, officially to revise some of the most controversial provisions of the 2001 reform (Neumann 2004, 17; Tóth and Neumann 2005). In reality, this amendment was more a symbolic attempt of the new government to satisfy the electorate and the trade unions and, in actual fact, changes were minor (Interview HU2, Interview HU9B). The new working time legislation is still seen as too liberal by many experts and as too inflexible by others.[4]

All in all, national authorities seem to believe that EU working time provisions have been correctly implemented and that the 2003 Working Time Directive, which brought only some tiny changes, did not necessitate amendments of the national legislation. However, when one looks at the national legislation and the Labour Code more precisely, several aspects of the Hungarian working time legislation are not in compliance with the Working Time Directive or its spirit.

First, Section 124 (1) of the Labour Code stipulates: 'employees shall be entitled to two resting days each week, one of which must fall on a Sunday'. This provision is in perfect accordance with the minimum 35 hours weekly rest period provided for in Article 5 of the Working Time Directive. Experts deplore, however, the fact that the Labour Code does not ensure that these two days have to be consecutive, as prescribed for by the 35 hours weekly rest period provided for in the Working Time Directive (Interview HU9B). Moreover, the Labour Code differentiates, in opposition to the directive, between ordinary working time and overtime. This means that in practice an employee can be required to perform overtime during his/her weekly rest period, which contradicts the logic of the directive.

Secondly, Sections 117/B (1) and 119 (3) of the Hungarian Labour Code, which stipulate that the working time of full-time employment shall be 40 hours and shall not exceed 48 hours, are not based on employee working time calculation but on employment working time calculation (Interview HU3A). Thereby, they do not prohibit that an employee works more than 48 hours provided that the employment is split up between different work contracts. However, this interpretation is not in opposition to the directive, which is silent on the subject. Furthermore, as pointed out by a labour law expert, Section 103 of the Labour Code limits this practice,

---

4   Some further minor changes were made later. Among them was the 2003 Act XX transposing the Working Time Directive of 2000 (directive 2000/34/EC) and creating some specific new regulations for healthcare workers and for mobile road transport workers (Act LXXXIV of 2003 on certain aspects of healthcare activities and Act XI of 2005 on road traffic).

since it stipulates that an employee has to be fit for work, which is hardly the case if someone has two full-time jobs (Interview HU9A). Moreover, while under Socialism multiple jobs were not an infrequent phenomenon, formal second jobs seem to have mostly disappeared from the Hungarian market to represent only about 1.7 per cent in 2002 (Köllô and Nacsa 2005, 32).

Finally, like in many other EU member states, Hungarian legislation is not in compliance with the changes brought by the ECJ in the definition of working time and on-call work. In several of its rulings, notably the *Simap* case of 3 October 2000 and the *Jaeger* case of 9 October 2003, the Court stated that on-call duty should be considered working time, even where the employee is provided with a bed to sleep on the employer's premises. This case law, as part of the *acquis communautaire*, should be implemented at the national level. The reality in Hungary, like in most EU member states, is quite different. On-call duty – defined as the period when an employee is required to be present 'at a place and for a duration specified by the employer' – is limited to 72 hours a week and 168 hours a month (Section 129 (4) of the Labour Code) and is paid at 40 per cent of the basic wage (Section 148 (1)). However, it is not as such considered working time. The Labour Code stipulates indeed that if the time used for actual work during on-call duties is not measurable, the whole period of on-call time qualifies as working time. As a consequence, in the opposite case, on-call duties as a whole are not treated as working time, contrary to ECJ case law (Interview HU9B, Focus Group HU3).

However, several cases, mainly concerning the payment of doctors' on-call duties, have recently been decided. The Hungarian Supreme Court ruled on 14 June 2006 that all hours spent on-call by doctors must be counted as working time and are subject to monetary compensation, even if they were not required to carry out any duties during that period. This judgement upholds several labour court decisions and is in line with the European Court of Justice's *Simap* and *Jaeger* jurisprudence. If such a decision is seen as an important step towards the recognition of on-call as working time, the government seems to be reluctant to modify the legislation and support the recognition of on-call duty as working time in EU negotiations on the amendment of the Working Time Directive.[5] In order to find a solution to this dilemma, trade unions would like to negotiate the payment of an average time for doctors on on-call duty with their counterparts 'since it is currently rather hard to differentiate what can or cannot be considered as working time' (Focus Group HU3).

Given the above-mentioned shortcomings, the Hungarian working time legislation does not fully comply with European regulation on the subject. In the field of equality in the workplace, similar remarks can be made concerning the compliance of Hungarian legislation with the Equal Treatment Directive and the Employment Equality Directive.

---

5   See, for example, the position of the Hungarian government as expressed in the European Commission Memo on the 'Frequently asked questions about Working Time', MEMO/04/1, Brussels, 5 January 2004.

Equality in the Workplace

With regard to equality, the most important and comprehensive realization in the Hungarian legislation was the adoption of Act CXXV on Equal Treatment and the Promotion of Equal Opportunities in December 2003 (Krizsán and Pap 2005, 11). Nevertheless, the prohibition of discrimination was not a new concept introduced by the *acquis communautaire*. Anti-discrimination clauses already existed during Socialism. However, this interdiction was theoretical since no legal action was possible due to the lack of procedural rules, sanctions and institutions, but also due to the absence of political will. After 1989, the protection of equal treatment and the prohibition of anti-discrimination were reinforced. Therefore, prior to 2003 and the new Act, Hungarian law already contained a certain number of legal references to anti-discrimination in its Constitution, Labour Code, Civil Code and procedural laws.

The cornerstone of the anti-discrimination legislation is Article 70/A of the Hungarian Constitution, which stipulates that the Republic of Hungary shall respect the human rights and civil rights of all persons in the country without discrimination on the basis of race, colour, sex, language, religion, political or other opinion, national or social origin, financial situation, birth or upon any other grounds whatsoever (1). The law shall provide for strict punishment of discrimination on the basis of Paragraph 1 (2). The Republic of Hungary shall endeavour to implement equal rights for everyone through measures that create equal opportunities for all (3). Article 66 (1) adds, the 'Republic of Hungary shall ensure the equality of men and women in all civil, political, economic, social and cultural rights'.

The Hungarian Constitutional Court has interpreted Article 70/A broadly. It stated that unequal treatment is not unconstitutional if a well-based social objective or a constitutional right may only be achieved by this measure. This 'positive discrimination' is, however, limited by the prohibition to restrict the core regulations of human dignity and basic individual rights (Decision 9/1990 [IV. 25.] AB). Moreover, the Constitutional Court has established that the anti-discrimination clause applies equally to natural and legal persons (Decision 59/1992 [XI. 6.] AB) and to the entire legislative system, including the rights that do not form part of human rights or essential citizens' rights (Decision 61/1992 [XI. 20.] AB). Finally, in two decisions the Constitutional Court also 'established that discrimination on the basis of sexual orientation was discrimination on 'other grounds' according to Article 70/A Paragraph (1) of the Constitution' (Decision 14/1995 [III. 13.] AB and Decision 20/1999 [VI. 25.] AB) (Kádár and Farkas 2005, 5).

There has been an on-going debate whether the Constitution's provision formulates an obligation only for the state or for private actors as well. On the one hand, if the term 'discrimination described in Paragraph (1)' included in Paragraph (2) of Article 70/A is taken to refer to the whole Paragraph (1), the requirement of strict punishment concerns only the Hungarian Republic's violation of its obligation to guarantee the given rights without any discrimination. On the other hand, if the term is interpreted as referring to only the second part of Paragraph

(1) listing the grounds of discrimination, Paragraph (2) provides for the severe punishment of any kind of discrimination committed by any actor, including private ones (Kádár and Farkas 2005, 6).

In addition to the Constitution, other legal texts prohibited discrimination, e.g. the Labour Code in its Section 5 (1). Therefore, the European Commission stated in its 1998 *acquis* screening that Hungary complied with six equality directives (European Commission 1998). Remaining directives at that time were implemented by inserting two new paragraphs in the Labour Code in the 2001 amendment (Act XVI of 2001) (Bitskey and Gyulavári 2005, 3). Still, there was no clear and unified set of rules on equal treatment and anti-discrimination issues. The first wave of transposition was reached by sectoral law rather than by comprehensive anti-discrimination legislation (Krizsán and Pap 2005, 9).

In order to comply with the new requirements of the Racial Equality Directive and the Employment Equality Directive (directives 2000/43/EC and 2000/78/EC respectively), clear definitions, specific institutions and effective, proportionate and dissuasive sanctions were needed. The necessity of a new wave of transposition led to an intensive debate in Hungary between those in favour of branch level regulations and those more in favour of the adoption of a comprehensive general act. In November 2002, soon after the change from the centre-right government to the socialist-liberal government, the new Ministry of Justice (*Igazságügyi Minisztérium*) – in charge of equal treatment questions – finally recognized the need for a comprehensive anti-discrimination policy. Under the pressure of some NGOs and human rights activists, the ministry decided that it was necessary to adopt a general rule that would comprehensively transpose the Employment Equality Directive, the Equal Treatment Directive and the Racial Equality Directive. The Ministry of Justice prepared a legal concept in autumn of 2002, which was transmitted to all ministries, NGOs and the general public via the ministry's website. Taking into account the submissions made during this first phase, the ministry prepared a draft version, which was finally voted on by the parliament on 27 December 2003 and which became Act CXXV on Equal Treatment and the Promotion of Equal Opportunities. It entered into force in January 2004.

The new Act defines several ways of violating the equality principle: direct and indirect discrimination, harassment, unlawful segregation, victimization and instruction to discriminate (Article 7 (1)). It also gives a very broad list of characteristics in relation to which discrimination is prohibited, and it even provides for further grounds to be included. The list in Article 8 includes: 'sex, racial origin, colour, nationality, national or ethnic origin, mother tongue, disability, state of health, religious or ideological conviction, political or other opinion, family status, motherhood (pregnancy) or fatherhood, sexual orientation, sexual identity, age, social origin, financial status, part- or fixed-term employment relationship or other relationship related to employment, membership of an organization representing employees' interests, or any other status, attribute or characteristics'. The Hungarian legislation thus goes well beyond the minimum requirements laid down in the European directive.

The concept of covering all grounds of discrimination in one piece of legislation was subject to strong criticisms by both women and Roma organizations, which stressed the risk of diluting the effective protection of the different individual categories (Krizsán and Pap 2005; Bitskey and Gyulavári 2005, 10). Other criticisms focused on some specificities of the Act itself. Three of these criticisms are linked to the lack of total compliance with the Equal Treatment Directive and the Employment Equality Directive.

Turning to the first transposition problem, Article 7 (1) of Act CXXV prohibits harassment, but it does not prohibit sexual harassment explicitly, thus contradicting the 2002 Equal Treatment Directive. In the Act, harassment is defined as 'a conduct violating human dignity with the purpose or effect of creating an intimidating, hostile, degrading, humiliating or offensive environment around a particular person' (Article 10 (1)). No specific definition or even reference is made to sexual harassment. NGOs and members of the Equal Treatment Authority see this absence as a major problem endangering the protection of victims of sexual harassment (Interviews HU4, HU11, HU13), while representatives of the Ministry of Justice justify it. According to them, 'the difference between this Act and the 2002 Equal Treatment Directive is that the directive is explicitly limited to equal treatment between men and women, while the Hungarian act has a far larger scope' (Interview HU12). They add that the Act prohibits discrimination not only against women, but also against homosexuals, older people, persons with disabilities, people from different religions, Roma, foreigners, and so on. If they had made a 'specific reference to sexual harassment in the Act, [they would also] have had to integrate explicitly the prohibition of harassment against Roma, people with disabilities, people with different belief, etc.'. Hence, they stress that 'the definition of harassment incorporated in the 2003 Act is a general one, which is intended to include all types of specific harassments and, implicitly, also sexual harassment' (Interview HU12). Given the implicit rather than explicit character of the legal measures against sexual harassment, we are not sure whether this interpretation would be confirmed by the ECJ.

Although the deadline to transpose the 2002 Equal Treatment Directive – which includes the definition of sexual harassment – expired in October 2005, the European Commission has so far not launched any infringement procedure against the Hungarian government on that specific issue. The Commission has indeed asked for explanations and has, as it seems, accepted the reasons stated by the Hungarian Ministry of Justice (Interview HU12). During a meeting in Brussels between the ministries in charge of equal treatment questions and the European Commission in June 2005, this question was once again raised. It was reported that representatives from the Commission themselves have stated that the 'definition of general harassment and its prohibition offer enough protection and that they do not expect more' (Interview HU6). However, one should mention that the government is planning to amend Act CXXV. The draft bill submitted to parliament in December 2005 could be a first attempt to bring the law into line with the directive without referring to it, since it proposes, among others, to define harassment as 'offensive behaviour of a sexual or other nature'. If adopted, this amendment will, however, not provide full harmonization with the directive (European Commission 2006a, 29). So far, the bill has been approved by the parliament, but the President of the Republic has referred it back to the parliament for modifications (European Commission 2006b, 33).

The second transposition problem is related to the exemption clause in Act CXXV, which concerns all types of discrimination while the exemption included in the two directives is only applicable in cases of indirect discrimination. Article 7 (2) of the Act stipulates that 'the principle of equal treatment is not breached by behaviour, measures, conditions, omissions, instructions or practices based on a characteristic related to any of the grounds referred to …, provided that they are found by objective consideration to have a reasonable explanation directly related to the relevant relationship'.

This larger exception scope makes it possible that more potential cases are exempted from the principle of anti-discrimination than permissible under the two EU directives. The drafters of the Act justify this provision once again citing its large scope. According to them, 'the Act covers more areas and more social 'groups' than the directive, therefore there was a need to strike a balance between reasonable cases and prohibition' (Interview HU12). They add that direct unequal treatment is sometimes needed, for example, in school or classes reserved for persons with disabilities. Such unequal treatment must however have a reasonable explanation founded on an objective consideration (Interview HU1). This solution seems acceptable to the European Commission, which so far has not commented on this specific question.

Turning to the third transposition problem, the shift of the burden of proof is limited by the provision included in Article 19 (1) of Act CXXV. Instituted by the Burden of Proof Directive,[6] the Employment Equality Directive and the Equal Treatment Directive, it aims to put an end to one of the most difficult obstacles victims of discrimination have to overcome: how to prove alleged discrimination. Therefore, the directives state that the plaintiff has to establish only 'facts from which it might be presumed that there has been direct or indirect discrimination' (Article 10 Employment Equality Directive). If s/he does so, then the burden of proof shifts to the defendant. Such a provision has existed in Hungary since the adoption of the Labour Code in 1992 (Section 5 (8) of Act XXII on the Labour Code). However, it was limited to labour disputes and raised serious problems in legal practice because it was not clear which facts or evidence the plaintiff should provide to the court (Bitskey and Gyulavári 2005, 15). Therefore, Act CXXV aimed to clarify this rule. Article 19 (1) states that 'the injured party or the party entitled to assert claims of public interest must prove that:

1) the injured person or group has suffered a disadvantage, and
2) the injured party or group possessing characteristics defined in Article 8'.

If these two elements have been established, the burden of proof shifts to the other party. In the eyes of some anti-discrimination activists interviewed, this

6   Council directive 97/80/EC of 15 December 1997 on the burden of proof in cases of discrimination based on sex.

provision is too strict for the plaintiff, since the burden of proof shifts only when s/he has already proven that s/he has suffered a disadvantage and not only established 'facts from which it may be presumed' so, as stated in the directive (Focus Group HU1, Interviews HU5, HU13, see also Kádár and Farkas 2005, 46). This provision might raise application difficulties (Tünde 2003; Kádár and Farkas 2005, 46), for example, in harassment cases where the anti-discrimination principle may be violated, even without obvious disadvantage or detriment (Interview HU5).

For all these reasons, the Hungarian legislation on anti-discrimination and equality, although very developed, is not in full compliance with the European directives. In both areas, equality at the workplace but also working time, some minor transposition problems exist. However, while these defects need to be solved, seen from a larger perspective, Hungary is respectful of EU social law, at least on paper. Looking at practical application, a different picture emerges.

Application and Enforcement

It seems that the practical application of the legislation on equal treatment and working time is rather problematic in Hungary. This is mostly due to serious enforcement deficiencies.

Application Problems

The transposition of the Working Time Directive, the Equal Treatment Directive and the Employment Equality Directive has lately generated important changes of national law. In spite of their recent introduction, the new national laws have been the subject of serious application problems. Breaches of working time and equal treatment legislation are still rather common.

Working time   Concerning working time, the Hungarian legislation is largely respectful of EU law. Paradoxically or maybe consequently, it is also the field where a multitude of serious application problems occur. According to the labour inspectorate's representative, the violation of labour law in general and working time provisions in particular 'occurs most of the time in small companies employing less than twenty employees' (Interview HU14A). However, some larger companies seem to neglect working time provisions, too (Interview HU3A, Focus Group HU3). The majority of cases of non-respect of working time regulations are concentrated in a few specific sectors, namely commerce, catering and tourism, building, transport, agriculture and seasonal work as well as health care. The types of breaches occurring are diverse and sometimes hard to report (Interview HU14A).

Violations of the working time legislation are, for example, made possible because of the practice of direct informal agreements between employers and employees, which are rather common in Hungary particularly in small businesses. Managers or local supervisors ask their employees verbally to work extra hours.

Often, these hours are not registered in working time records and are thus hard to monitor. The question is then whether the employee receives the amount of surplus work as time-off, since remuneration for this work surplus is not common. Other breaches occur when employees do not receive as much annual leave as they are entitled to under the Labour Code. Problems also exist when employees are not allowed a break when their work duty exceeds six hours or when they do not have two rest days a week or the prescribed daily rest (Focus Group HU3, Interview HU9B). Moreover, in some rare cases, employers disrespect the deadline for informing employees of their working schedule, even failing to produce any schedule at all or using reference periods to deny an employee the right of a day off in compensation for working on a Sunday (Neumann 2004, 19). Although the labour inspectorate sanctions these practices, they still exist.

Due to a lack of staff and resources, the health care sector is often identified as the most problematic with regard to working time (Focus Group HU3, Interview HU9B). Health care employees may work under a variety of legal statutes since they can be employees in the private sector, self-employed, civil servants or members of the armed forces. Therefore, working time in this sector is regulated by a combination of legal instruments.[7] Legally, the normal weekly hours are forty hours a week and forty-eight hours maximum including overtime. But this overtime limit can be exceeded in cases of emergency, and additional 'voluntary' twelve hours can be added via the individual opt-out provision of Article 22 of the Working Time Directive, which applies exceptionally in this sector.[8] Therefore, the maximum weekly working time, adding overtime and voluntary hours, can be as much as sixty hours a week (Fodor and Neumann 2004, 2). This leads, in practice, to major problems, especially because it does not include on-call time, which is not qualified as working time. Government Decree 233/2000 goes further and provides a system of lump sum calculation of working hours within on-call duties: if there is no collective agreement provided, the work done is not measurable. Adding up all the possibilities offered by the legislation, it does not come as a surprise that the weekly aggregate of working and on-call hours of health-care employees may easily reach eighty hours a week (Interview HU9B).

Similar application problems in the field of equality in the workplace have been reported.

Equality in the workplace   Our study confirms various breaches of equal treatment between men and women and anti-discrimination legislation in Hungary.

Employment of women is characterized by both vertical and horizontal segregation. Horizontal segregation means concentration and over-representation of female labour in services and in certain low prestige, low paid and conventional

---

    7   In this field the Labour Code, Act XXXIII on Public Service Employees of 1992, Government Decree 233/2000 on application of the Public Employees Act in the Health Sector and finally Act LXXXIV on Certain Aspects of Health care Activities of 2003 can apply.
    8   In Hungary, an individual opt-out is possible only in two cases: the healthcare sector and for stand-by workers (Interviews HU8; HU9A, Focus Group HU3).

'women' jobs. The vertical segregation is indicated by an unfavourable employment structure, showing strong under-representation of women in higher positions, despite the fact that the female educational level is on average higher than that of men (Halmai 2005a, 73; Hungarian Ministry of Employment and Labour 2004, 4). Women are often discriminated against because they are considered to be less competent, less dedicated to their career or because of potential pregnancies and subsequent childcare obligations. Although it is prohibited to ask a woman during a job interview whether she intends to have children, the question is often asked indirectly. In cases of equal qualification and experience a man is still more likely to receive a job offer. The lack of women in key positions is deemed to be due to their lack of ambition, although less acceptable motives might explain the situation (Focus Group HU1; HU2). Evidence of gender bias has been reported in the recruitment practices of some employers in Hungary. Private-sector employers who face a competitive business environment may associate higher non-wage costs, such as maternity leave, with women because of their family responsibilities (UNICEF 1999, 31).

Gays, lesbians and bisexuals often prefer not to disclose their sexuality in order to avoid discrimination in their professional life. Law CXXV of 1995 on the national security special services stipulates that those who work in certain public service offices[9] have to complete the so-called 'C questionnaire'; the questionnaire asks specifically about extra-marital relationships, including sexual orientation. The legislators' justification is that if the person responds truthfully, s/he will not be the subject of blackmail due to sexual orientation. It is held against that revealing their sexual orientation could expose minorities to discrimination or harassment in the workplace (Sándor 2001, 10).

Although only few problems of discrimination based on religious belief are reported in employment and vocational training, the different religious communities' right to observe rest days and celebrate holidays in accordance with the precepts of their religion is not without problems. In 1993, the Constitutional Court stated that the regulation of public holidays is only based on traditions and is the result of a historical process. The court also stressed that Article 134 of the Labour Code guarantees employees to take at least one quarter of their days off (twenty to thirty a year depending on the employee's age) whenever they want. This enables them to exercise their religious duties (Decision 10/1993 [II. 27.] AB). However, five days a year may not be enough to celebrate all the religious holidays.

Given these breaches, a certain number of cases are adjudicated every year. According to a document communicated by the Equal Treatment Authority about its most relevant cases in 2005,[10] certain assertions can be made. A large majority of cases concern discrimination on the grounds of national and ethnic origin, mostly discrimination against Roma. Interestingly, there have been no cases linked to sexual orientation, religious or ideological conviction in the workplace.

---

9   This is the case for ambassadors, state secretaries, deputy state secretaries, leaders of the parliament's offices, the heads of the armed forces or the leaders of economic organizations, insurance companies and banks fully or partly state-owned.

10   The document was communicated on 3 April 2006.

One case can be classified as discrimination against a woman as provided in the directive – even if the Equal Treatment Authority defined it as discrimination on the basis of motherhood.[11] In that case, employment was refused to a woman because she was planning to have a baby and was participating in a test-tube program (Interview HU11B).

In courts, few cases concerning discrimination against women in the workplace have been filed. The majority of them are related to discriminating employment conditions and advertising. The media have reported about a few cases. One of them concerned a shooting-range commander who was found guilty of insulting a subordinate. The Supreme Court reduced his punishment from imprisonment to a simple fine. Another case took place in a country hospital but the media did not cover the judgement (Krizsán and Pap 2005, 45). A third one, and maybe the most high profile one, involved the ministry responsible for equal opportunities itself – the Ministry of Youth, Family, Social and Equal Opportunities Affairs. According to our interviews, 'the case was resolved through an internal procedure and ended in the dismissal of both parties' (Interviews HU6, HU13, Focus Group HU1).

Moreover, one judgement related to the alleged violation of Act CXXV has been largely commented on. In the case *Háttér Support Society for LGBT People versus Károli Gáspár Reformed University*, the university declared in a public statement that educating homosexual persons in minister or theology-teacher courses was unwanted and made heterosexuality a precondition to participate in education. The plaintiff asked the court to rule that certain wordings of the public statement, which had legal consequences and were the basis for the exclusion of a student from the university, offended the right of equal treatment of homosexuals on the basis of Act CXXV. The respondent explained that the Church had established this university on prohibitions and dogmas included in the Bible and that on this basis homosexuals were not welcome among religion-teachers and ministers. The Regional Court of Appeal in Budapest stated that the declaration resting on the religious and moral belief of the Reformed Church was not illegal on the basis of the voluntary oath of the theologian and religion-teacher to keep the dogmas of the Church, of the freedom of expression and of Article 28 (2)b of Act CXXV.[12] This Article states that the principle of equal treatment is not

---

11   More discrimination grounds are prohibited in Act CXXV than in the directives. The Equal Treatment Authority classifies this case as a discrimination against motherhood, while under the directives it could have been classified as discrimination against women.

12   Article 28 (2) of Act CXXV states that 'the principle of equal treatment is not violated,

      a) in elementary and higher education, at the initiation and by voluntary choice of the parents

      b) at college or university by the students' voluntary participation, education based on religion or other ideological conviction, or education for ethnic or other minorities is organized whose objective or programme justifies the creation of segregated classes or groups; provided that this does not result in any disadvantage for those participating in such education, and the education complies with the requirements approved, laid down and subsidized by the State'.

violated if in a university, where the student participates voluntarily, education based on religious conviction justifies segregation. This case, which is linked to education and training but more largely, to the possibility for homosexuals to work as theology teachers or to be pastors, was not considered discrimination because it was based on doctrinal reasons. This judgement fully satisfied the drafters of Act CXXV, who wanted religious issues to remain outside the scope of the law (Interview HU12, see also Kádár and Farkas 2005, 4; European Network of Legal Experts in the Non-discrimination Field 2005b, 63). We believe that such conclusion might be rejected by the ECJ and the relevant legal provision could possibly be viewed as not complying with the Employment Equality Directive.

In spite of the theoretical possibility for legal remedies, discrimination cases hardly ever reach the courts (Vajda 2006, 14) and/or are made public. The question arises, why this is the case?

Lack of Complaints

Two reasons explain why discrimination victims are rather reluctant to submit their case to enforcement institutions. First, plaintiffs sometimes ignore their rights and lack information about legal redress possibilities. Secondly, they refrain from court proceedings and even from reporting their problem because of the general indifference as well as fear of the consequences (Vajda 2006, 15).

In the field of equality, the lack of willingness to seek rights enforcement is particularly critical. The new Act CXXV never became a 'hot topic' in the Hungarian media, mainly because the government, scared of the possible opposition of the general public, was reluctant to support large media coverage (Interview HU12). This might explain why employees are not necessarily aware of this new legislation. Nevertheless, the situation is improving. The government has distributed leaflets with information on equality legislation (Interview HU12). The President of the Equal Treatment Authority has been actively seeking media coverage to raise people's awareness about the existence and the role of the institution (Interview HU11A). But even if the situation is slowly changing and if people start to be aware of the existence of legislation on the subject and of institutions in charge of its enforcement, 'they still do not necessarily understand that they are or have been discriminated against' (Interview HU11A). Besides, the old social and geographical cleavages continue to exist. Unqualified employees and employees from rural areas are far less informed than highly qualified employees and employees residing in urban areas.

If the lack of 'legal awareness' seems to be particularly problematic in the field of equal treatment and anti-discrimination, it also exists in the field of working time even though the situation is rather different. The lack of knowledge, in that respect, is largely due to the complexity of the legislation, which provides that different legal regimes apply to employees in the same vicinity. Labour Code provisions and other sectoral working time legislation are very complicated and often tricky. A novice will not be able to understand his/her rights and will require the assistance of a lawyer. Even legal experts consider some provisions controversial, and competing interpretations are possible. Moreover, employers' obligations to inform their employees about the applicable labour law and to ensure easy access to the text of the law is not always respected (Interview HU9A, Focus Group HU3).

The risk of dismissal when reporting on unlawful treatment or suing their superiors exists and is intensified in certain sectors or regions with high levels of unemployment. Workers prefer to endure discrimination, harassment, longer working hours or fewer days off to being unemployed. Besides, employees are often willing to accept breaches of working time regulation as long as this guarantees a better salary. If they dare to sue their employer or report a violation, they often do so after the end of their work contract. The enforcement of working time and equality based on the principle that people will be brave enough to seek legal action therefore cannot work effectively.

Thus, the role of enforcement institutions is essential to cope with employees' lack of legal awareness and courage to defend their rights.

Labour Courts

It is a problematic feature of the Hungarian enforcement system that court proceedings are relatively long, as is evident from judgements of the European Court of Human Rights.[13] But in comparison with some 'old' EU member states and the Czech Republic, there are fewer cases relative to the procedural length lodged with the European Court of Human Rights. Labour courts generally take about one to two years to decide in the first instance, which is within the European average. This timeframe is nevertheless subject to criticism and is principally due to the lack of judges and other resources necessary to ensure the swiftness of the judicial system (Interview HU12).

Although the number of cases in labour courts has more than doubled since the 1980s – reaching 29,000 in 2003 – it is rather low in comparison with other industrialized countries. Experts think that this is due to cultural factors, to the weaknesses of interest representations and to a labour market more favourable to employers than to employees (Tóth, Nacsa and Neumann 2004, 2). Starting legal action entails a rather long procedure, substantial personnel and financial investments – even if support from NGOs or trade unions is provided – and the risk of job loss and/or of gaining a reputation that makes it difficult to find a new position. Therefore, in 70 per cent of labour court cases, employees seek legal redress after the end of their work contract. In the public sector, employees are better protected against dismissal and with higher job security they are more willing to seek legal redress (Focus Group HU3).

------

13   See for example recent cases on the length of civil proceeding such as *Szilágyi versus Hungary* (No. 73376/01), 5 April 2005 [Section II]; *Earl versus Hungary* (No. 59562/00), 20 January 2004 [Section II] or *Lovász versus Hungary* (N° 62730/00), 20 January 2004 [Section II]. See also cases on length of criminal proceeding such as *Németh versus Hungary* (No. 60037/00), 13 January 2004 [Section II] or *Csanádi versus Hungary* (No. 55220/00), 9 March 2004 [Section II].

Judges also lack the necessary knowledge of anti-discrimination law and maybe even more so of equal treatment between men and women and sexual harassment. Despite the fact that in order to change this situation, helpful training programmes have been organized for judges, they have not been systematic and are insufficient to change mentalities (Interviews HU4, HU13).

Labour Inspectorate

The state authority in charge of supervising employment conditions as well as health and safety issues in the workplace is the National Labour Safety and Labour Affairs General Inspectorate (*Országos Munkabiztonsági és Munkaügyi Főfelügyelőség – OMMF*), created in the mid-1980s.

It controls the compliance with legal provisions on working time and equal treatment (Act LXXV of 1996 on Labour Supervision), but none of these issues is a priority. Labour inspectors concentrate on the main objectives instructed by the Ministry of Employment and Labour, i.e. mainly illegal work, which is a severe problem in the Hungarian labour market (Interview HU14A). Trade unions have also criticized the tendency to focus on health and safety issues, paying too little attention to controlling the compliance with general employment regulations (Bodnár and Neumann 2005, 1). Added to the lack of inspectors, these problems need to be addressed.

Several measures were taken in 2005. Act CLV of 2005, which entered into force on 1 January 2006, recently amended Act LXXV of 1996 on Labour Supervision. It aims at improving the effectiveness of the Inspectorate. Seven regional labour inspectorates have replaced the twenty county offices. Safety and health services (National Public Health and Chief Medical Officer's Service, *Állami Népegészségügyi és Tisztiorvosi Szolgálat – ÁNTSZ*) and the labour inspectorate have been separated. The number of labour inspectors has been increased. While there were 175 in August 2005 inspecting labour and employment issues only, their number has risen to 285 in 2006 (Interview HU14B). Previously considered as too low to persuade employers – and in particular big companies – to respect labour law, fines have been raised. The minimum fine was increased from €80 to €113 and the maximum from €8,000 to €56,543 depending on the nature of the infringement and/or the number of workers, whose rights have been violated. It can reach €75,403 in exceptional cases (Interviews HU14A, HU14B).

There is no doubt that these recent changes should improve the position of labour inspectors in the enforcement of social legislation. However, the primary aim of the reform of the inspection system is to combat illegal work (Bodnár and Neumann 2005, 1). Therefore, there is a risk that the focus on this issue undermines the other functions of the Inspectorate, including ensuring compliance with working time and equal treatment law.

Also, dissimilarities exist between the power of labour inspectors with regard to working time and equal treatment. On issues of working time, labour inspectors can act *ex officio* or following a complaint. However, they can only control the respect of working time legislation on the basis of an existing work contract and not after the contract's termination or after the dismissal of the employee.

Under Article 3 (1) (d) of Act LXXV of 1996 on Labour Supervision, the labour inspectorate is also competent to examine compliance with anti-discrimination provisions. However, investigations in that field can only be conducted following a complaint and not *ex officio*. Hence, without the willingness of the victim, labour inspectors are unable to act (Kádár and Farkas 2005, 39). Every year, there are only few complaints concerning alleged violations of anti-discrimination legislation (Interview HU14A). Also, after the adoption of Act CXXV, training of inspectors necessary to familiarize them with the new legislation was limited (Interview HU14A). Hence, the role played by the labour inspectorate in the enforcement of equal treatment legislation is limited in the eyes of many experts (Focus Group HU1).

Equal Treatment Body

There are, however, other possibilities offered to victims of discrimination in order to defend their rights. Article 15 (1) of Act CXXV stipulates that victims can, alternatively to public administration bodies and the labour inspectorate, choose to turn to the Equal Treatment Authority (*Esélyegyenlőségi Hivatal*). In that case, the Act stipulates strict rules in order to avoid double procedures. The Equal Treatment Authority shall inform other bodies about the initiation of a procedure into a case of discrimination and *vice versa* (Article 15 (2)). Furthermore, if a procedure has been initiated before any public administrative body, then other public administrative bodies may not proceed in the same matter against the same person and shall suspend their procedure initiated in cases related to the same matter but concerning another person (Article 15 (3)). Once the case has been decided, then other bodies may not proceed in the same case with regard to the same person and shall proceed with regard to other persons 'using the facts of the case established in the binding decision in its procedure' (Article 15 (4)).

The Equal Treatment Authority is without doubt one of the main improvements brought about by Act CXXV. However, its creation was disputed during the drafting process. The question was whether it was necessary to create a new institution or enough to modify one of the existing ones. The existing institutions, including the Parliamentary Commissioners, did not comply with the requirements of Article 8a of the Equal Treatment Directive and Article 13 of the Racial Equality Directive. The difficulty of reforming the competence of the two bodies which seemed appropriate for this role – the Parliamentary Commissioner for Civil Rights and the Parliamentary Commissioner for National and Ethnic Minorities' Rights – and the legislator's desire to introduce public administrative sanctions backed up the second option: the establishment of a new body (Bitskey and Gyulavári 2005, 17–18). Its creation was problematic, mainly because the Ministry of Finance did not want to allocate funds to it in the 2004 budget (Interview HU1). Therefore, the institution did not start to function before 1 February 2005, after the adoption of its rules of procedure in December 2004 (Act 362/2004 (XII. 26)).

The new body was vested with more power than required by EU legislation. The Equal Treatment Directive stipulates that member states should designate a body 'for the promotion, analysis, monitoring and support of equal treatment of all persons without discrimination' (Article 8.a.1. of the Equal Treatment Directive). Act CXXV goes further. Not only can the Equal Treatment Authority 'initiate a lawsuit with a view to protecting the rights of persons and groups whose rights have been violated' and accomplish the other functions set in the directive, it can also 'conduct ex-officio an investigation to establish whether the principle of equal treatment has been violated, and make a decision on the basis of the investigation' (Article 14 of Act CXXV). In other words, the Equal Treatment Authority has the competence to impose administrative sanctions, i.e. fines from €220 to €26,000 (Interview HU11A, see also Kádár and Farkas 2005, 47).

This provision not only gives the Equal Treatment Authority a more effective and active role than many of its EU counterparts, but it also provides victims with more options to protect their rights. They can initiate a procedure with the Equal Treatment Authority parallel to a lawsuit in the labour court. In such cases, both the court and the Authority may suspend its procedure, but neither is obliged to do so.[14] As indicated, victims seem to be more willing to complain to the Equal Treatment Authority, because the procedure is easier and faster than court proceedings. 'A decision by the Equal Treatment Authority has to be taken within two and a half months, while the labour courts can take about two years' (Interview HU11A).

Although in comparison to the equivalent institutions in many other EU member states, the Hungarian Equal Treatment Authority is in a rather good position, the body lacks adequate resources. There were more than 300 complaints in the first five months of its existence[15] and the number of cases 'will most likely increase within the next years' (Interviews HU1, HU5, HU11A). However, the body employs only seven legal advisors, excluding the President, the Deputy President and administrative staff.

Stronger criticism concerns the supervision by and financial dependence on a ministry – presently the Ministry for Social, Family Affairs and Equal Opportunities. It is considered to be 'in opposition with the independence of action of such a body required by Article 8a of the Equal Treatment Directive' (Interviews HU1, HU5). However, the legislator had no choice, as a public authority has to be part of a given structure in the public administration (Bitskey and Gyulavári 2005, 18). To counterbalance this lack of structural independence within the administrative institutional framework, Article 13 (3) of Act CXXV states that 'the Authority cannot be directed at the exercise of duties'. Only practice will show whether this lack of budgetary autonomy influences the actions of the Equal Treatment Authority.

---

14   See, as quoted by Lilla Farkas and András Kádár, Article 37 of Act IV of 1957 on the General Rules of Administrative Procedure and Article 152 of Act III of 1952 on Civil Procedure (Kádár and Farkas 2005, 41).

15   80 per cent of them had to be rejected because they were not perceived to be discrimination cases or outside the scope of the law.

Other Aspects of Enforcement

The Parliamentary Commissioners (Ombudspersons) are entitled to conduct individual and comprehensive investigations into discrimination cases (Kádár and Farkas 2005, 43). Article 32/B of the Constitution states that Ombudspersons investigate violations of constitutional rights and initiate general or individual measures to remedy such violations. According to Act LIX of 1993, they can investigate any public authorities *ex officio*, including armed forces and police services. Any victim of acts or omissions of public services can complain to the Ombudspersons' office, provided that administrative remedies do not exist or are exhausted. When finding a violation, Ombudspersons issue recommendations or a petition to the Constitutional Court, initiate that the prosecutor issues a protest and propose legislative amendments. They can also repeal, issue or initiate disciplinary or criminal proceedings. All in all, they are competent only for controlling the action of the public administration and their main activity is to publish reports (Interviews HU11A, HU12). Therefore, their role in the enforcement of anti-discrimination legislation is limited and their actions do not really compete with those of the Equal Treatment Authority. Act CXXV fails anyway to settle potential conflicts between the two institutions and does not contain any solution for cases in which the conclusion of and the sanction imposed by the Equal Treatment Authority is not in line with the opinion of the Ombudsperson (Kádár and Farkas 2005, 43–4).

Another possibility to resolve individual disputes is the use of mediation. The workplace-level resolution of individual rights disputes was reformed comprehensively during the transition period. Under the Communist regime, company-level grievance boards run by trade unions were first instance juridical fora for individual disputes. Workplace-level grievance boards were abolished in 1992. Instead, the new Labour Code established a pre-court conciliation procedure at the labour court between employee and employer (Tóth, Nacsa and Neumann 2004, 3). It was a simple formality and such a step is not compulsory anymore.

A Labour Mediation and Arbitration Service (*Munkaügyi Közvetítő és Döntőbírói Szolgálat, MKDSZ*) was also created, but only to facilitate agreements in collective labour disputes and not to provide conciliation, mediation and arbitration service in pre-court reconciliation processes of individual legal disputes (Tóth, Nacsa and Neumann 2004, 3).

Additionally, conciliation can still be provided at company level via collective agreement or a joint decision of the parties. Due to the absence of legal regulations and well-established traditions in this area, only a handful of large companies established the use of conciliation procedures. To be effective such procedures require a certain balance of power. The employers' position is often stronger than that of trade unions, which suffer from a lack of members and thereby weight in company-level bargaining (Tóth, Nacsa and Neumann 2004).

Finally, in 2002, the adoption of the Act on Mediation allowed private agencies, legal advisors and lawyers to offer conciliation and mediation services for companies (Tóth, Nacsa and Neumann 2004, 3). The effectiveness of such services, however, depends on companies' willingness to involve mediation and conciliation services in the dispute with their employees (Interview HU2).

The right of associations, organizations or other legal entities with a legitimate interest to engage, either on behalf or in support of victims of discrimination in judicial and administrative procedures, was hardly guaranteed before 2003. Act CXXV changed, to a certain extent, the situation by claiming that any 'social and interest representation organization' with a legitimate interest as well as the Equal Treatment Authority, may 'act as a representative authorized by the party who suffered a violation of law in procedures initiated because of a violation of the principle of equal treatment' (Article 18 (1)). Furthermore, according to Article 18 (2), the 'social and interest representation organization is entitled to the rights of the client'. Different interpretations have been offered as to whether this Article includes the right to initiate procedures in the absence of a complaint from a victim, or whether it only provides organizations with the possibility of 'joining in' once a complaint has been made. The second interpretation seems to be more likely. But it is too early to draw any conclusions, as jurisprudence is pending (Kádár and Farkas 2005, 44–5).

Another important innovation, introduced by Article 20, is the possibility of initiating an *actio popularis*. If the principle of equal treatment is violated, a lawsuit against the infringement of rights or a labour lawsuit may be initiated by social and interest representation organizations – or the Public Prosecutor and the Equal Treatment Authority – provided that 'the violation of the principle of equal treatment was based on a characteristic that is an essential feature of the individual, and the violation of law affects a larger group of persons that cannot be determined accurately' (Article 20 (1)). In other words, it seems that in this case the possibility of initiating a lawsuit only exists if an individual victim cannot be identified. This provision is relatively important and has already generated cases. Among them is the famous *Háttér Support Society for LGBT People v Károli Gáspár Reformed University*, where the court stated that homosexuality is an inherent feature of one's personality and that the future possibility of an infringement of rights is a sufficient ground for initiating an *actio popularis*. Although Háttér organization's claim was rejected, this case was an important decision for future action, stressing the possibility for active NGOs not only to act on behalf of or in support of a victim, but also to act on their own initiative as long as one of the inherent characteristics of a group of individuals is violated (Jaichand, Sembacher and Starl 2006, 13). An interesting question, which is not yet resolved, is whether the court will consider religion as an 'essential feature of an individual'. This provision would certainly ensure a better respect for equal treatment legislation in Hungary. Active NGOs are less intimidated by a formal procedure than individuals might be, as long as they have the activists to initiate such action and can afford it.

One should emphasise that Act CXXV defines 'social and interest representation organizations' as social organizations or foundations whose objectives include the promotion of equal opportunities of disadvantaged groups or the protection of human or individual rights, as well as the minority government and trade unions

(Article 3e). Trade unions' actions in this field are, however, rather limited (Focus group HU1).

More generally, trade unions and works councils have no statutory role in individual legal dispute procedures but they can assist their members with legal advice or by providing legal representation in the court procedure. Legal advice is deemed to be the most important service that unions provide to their members. However, they cannot initiate action since the employment relationship is regulated by a private contract between the employer and the employee (Interview HU3A). Therefore, trade union action in the field of working time is dependent on the willingness of the employee to act and to seek legal redress. In other words, trade unions cannot act if their members are not ready to fight (Focus Group HU3A).

In order to increase employees' readiness to defend their rights, trade unions understood that it was necessary to increase the legal knowledge of their members. Therefore, one of their successes was the publication of booklets for workers explaining the Labour Code and equal treatment legislation (Focus Group HU1). Such initiatives are not isolated and often supported by the EU.

Conclusions and Improvement Strategies

As the above discussion of Hungary's implementation of the three selected EU directives has shown, the transposition record is relatively good, with only a few legal details remaining open. However, full compliance is hampered by serious shortcomings in the Hungarian enforcement system. While possibilities and fora for legal redress exist and are well established, they face important practical difficulties that need to be addressed.

In the field of equality in the workplace, measures have to be taken at the legislative, institutional, policy and practical level. Further legislative amendments are needed to include specific provisions on sexual harassment (Interviews HU13, HU4), and to reduce the scope of the exception clause to indirect discrimination as foreseen in the directive (Interview HU1). Legislation referring to the burden of proof in cases of discrimination should define the *prima facie* case, which will not include as a requirement the proof of suffering disadvantage, but only the criteria to make a presumption that there has been discrimination (Interview HU13). Finally, the Act on Labour Inspection should be modified to enable *ex officio* investigation of discrimination cases (Krizsán and Pap 2005, 48–9).

Legislative amendments would not, however, efficiently ensure a better protection of discrimination victims if improvements are not made in institutional mechanisms. The budget and staff of the Equal Treatment Authority should be increased and its financial independence should be better safeguarded (Interviews HU1, HU5). Similarly, in the fields of equal treatment but also working time, the resources (budget, personnel) and sanctioning capacities of labour courts and labour inspectorates should be increased to ensure a faster resolution of conflicts and an adequate control of the compliance with labour law provisions. Parallel thereto, the labour inspectorate should increase its control and actions in the field of anti-discrimination and equal treatment as soon as it would be allowed to act *ex officio* (Strategy Workshop). Then, the Council for Women's Affairs, instituted between 1998 and 2002, which was a forum for discussion between experts, NGOs and government representatives, should be re-established (Interview HU13).

Finally, efforts should be made through better and additional policies, programmes and awareness campaigns. A better protection of victims of discrimination should be established and complaint units should be created in private enterprises (Interview HU4). More training courses on the subject of anti-discrimination and equal treatment between men and women have to be organized for civil servants, judges and labour inspectors (Strategy Workshop) as well as programmes in private and public companies to ensure that employees, but also employers are aware of their rights and obligations in the field of equal treatment (Strategy Workshop). The programmes and projects launched by the government offices dealing with equal treatment issues should be more visible. Awareness-raising campaigns on the role and existence of the Equal Treatment Authority, labour courts and the labour inspectorates in such matters should be organized to ensure that employees know about the possibilities offered to them (Strategy Workshop). Moreover, the creation of an Equal Opportunities Action Plan for public bodies and legal entities in state ownership that have more than fifty employees should be made effective as is provided in Act CXXV (Interview HU4). The reintegration of women in the labour market should be facilitated via the promotion of flexible work, certain forms of childcare benefits and facilities (Krizsán and Pap 2005, 51). Instituting childcare benefits for fathers, longer paternity leave or awareness campaigns should guarantee that family obligations are better shared between parents. Finally, research should be encouraged to ensure a better understanding of discrimination problems, explanations and solutions.

Similar measures have to be taken to improve the implementation of the Working Time Directive. In that field, legislative amendments are also needed. Labour legislation should be simplified and made more comprehensive (Interview 9A, Focus Group HU3, Strategy Workshop). The Labour Code and branch legislations should be amended to clearly stipulate the limitation of the maximum weekly working period to forty-eight hours for each employee and not for each employment relationship (Interview HU3A, Strategy Workshop). The Labour Code and more specific legal texts – such as Act LXXXIV on Certain Aspects of Health Care Activities – should be amended to be in conformity with the jurisprudence of the ECJ concerning the definition of on-call duty (Focus group HU3, Strategy Workshop). Rest period and rest day provisions of the Labour Code must clearly stipulate that no distinction should be made between usual working time and overtime, that such periods should be respected in any case and that no overtime should diminish the rest period an employee is entitled to. The legislation should allow trade unions to enact an *actio popularis* in working time matters. Better protection against dismissal and mobbing should be ensured for employees who dare to seek legal action.

Changes at the institutional level could also complement the legislative amendment to ensure a better application of working time provisions. The focus on working time related inspections should be increased.

Finally, practical changes have to be made via new policies, programmes and awareness campaigns. Mediation procedures to resolve labour disputes should be better promoted. A greater priority should be given to working time in the action of the labour inspectorate. Awareness campaigns on employees' working time rights should be organized by the responsible ministry. And finally, trade unions, in that respect, should intensify their role.

These recommendations might be useful to improve the implementation of Hungarian legislation on working time, equal treatment between men and women and anti-discrimination. However, impressive changes will hardly be possible without first coping with unemployment, although the unemployment rate is below the EU average. Hungarians see it as one of the main curses of their modern state, in particular in regions where this rate is multiplied by a factor of two or higher. Most Hungarian specialists agree therefore that 'as long as unemployment remains high, employees would still be unwilling and scared to fight for the respect of their labour rights' (Focus Groups HU1; HU3).

In conclusion, the three Hungarian case studies have been marked by a combination of politicized transposition processes, which were completed successfully and within the given time constraints, on the one hand, and flawed enforcement and application of the laws on the other hand. This pattern is similar to what we have found in the Czech Republic.

The subsequent chapters will show if similar processes may be found in Slovakia and Slovenia. On this basis, the concluding chapter will finally discuss – from a comparative perspective – to which 'world of compliance' the observed modes of implementation belong.

Chapter 4

Slovakia

Marianne Schulze

Background Information

Political System

Slovakia's history is rooted in the Middle Ages: It once formed part of the Moravian Empire and – following the Ottoman Turkish victory – fell under Habsburg rule. Heavily influenced by Hungarian power, nationalism was a recurring theme: first the Germanization under Maria Theresia and Joseph II, who brought about social reform and some religious tolerance, and later the Magyarization following the *Ausgleich*, which established the Austro-Hungarian Empire in 1867 and was part of a general nationalist wave in Europe. Catholic clergy, the pillar of Slovak intelligentsia, has always been a major nationalistic force. Deeply imbedded seems the resentment towards Czechs, which was invigorated during the rise (1948) and to some degree during the fall (1989) of the Communist regime. Despite rigorous persecution under the Communists, the Catholic Church is still a decisive influence; in recent years a concordat between the Slovak Republic and the Holy See has been a hot political issue.

The Slovak Republic is a parliamentary democracy based on the rule of law. The preamble to the Constitution makes a distinctive reference to the country's heritage and proclaims the protection of minorities and ethnic groups. In addition, Article 1 of the Slovak Constitution emphasizes that the State has no ideological or religious commitments whatsoever.

The president is the head of state: since 1999 presidents have been elected by popular vote (amendment to Chapter VI, Part 1 Slovak Constitution). The government complements the executive powers of Slovakia; it is headed by the prime minister, who can be appointed and recalled by the president. The government as a body and its individual members, respectively, are accountable to the National Council. Its tasks include *inter alia* the elaboration and implementation of Slovakia's economic policy, the drafting of laws – including the state budget – and governmental decrees (Chapter VI, Part 2 Slovak Constitution).

Legislative power is solely invested in the National Council, a single chamber body with 150 elected representatives who exercise their mandate 'personally according to their conscience and conviction and are not bound by orders' (Article 73/2 Slovak Constitution). Stringent constitutional immunity and indemnity provisions protect the members of the National Council. Their duties include the passing of constitutional and other laws and monitoring their implementation, respectively.

Also, the National Council gives consent to the ratification of international treaties of a political and economic nature as well as those that require the passing of national legislation prior to ratification. In addition to controlling the government's activities, the checks and balances of the Constitution require that the National Council elect the judges of the Constitutional Court, the Supreme Court as well as the chairperson and deputy of the Supreme Control Office of the Slovak Republic (Chapter V Slovak Constitution).

The growing constitutional and democratic stability in Slovakia was earned the hard way. The charismatic then-Prime Minister, Vladimir Meciar, imposed the so-called 'Velvet Divorce' – the separation from the Czech Republic. The majority of Slovaks was opposed to this but various factors such as the inability to create a mutually enforcing social fabric, the failure of the elite and spasm of a post-communist panic are reportedly to blame for the split (Bútorová and Bútora 1995; Bútora, Bútorová and Gyárfásová 1994; Szomolányi 2004). A crucial factor was ongoing discussions over economic resources: federal and national monies for Czechs and Slovaks, respectively, were a key issue as the government(s) moved to privatize industries. On the international level, the aftermath of the collapse of the Soviet Union created a special atmosphere for former Socialist countries.

Slovak society stumbled from subdued political interest, which prevailed while under Communist rule, into a sense of being abandoned, following the split from the Czech Republic only a few years later. Not surprisingly, Slovak society lacked a firmly rooted political interest. Thus, a significant factor in these developments was also the insufficient participation of civil society, which was almost non-existent in the early 1990s, shortly after the fall of the authoritarian regime. In contrast to those days – when opposition was the weakest and least visible in all of the Communist countries – civil society today is one of the most dynamic and self-sustaining (Freedom House 2004; Szomolányi 2004). The majority of civil society actors are, however, only active in Bratislava.

The fragility of the political and, even more, the constitutional culture was the breeding ground for the populist support for Vladimir Meciar, who stepped right into the leadership void that was readily available for populist-charismatic politicians of his sort who ably presented themselves as objects of popular identification after a long absence of partisan attachments (Pridham 1995; Szomolányi 2004; see also Baer 2001). Lacking a decisive formal opposition, Meciar and his followers ruled with a 'tendency toward unchecked majority rule', displaying significant signs of 'illiberal democracy' (Szomolányi 2004), and the Slovak government can be seen to have lost five years of valuable reform time (Interview SK12).

Meciar's charisma and power crumbled as forces within the populace demanded a more democratic style and the strongest outside force, namely the European Union, insisted on a radical overhaul in preparation for a possible EU accession. 'Slovakia is a compelling example of how the EU's conditionality affects democratization from beyond the nation-state and the EU's capacity to function as a democratizing force' (Harris 2004, 190).

Table 4.1   Governments of Slovakia (1993–2006)

Period	Government	Parties	Political orientation
Jan. 1993– March 1994	Meciar	Movement for a Democratic Slovakia (HZDS) Slovak National Party (SNS)	Right-wing, populist
March 1994– Dec. 1994	Moravčik	Defectors from SNS, HZDS, KDH and Party of the Democratic left (SDL) – continued fragmentation	'Against Meciar'
Dec. 1994– Oct. 1998	Meciar	HZDS, SNS, Association of Workers of Slovakia (ZRS)	Right-wing, nationalist, populist
Oct. 1998– Oct. 2002	Dzurinda	Slovak Democratic Coalition (SDK), Party of Civic Understanding (SOP), SDL, Party of the Hungarian Coalition (SMK)	Broad left-right-centre
Oct. 2002– June 2006	Dzurinda	Slovak Democratic and Christian Union (SDKU), (SMK), (KDH), New Citizen Alliance (ANO)	Centre-right
June 2006–	Fico	Direction-Social Democracy (SMER), HZDS, SNS	Left and nationalist right

Source: Deegan-Krause (2004); own internet research.

Ever since Meciar was ousted in 1998, the Slovak government has steadily improved its constitutional and economic performance, placing it in the international limelight as a model post-communist country and making it a favourite of the World Bank. However, Slovakia is among the countries where the level of inequalities has broadened and deepened and where poverty 'has become more deeply entrenched and much more visible' (Kornai 2005, 27).

EU membership was the political mainstream's prime ambition. The accession process, however, was curtailed by national problems and the first attempt at joining – under Meciar's rule – failed in 1997. Henderson (2004, 158) states very pointedly: 'The key question was not whether Slovakia wanted to join the EU, but whether the EU would accept it.' Once Meciar and his party had been forced to resign, the negotiations started in earnest, and during the accession process 80 per cent of the *acquis* were adopted in record time. The campaign for a 'yes' vote was mutually endorsed across party lines and produced the highest approval ever in a EU referendum: 93.7 per cent. A critical discussion of the accession was hardly visible and campaigns for a 'no' vote were almost non-existent. The constitutional requirement of 50 per cent participation of eligible voters, however, was barely met: 52.2 per cent cast their vote. There are indicators that potential 'no' voters deliberately stayed at home (Henderson 2004).

The accession to the EU fulfilled, amongst others, a need to 'belong', also because after years of rejection Slovaks could feel as equals among countries like Poland and the Czech Republic, which acceded at the same time. The European Union is generally seen as more open, tolerant and also socially more advanced, caring for socially disadvantaged people such as persons with disabilities and women (Interview SK21).

In the first European Parliament election, just six weeks after accession, however, only 17 per cent of Slovakia's electorate cast their votes. Experts assert that this is possibly a harbinger that some of the illusions about the 'West' and 'democracy', which people had prior to the downfall of Socialism, are slowly becoming undone (see also Kornai 2005).

Legal System

The Slovak court system as prescribed in the Constitution is the decisive framework in which the implementation of EU directives takes place. The Constitutional Court (*Ústavný súd Slovenskej republiky*) and the Supreme Court are the only courts explicitly foreseen. The 'detailed arrangement of the court system', however, is set out in basic legislation (Article 143). In addition, the Constitution enumerates the universal standards for a fair trial and customary guarantees for judges (Chapter VII, Part 2 Slovak Constitution).

Judicial independence is a novice in Slovakia. Basically non-existent during the era of the Austro-Hungarian-Empire, the transition in 1989 and the subsequent 'Velvet Divorce' were not helpful to the development of Western-style judicial culture. It was only after the end of the Meciar government that a constitutional culture began to flourish. The fragility of the situation is highlighted by a recent crisis surrounding the then-President of the Supreme Court, Stefan Harabin, whom the government accused of severe wrongdoings such as hampering efforts to fight corruption in the judiciary (Cumaraswamy 2001).

The centre-right government under Prime Minister Dzurinda, incumbent from 1998 to 2006, revamped the judicial system, amongst others by establishing a Judicial Council. Its inception is a response to the harsh criticism of the lack of judicial independence voiced by the EU. In effect since 2002, it is a body that aims at strengthening the judicial self-governance and has the right to propose judicial candidates, determine the transfer of judges, and is involved in disciplinary issues of judges. The Judicial Council is comprised of 18 members: eight are elected by the judges, and three each by the President, the National Council and the government, respectively. The President of the Supreme Court chairs the Council. In 2005, the Judicial Council had to nominate three candidates for the European Court of Human Rights. The Council did not nominate any women and thus failed miserably in complying with international standards, particularly with obeying the affirmative action rule set out by the Parliamentary Assembly of the Council of Europe (Fialová 2005, 154; International Helsinki Federation 2006).

Currently, there are 55 district courts and 8 regional courts; the latter function both as courts of appeal for the district courts and as courts of first instance. Administrative acts can be challenged in civil courts. There are no special courts for labour law matters; special senates within the civil court system take on these issues.

The judicial system is under heavy scrutiny also because of the length of procedures: in 2002 an average civil proceeding took 14 months. Lately, plaintiffs have turned to the Constitutional Court to fight unjustly long procedures. In 2004, 968 complaints were filed; in an unspecified number of cases the Court awarded compensation (Jurinová 2005; Meseznikov 2005, 47). Approximately two thirds of the applications lodged against the Slovak Republic with the European Court of Human Rights in Strasbourg concern 'judicial procrastination' and claim a violation of Article 6, the right to a fair trial (Fialová 2005, 151).

In its 2002 Report (European Commission 2002a), the EU Commission welcomed changes being made but urged that funding had to be provided to ensure 'proper implementation' (European Commission 2002a, 24). In response, the number of judges has been slightly increased and the Code of Civil Procedure was amended to accommodate the need for more efficiency. In addition, arbitration measures such as mediation have been introduced in some areas and meanwhile have been expanded to include foreign entities. It is noteworthy that such procedures existed prior to 1989 and functioned better than courts at the time. Because they primarily dealt with cases between state-owned companies, they were branded as 'socialist elements' and abolished. Hopes are that the current backlog of approximately 900,000 cases will subsequently decrease. However, there appears to be a lack of appreciation for the important role the judiciary plays in the ongoing reforms of both the political framework but also the economic reforms (Open Society Institute 2001, 401). The self-perception of judges is still in flux and very much in need of further improvements, both institutionally and individually. For one, many judges mistake independence for 'immunity from any criticism'; on the other hand public opinion concerning judges is generally negative – the trend being more downward, even in the Justice Ministry's own findings. As one assessment states, judges seem to believe that fulfilling the wishes of the political branch is their primary duty: they have not yet embraced their role as an independent watchdog (Open Society Institute 2002a, 403).

Socio-economic Background

Once one of Europe's poorhouses, Slovakia quickly revamped its economic landscape to market-economy mechanisms in the late nineties. Hence, the European Commission declared the Slovak Republic a 'functioning market economy' (European Commission 2002a, 45). Large-scale privatizations are the pillar of the recent economic success (Höferl 2004), combined with the far-reaching business-friendly policies such as downgrading the labour standards and introducing an industry-friendly flat tax system of 19 per cent.

In addition, the fairytale success story has to be seen against major backdrops such as a growing disparity between the well-developed region around Bratislava and the manifold grievances of the eastern part of the country, where heavy industry collapsed after the downfall of Communism (Weiss 2006). The main eastward connection runs through the northern part of the country, which has left the South, another 'problematic region', comparably underdeveloped. The unemployment rate there exceeds 30 per cent, and an unusually high ratio of people is retired (Kling 2003, 470). The East is home to the Roma minority with its manifold structural problems, which are particularly prevalent in the areas of housing, education, health care and employment.

Table 4.2   Basic economic developments in Slovakia (1993–2004)

	1993	1994	1995	1996	1997	1998	1999	2000	2001	2002	2003	2004
Real GDP growth (%)	1.90	6.21	5.84	6.15	4.61	4.21	1.47	2.04	3.79	4.62	4.46	5.50
Unemploy- ment rate (%)	-	13.70	13.10	11.30	11.90	12.60	16.80	18.70	19.40	18.70	17.50	18.20
Inflation rate (%)	15.37	13.45	9.89	4.33	6.71	5.22	6.45	8.45	4.17	3.99	4.66	4.59
General government balance (% of GDP)	-	-6.13	-0.86	7.40	-6.18	-3.77	-7.14	-12.31	-6.58	-7.77	-3.78	-3.15

Source: OECD.

It is noteworthy that the Slovak Constitution contains a substantial section on economic, social and cultural rights. In Part 5 it enumerates the right to work and adequate working conditions – Articles 35 and 36 respectively – as well as the right to freely associate to protect economic and social interests.

Tripartism, which was set up within the framework of the Council for Economic and Social Concertation in 1991 and modelled after the Austrian *Sozialpartnerschaft*, is undergoing changes, which appear to be influenced by economic developments.

First of all, both employees and employers had to build their organizational structures from scratch, given that the state had previously been the only employer. Although the Confederation of Trade Unions of the Slovak Republic, KOZ, still represents a majority of the employees' interest groups, its membership has plummeted significantly: union affiliation stood at 2.4 million in 1990 and only at 655,000 11 years later (Czíria 2002). In 2004, less than one third (31 per cent) of all Slovak employees were affiliated with a trade union (European Commission 2006g, 25).

The overhaul of the Labour Code in 2002, just a few weeks after the centre-right coalition of Dzurinda II came to power, also included a drastic change of the Tripartite system. Giving in to demands by the employers' associations, the existing Council was replaced by the Council of Economic and Social Agreement (RHSD) and was later scaled down to an advisory body, namely the Council of Economic and Social Partnership (RHSP) in 2004 (Interviews SK6, SK12, see also Malová and Rybár 2005). The Justice Minister, Daniel Lipšic (Christian Democratic Movement), who originally proposed this latest downgrading, stated that the old model had not provided sufficient room for 'other interest groups', but also that trade unions 'had begun to pursue an anti-government policy' (Malová and Rybár 2005, 238).

Tripartism is now reduced to a largely formal process, which is in no small parts due to the fact that it is not an organically grown process and institution but rather a top-down imposed measure. In addition to the Dzurinda II government's clear pro-employers stance, however, there are also major internal issues that both employees' and employers' representatives have to deal with.

The employees, who were organized under Communism, appear to have been offered a 'deal' that enabled the trade unions to retain their substantial property, which consists mainly of real estate accumulated during Communism, in exchange for consenting to the large-scale privatizations after the downfall of Communism. At the time, trade unions allegedly had the power to oppose such privatizations at company level. Also, a personal friendship between trade union leader Alojz Engliš and Vladimir Meciar added to the dynamic (Interview SK6, see also Malová and Rybár 2005).

Based on sound and solid economic means, the trade union leadership, the majority of whom were socialized under Communism, has very little incentive to embrace change of any sort. As a consequence, the management appears somewhat detached from both its goals and its membership. A case in point is the Confederation's unwillingness or inability to defend the wage demands of its members. Both the method of transformation and the quality of the leadership 'were strong factors affecting the trade unions' debilitation, at both the national and corporate level' (Malová and Rybár 2005, 236).

Despite the aforementioned dramatic decline in membership, which has in fact caused a gradual deterioration of their power, trade unions continue to be recognized as a political player. The expected embrace of the left-wing 'Direction – Social Democracy' (SMER) as its natural partner in the run-up to the June 2006 elections is rooted in a statement made prior to the 2004 European Parliament elections, in which the Confederation stated that SMER 'knows what social policy is' (Malová and Rybár 2005, 235). However, the unconditional support is not only principally problematic but also because 'SMER policies include the adoption – in parts – of Meciar's populist appeal' (Interview SK12). Cautious expectations of Fico's government, which was sworn in in June 2006, included a renewal of the social partnership dialogue.

The employers had to start from scratch and until 2004 were represented solely by the Slovak Association of Employers' Unions and Federations (AZZZ), when an alternative, namely the Republican Union of Employers (RÚZ), emerged. The primary motivation for the split remains unclear. However, it appears that the leadership was too focused on businesses that derived from Communist times rather than the establishment of new businesses and the strategies necessary for such developments. Also, personal issues appear to have been a factor (Malová and Rybár 2005). Meanwhile, most of the representative organizations have become members of EU-wide organizations.

The Slovak welfare system is founded on the Constitution's provisions: Article 35 (3) protects the right to work, Article 39 safeguards 'adequate material provision in old age', and Article 41 guarantees assistance for parents of children. The enforceability of these rights is, however, limited: Article 51 states that these rights 'can be claimed only within the limits of the laws that execute those provisions'.

The introduction of a new pension scheme provoked a huge controversy as the '1968 baby boomers' are now disproportionately affected by the consequences of the privatizations in the 1990s and the employment crisis. A governmental information campaign propelled the public approval to 60 per cent (European Forum for Democracy and Solidarity 2005). The welfare reforms following the 'Velvet Divorce' also revamped the insurance scheme – introducing separate funds for health insurance, sickness and pension – and were later added to the wave of privatizations. Originally, only pharmacies were privatized, but by 1996 the entire primary health care was in non-communal ownership. A 'radical' reform, again focused on the business aspects of the system, was initiated by the new government starting in 2002. The latest changes take the high level of corruption – that still prevails throughout the system – into account and foresee, *inter alia*, the introduction of direct payments for healthcare services (Hlavacka, Wágner and Riesberg 2004, 99).

Corruption generally continues to be a serious social problem. According to observations, it is continuously changing forms and is now spilling over from the central levels of government to regional and local levels (Sicáková-Beblavá 2005, 681). While a number of officials were put on trial, it appears that 'the intense media interest in cases of political corruption has resulted in a paradoxical effect: people are becoming increasingly tired of political scandals' (Bútorová, Gyárfásová and Velsic 2005, 257).

Relevant Aspects of Societal Order

Particularly with a view to EU standards in the field of minority protection, it should be mentioned that apart from the Romani, Hungarian and other, smaller, ethnic minorities, Slovak society is comparably homogenous. There is little or insignificant immigration, mostly international students from Middle Eastern countries and a few Albanians. 25 asylum applications were approved in 2005 as the vast majority of asylum seekers transit further west (International Helsinki Federation 2006).

The transformations since the 'Velvet Revolution' have also left a distinctive mark on the societal order. The private sphere – the family – came under especially heavy pressure following the transition phase. One of the first initiatives of women's NGOs (as in other CEECs) was a domestic violence campaign that increased awareness.

The frequently patriarchal nature of family settings is also prevalent in Slovakia, but nevertheless the burden of adjusting to the new political, economic and related circumstances was often left to women. The 'transition' phase seems to have consolidated the reality of formal equality and real inequality, and the decline of social support and increasing unemployment affected women far more than men.

While official statistics would give the impression of 'gender balanced' unemployment, it appears safe to say that women's unemployment is often hidden. Women stay at home for a number of reasons: there is a lack of affordable childcare, and a woman who stays at home is not necessarily eyed negatively, as 'keeping house' is a valid purposeful statement (UNIFEM 2006, 33). There is no systematic information on the level and quality of informal work; women are the predominant care-takers for an increasing number of ill male family members (UNIFEM 2006, 10). In 2005 the activity rate of women was 50.9 per cent. This constitutes a decrease in women's activity, since the respective share in 1998 was 53.5 per cent. In 2005, the unemployment rate of women was 17.2 per cent, 1.7 per cent higher than that of men (Eurostat 2007).

The post-socialism phase has also reinforced the divide between the public and private spheres into a male and female world, respectively. The formal equality of Socialism has been particularly undermined in the political realm, in which women participate significantly less than men. Added to that, the public sphere is thought to be not very desirable, also because it is prone to corruption. As a result of this and other factors, men largely dominate public discourse and women are by and large absent. The participation of women in politics plummeted after 1989 and is only slowly making a resurgence. Based on the patriarchal-socialist structure, there is a pretty solid knowledge of workers' rights and related issues, but there are significant gaps in the knowledge of women's rights or the 'human rights of women', as they are preferably termed. Discussions also revealed the appearance of a peculiar, seemingly endless ability to put up with grievances (*Leidensfähigkeit*), a cultural disposition that is more ubiquitous among women than men. The classic Socialist woman's dream of having a 'right to choose not to work' (Bitusikova 2003) has been replaced with a struggle to get access to the employment market and to maintain the position after maternity leave, not in the least because the so-called 'feminization of poverty' is lurking.

It is promising to see that public awareness is comparatively high in that three in five Slovak citizens (61 per cent) believe that the social status and opportunities for women are worse compared to those of men. Respondents view Slovak society's attitude toward women as significantly less accommodating when compared to other EU countries. Public opinion is most critical of discrimination of women in the labour market as well as the low status of women in politics, namely their inadequate inclusion in the political decision making process at the highest levels (Bútorová, Gyárfásová and Velsic 2005, 264).

Save the last nine months of the Dzurinda II government, when Iveta Radičová of the Slovak Christian and Democratic Union (SKDU) was made Minister for Labour, Social Affairs and Family, the Slovak cabinet consisted entirely of male members. However, this appointment appears to have been a token suggestion, given that at the same time, the specialized department within that very Ministry devoted to women's issues, the Department of Equal Opportunities and Anti-discrimination, was replaced by a new Department for Family and Gender Policy. The government's policy documents in this area are too general to be translated into meaningful programmes (see also International Helsinki Federation 2006).

As a consequence, the government's report on the implementation of the Beijing Platform for Action[1] (Ministry of Labour Social Affairs and Family of the Slovak Republic 1999) was criticized as relying on NGO activities and selling those wide-ranging programmes as governmental achievements. One such programme was the 'Fifth Women' campaign, which highlighted gender based domestic violence (International Helsinki Federation 2006). Also, the government states quite pointedly that 'there is a strong will of the Government of the Slovak Republic to support issues of gender equality in Slovakia. Problems with economic transition, strong traditional thinking of the society, stereotypes concerning the role of men and women in the society and in the family create an important barrier in regard of this will' (Ministry of Labour Social Affairs and Family of the Slovak Republic 1999, 5). Furthermore, the government correctly states in its report that a National Programme on Sexual and Reproductive Health was drafted for the years 2004–2010, but fails to mention that it has been stalled due to the resistance of the Christian Democratic Movement and the Catholic Church (International Helsinki Federation 2006).

With regard to the realm of religion in Slovakia, a crucial point is the wide-ranging influence of the Catholic Church, which found its most visible expression in a treaty between the Slovak Republic and the Holy See. Signed in 2001, the treaty enshrines the legal framework of the country's relationship with the Holy See.

Four corollaries have been proposed within that framework. The first two govern access to military service and religious education in schools and have already been approved. The treaty is hotly contested for various reasons. The agreement gives way to collaboration between the government and one church, the Roman-Catholic denomination, and thus allows for decisive influence of one religious group. This can be questioned in light of the basic democratic principle of separation of church and state. Also, the text appears to be a copy of the agreement reached between Mussolini and the Holy See in 1929 (Interview SK2). Further, the Slovak Constitution was amended in 2001, placing international agreements above national legislation (Article 7 Paras. 4 and 5 Slovak Constitution). Therefore, the agreements stemming from the framework may take precedence over national Slovak law because the basic agreement is an international treaty. The attempt to foresee that religious marriages could only be divorced civilly after a church divorce was stalled, as was the proposal to make religious instructions mandatory in all schools. The latter was replaced with an optional class on ethics, which creates implementation problems, particularly in rural areas.

The corollaries reached thus far include substantial influence for the Catholic Church on education and permitting the inclusion of priests in the military. The latest proposal is an agreement that would also provide an option for conscientious objection, which would include the right to refuse to carry out abortions on religious grounds. Thus, doctors and other medical staff, both in public and

---

1   The Beijing Platform for Action is an agenda for women's empowerment to achieve the removal of all obstacles to women's active participation in all spheres of public and private life through a full and equal share in economic, social, cultural and political decision-making.

private hospitals, could turn down requests for abortions. According to the EU Network of Independent Experts on Fundamental Rights, this could amount to inhuman and degrading treatment in violation of the International Covenant on Civil and Political Rights (ICCPR), which the Slovak Republic has ratified (EU Network of Independent Experts on Fundamental Rights 2005, 19).

On the whole, religious freedom seems to be healthy in the Slovak Republic, as the relationship among the various religious groups is amicable. According to the census, 68.9 per cent are Catholics, 6.9 per cent Lutherans, 4.1 per cent are Byzantine Catholics and the remainder consist of various other, smaller religious groups. The number of Jews and Muslims is based on estimates, the former have a community of about 3,000. Data on the size of the latter varies between 300 and 3,000 (Interviews SK2, SK13, see also Bureau of Democracy, Human Rights, and Labor 2006).

However, our country experts outlined that Jewish cemeteries are quite regularly desecrated and that it cannot always be discerned whether the motivation is really racism or possibly 'simple' vandalism. The members of the Muslim community appear to be integrated. However, Bratislava is one of the few European capital cities – including Athens and Ljubljana – without a mosque. Efforts to build an Islamic Centre in the capital were originally approved by local officials but later stalled, according to representatives of the Muslim community (Interview SK13).

A different affair is the relationship between the majority and its ethnic minorities; it is 'the' contentious issue, which parties use in self-serving attempts to mobilize their electorate. The fragility of Slovak democracy is most visible when nationalism plays into the political environment (see generally Harris 2004).

Most Roma live in the country's economically underdeveloped East. Notwithstanding official census, which states that 1.7 per cent of the population are Roma, estimates are that 4.6 per cent or possibly even 10 per cent of the population belong to this minority. There are far-ranging issues regarding child-education, housing and, most significantly, segregation, which are barely covered by a political lid and remain explosive, as the so-called 'Romani riots' in early 2004 indicate (see also World Bank, Foundation SPACE, INEKO and Open Society Institute 2002). The unemployment rate reaches more than 80 per cent in some Roma communities. Even though, according to opinion polls, the public perception is improving, the numbers are still staggering: while 74 per cent did not think in 2004 that Roma were discriminated against, there were still 68 per cent who stated that they would mind if a Roma were to move to their neighbourhood. However, the latter figure is seen as a significant improvement, given that it was 76 per cent ten years earlier in 1994 (Bútorová, Gyárfásová and Velsic 2005, 266).

The integration of the Magyar minority – about 9 per cent of the population – is also a lingering issue. In contrast to the Roma, however, they have a fairly well functioning political representation: the Hungarian Coalition Party (SMK) and the comparatively small Hungarian Federalist Party. They assess their social status and opportunities more critically than ethnic Slovaks: only 37 per cent of ethnic Hungarians believe to have conditions equal to the mainstream, while 55 per cent of ethnic Slovaks think that Hungarians enjoy full equality. Also, while 7 per cent of ethnic Slovaks perceive themselves as disadvantaged in comparison to the mainstream, 59 per cent of ethnic Hungarians consider themselves aggrieved (Bútorová, Gyárfásová and Velsic 2005, 267).

Concealment is a dominant factor among sexual minorities (lesbians, gays and bisexuals) in Slovakia. In a 2002 survey, a representational sample stated that they were hiding their sexual minority identity from their parents (46 per cent) and in public (50 per cent); the majority (55 per cent) felt that they needed to hide their identity in the workplace generally, whereas 34 per cent stated this to be the case in some jobs (Jójart, Siposová and Daucikova 2002, 17, 26, 31).

While exposure to persons of sexual minority identity has increased over the last decade from 35 per cent of respondents stating that they knew a homosexual in 1995 to 38 per cent in 2003, the public perception of sexual minorities is still highly ambiguous. The much-revered EU value system is seen as being out of sync on this point. Public awareness about the vulnerability of sexual minorities, however, appears to be comparatively high, with 43 per cent stating that they believed that persons of sexual minority identity were worse off than heterosexuals (Bútorová, Gyárfásová and Velsic 2005, 266–7).

To end our discussion of the relevant political, economic, social and societal framework conditions for the implementation of our sample directives in Slovakia, one further issue needs to be mentioned. As is the case in many other EU countries, discrimination based on age is a prevalent phenomenon, particularly in employment, and very manifest in some sections, such as teaching.

Transposition of EU Directives

Working Time

The Slovak Labour Code, amended in 2002, dates back to 1965 and was already quite advanced on the issue of working time. The economic reforms of the 1990s brought about an increase of liberalism and flexibility. However, the trade unions were able to hold up against it until 2002. Following the formation of the Dzurinda II cabinet, the Labour Code was overhauled significantly and speedily: the far-reaching reforms were put in place within eight weeks. It was the most important change since the inception of the Labour Code in 1965 (Barancová 2006).

The amendment was based on a significant change of notion: economic considerations defined the goals of employment relations. Flexibility as the key to attracting business was the overarching theme, and a focus on individual agreements was the way to achieve this goal. For one, the regime of dismissal was redesigned to cater to the needs of employers (Barancová 2006). Individual agreements were strengthened; at the same time trade union influence was weakened on various levels, most obviously by the subsequent changes to tripartism, which established the Council of Economic and Social Partnership (RHSP), and limited it to an advisory role only.

Opinions as to who really instigated the 2002 reforms are divided. The government, most notably the Ministry for Labour, Social Affairs and Family, claims that it pushed for the changes in order to make the adjustments necessary to conform with EU legislation (Interview SK8). On the other hand, the employers' association states that it took advantage of the change in government and, immediately following the formation of the new cabinet, prompted the overhaul of the Labour Code (Interview SK4).

Both the Ministry for Labour, Social Affairs and Family and the employers' association, AZZZ, consulted the International Labour Organization (ILO) to ensure compliance with international labour standards (see International Labour Organisation 2002). Due to the difficulties in obtaining comprehensive interviews with both employers and employees, the paper of the International Labour Organization is the primary resource for assessing the drafting process.

Despite the decline of trade union power and the comparably reduced influence of tripartism, negotiations took place. There were a number of meetings during which the substance was discussed. One interviewee complained that documents were only provided two days beforehand and that meetings were set at inconvenient times, such as Friday afternoon (Interview SK11). The negotiations are generally described as 'conflicted', but while both sides agree that there were contentious issues, they state that it was possible to reach a 'balance' between the various interests (Interviews SK4, SK8, SK16).

Negotiations were based on a draft prepared by the Ministry; but there was no involvement on the parliament's side (Interview SK8). It is noteworthy that in addition to the general question of increasing flexibility, the public discourse on the amendment of the Labour Code was dominated by the Christian Democratic Movement's refusal to include 'sexual orientation' among the grounds of discrimination (Paragraph 13 of the Labour Code, see below for more details). Changes with regard to working time – so as to comply with the Working Time Directive – were 'minimal' according to all sides.

The only provision of the Working Time Directive that was not incorporated was mandatory Article 22.1, namely the individual opt-out, which allows member states to institute exceptions to the maximum weekly working time on the basis of individual agreements between employers and workers (Interview SK8).

As regards on-call duty, the amendment only brought a specification for fire brigade workers. Paragraph 87 (5) Labour Code states specifically that 'the working time of an employee of a fire brigade unit may not exceed 18 hours in the course of 24 hours'. The Ministry stated that it was preparing the changes to comply with judgments of the European Court of Justice[2] and a possible revision of the Working Time Directive declaring on-call time as working time, but declined to discuss necessary amendments in the course of the interview for this project (Interview SK8). At the time of the interview, the government did not view on-call time as working time. Given the general approach to timely transposition

---

2   In particular Judgements of the Court of 3 October 2000, Case C-303/98, *SIMAP v. Conselleria de Sanidad y Consumo de la Generalidad Valenciana* and of 9 September 2003, Case C-151/02, *Landeshauptstadt Kiel v. Norbert Jaeger.*

of EU legislation, as one interviewee stated, 'the government is excruciatingly determined to adopt in time' (Interview SK10), and it can be expected that the on-call provisions will be incorporated.

The implemented changes are seen as an increase of flexibility more than anything else; it is viewed as a major achievement that collective agreements on overtime were replaced with oral agreements between employer and individual employee. Overall, there is 'a certain loss of security' (Interview SK18). This appears to be a reflection of a tendency to replace collective agreements adapting working-time rules to the circumstances of certain branches or individual companies, with plant-level agreements on these issues between employers and employees, without trade union involvement.

As in other countries, the maximum weekly working time applies only to one given contract and not one person. Thus, the current Labour Code has a loophole, which makes multiple contracts possible; each with a maximum weekly working time of 48 hours. Surprisingly, the European Commission called for a 'more flexible labour legislation' (European Commission 2002a, 45) despite the far-reaching amendments. It acknowledged the increase of flexibility with regard to 'extending maximum working time, the possibility to work under an external part-time agreement, during weekends and overtime in extraordinary situations and for emergency works' (European Commission 2002a, 79).

Equality in the Workplace

Anti-Discrimination Act　　The Slovak Republic embarked on a rather turbulent debate concerning anti-discrimination legislation on the basis of roughly 18 scattered provisions related to the issue and in particular Paragraph 13 Labour Code, which prohibits discrimination on various grounds. Reflective of the biggest point of contention, 'sexual orientation' was not among the grounds of discrimination in Paragraph 13. The second big issue was the insertion of an affirmative action clause. However, this only happened at the end of a roughly two-year process.

In its 2002 assessment, the ILO criticized the absence of 'sexual orientation' both in Article 1 of the Fundamental Principles, which precede the Labour Code, as well as Paragraph 13 of the Labour Code. This ground of discrimination is included in Article 2 Employment Equality Directive. The ILO also pointed to a possible compliance issue with Article 21 of the European Charter, which enshrines non-discrimination. It also suggested that – in accordance with European standards – 'equal treatment' in Article VI of the Fundamental Principles of the Labour Code be specified as 'equal pay' and 'equal treatment', respectively. As for Paragraph 13, which stipulates the prohibited grounds of discrimination, the ILO limited its comments to citing the relevant wording of the Employment Equality Directive, covered in Article 2. Also, the ILO suggested that legislative protection against 'sexual harassment' be added to the Labour Code (International Labour Organisation 2002, 4, 8).

The rift over anti-discrimination legislation was instigated over the very basic question whether such a law was necessary or not. The Christian Democratic Movement originally held the position that Slovak legislation provided sufficient safeguards against discrimination, while most other political parties argued for a completely new bill solely devoted to the issue of anti-discrimination. Otherwise, they contended, adequate victim protection would not be guaranteed (Interview SK 19). Described by one interviewee as possibly another attempt to 'slow down the process' (Interview SK 14), the Christian Democratic Movement proposed to amend several of the existing provisions related to the issue of discrimination. The Ministry for Justice, then led by Christian Democratic Movement member Daniel Lipšic, even wrote an expertise to that effect (Interview SK 19). However, this was seen as impractical and not particularly helpful for possible victims of discrimination. Thus the Deputy Prime Minister, Pal Csaky and the Department of Anti-discrimination in the Ministry for Labour, Social Affairs and Family pushed for a single anti-discrimination bill (Interview SK 19).

Just before the discussion started in earnest, two prominent members of the Christian Democratic Movement publicly stated their strong views against homosexuals, thereby reflecting the core issues of the ensuing anti-discrimination debate. The then Minister for Justice, Ján Carnogursky, stated, 'same sex marriages degrade the family', adding: 'As long as I am Justice Minister there will be no registered homosexual partnerships.' His colleague, the psychiatrist and former Minister for Health, Alojz Rakus, claimed that 52 per cent of homosexuals were 'curable' (Pisarova 2001a; 2001b).

About half a year after these comments were made, representatives of the gay and lesbian community met with members of parliament for the first time, lobbying to include 'sexual orientation' among the grounds of discrimination listed in Paragraph 13 Labour Code (Reynolds 2001). However, the amendments were passed without including the term 'sexual orientation' after only 43 of the 128 members present had supported the inclusion of this ground of discrimination in a rather chaotic vote (Pisarova 2001b).

Shortly after, in October 2001, a member of the ruling coalition party, the Democratic Left Party, submitted a proposal for life partnerships, including lesbians and gays. The initiators were aware that a passing of the bill was unrealistic, but felt that it was a necessary response to the Justice Minister's comments as well as a general support in the ongoing debate on anti-discrimination (Pisarova 2001a).

As the first draft for an anti-discrimination bill was tabled, the Christian Democratic Movement embarked on a new inroad against the proposed legislation. The Deputy Chair, Vladimir Palko, therefore stated that it was a 'myth' that passing such a bill was a necessary requirement before acceding to the EU. He added that the term 'sexual orientation' was the draft's most 'confusing expression', which, in his opinion, 'doesn't belong to politics but rather to the private sphere'. The Christian Democratic Movement at the same time maintained its stance that recognizing 'sexual orientation' as a ground of discrimination was a first step on the slippery slope toward having to grant homosexual couples the right to adopt children (*Slovak Spectator* 2002b).

After the first proposal for a reading of a draft single anti-discrimination bill fell through, the Deputy President of Parliament, Pavol Hrušovský (Christian Democratic Movement), removed the item from the parliament's agenda on 18 June 2002. NGOs responded with an open letter to MPs demanding the inclusion of all grounds of discrimination in the draft bill, and held protests outside the parliament. At the next session of parliament – the last before the elections – the MPs (including the Prime Minister's party, SDKÚ) vetoed the discussion of the draft. MPs, particularly from the Christian Democratic Movement, insisted that EU accession did not depend on passing such a bill. However, the EU's chief negotiator, Dirk Meganck, sharply criticized the refusal to discuss the draft (Fila 2002).

After the elections and the formation of the second Dzurinda government (centre-right), in autumn 2002, the EU increased its pressure on the Slovak government to pass anti-discrimination legislation, particularly to protect the Roma minority (*Slovak Spectator* 2002a). The European Commission joined the European Parliament in its criticism (Toft 2003a).

The debate was stirred again in early 2003, following the passage of amendments to the Labour Code without any changes to the discrimination provisions therein, i.e. again failing to include 'sexual orientation' as a ground of discrimination (Toft 2003a). A compromise was found when the Christian Democratic Movement's proposal for a provision (Paragraph 2) was added to Paragraph 13, according to which the sexual orientation of a (future) employee could not be queried: 'An employer may not investigate the sexual orientation of an employee.' The Christian Democratic Movement now started to single out homosexual teachers. The Christian Democratic Member of Parliament, Anna Záborská, argued that some jobs indeed had to be barred for homosexual persons because of their 'potential influence on children' (Toft 2003b). She added that homosexual persons suffered from a 'physiological defect' and that people who take part in love parades could not be trusted with working with children (Pisarova 2003b).

The insertion of the 'right' not to be asked about one's sexual orientation 'closed' the issue according to the Christian Democratic Movement, stating that 'the compromise is a good one' (Pisarova 2003c). Meanwhile, the EU insisted that Slovakia pass 'effective' anti-discrimination legislation (Pisarova 2003c).

Next, the Christian Democratic Movement resorted to the Constitution, stating that various grounds of discrimination were sufficiently covered therein (*Slovak Spectator* 2003c). At the same time, the party vehemently opposed a public information campaign aimed at supporting the adoption of the proposed anti-discrimination bill, which was to be launched in early September (Balogova 2003b). Reportedly, the general director of the public Slovak TV, Richard Rybnicek, halted the broadcast later that month because of a personal 'dislike' of the reference to homosexuals (Balogova 2003c). According to the Deputy Chair of 'Direction – Social Democracy' (SMER), Dusan Caplovic, Rybnicek is closely associated with the Christian Democratic Movement (Balogova 2003c).

At the same time, the draft bill was yet again brought to the forefront of the government's open legislative issues. The Chair of the Christian Democratic

Movement took another inroad against the proposed bill, this time stating that 'we have other, more serious problems in Slovakia, and I am asking: what do we need the anti-discrimination law for?' (Pisarova 2003a). In November, the Deputy Prime Minister for EU Integration, Pal Csaky, stated that as a future EU member, Slovakia had committed itself to passing an anti-discrimination bill prior to accession and announced that a proposal would be submitted to the cabinet in January 2004 (*Slovak Spectator* 2003a). At that point the Christian Democratic Movement was the only one of the four ruling parties opposing the proposed bill.

In a report released the same week Csaky made his announcement, the EU made clear its unequivocal support for a single anti-discrimination bill – particularly because it would ensure clarity (Balogova 2003a). In December 2003, the European Parliament warned Slovakia and other accession candidates that failing to pass the anti-discrimination provisions could result in sanctions (*Slovak Spectator* 2003b). Also, the EU Commissioner for Employment and Social Affairs made the EU's stance clear: 'This is not a matter of choice for governments, but an obligation' (Juhasz 2004).

Finally, on 15 January 2004 the cabinet agreed on adopting a single piece of legislation rather than amending the roughly 18 provisions. A committee was set up immediately to prepare a draft by early February (Juhasz 2004). The Minister for Justice, Daniel Lipsic (Christian Democratic Movement), was hopeful that the proposal would be both in compliance with EU requirements and the Slovak Constitution. Earlier he had criticized the law as an 'attempt at social engineering' (Juhasz 2004). The draft anti-discrimination bill passed the Cabinet without the votes of the Christian Democratic Movement in mid-February (Balogova 2004). Simultaneously, the Christian Democratic Movement proposed a constitutional law aimed at protecting the 'traditional family' (Pisarova 2004b). Questioned about the Christian Democratic Movement's opposition to the anti-discrimination law, the Minister for the Interior and Deputy Chair of the Christian Democratic Movement, Vladimir Palko, stated that he 'did not like the provision about sexual orientation' (Pisarova 2004a). 'It is difficult to tell the difference between real employment discrimination against a homosexual, which is something we all oppose, and a situation where we are confronted with the indecent behaviour of a homosexual who publicly declares his different orientation, whereby offending those around him', he declared (Pisarova 2004a).

In the run up to the vote in parliament, the member of the Hungarian minority party, Edit Bauer, proposed an amendment inserting an affirmative action clause. Its main aim was to provide special support for the Roma minority, in particular to ensure equal access to jobs and to education. The Anti-discrimination Act was finally adopted with a vote of 116 of the 150 MPs on 20 May, 2004. The law, Act on Equal Treatment in Certain Areas and Protection against Discrimination, amending and supplementing certain other laws (Anti-discrimination Act) (Act No 365/2004 Coll.), took effect on 1 July 2004. The delayed adoption of the Act – three weeks after accession – did not seem to raise any major issues; the experts stated that the passing of the Law was imminent and thus no political or diplomatic hairs were raised.

The Justice Minister immediately voiced his opposition to the affirmative action clause. In September 2004 he lodged a complaint with the Constitutional Court asserting that the affirmative action clause was unconstitutional. Lipsic held that the clause 'infringed the human dignity' of the majority (Interview SK19; Fila 2004; Jurinova 2004).[3]

At the same time, an opinion survey found that 85 per cent felt that the adoption of the Anti-discrimination Act was a step in the right direction (Bútorová, Gyárfásová and Velsic 2005, 263). 'The main reason for the positive public response to the adoption of the Anti-discrimination Act is a shared conviction amongst many people that disadvantaged social groups in Slovakia should be protected from discrimination' (Bútorová, Gyárfásová and Velsic 2005, 263).

The Anti-discrimination Act is in conformity with the two directives (Employment Equality Directive, Equal Treatment Directive), save that it lacks a definition of 'sexual harassment' (*compare* Paragraph 2 Anti-discrimination Act) (Interviews SK1, SK10). Generally speaking, the Act is perceived to emphasize issues of race – particularly with a view to the Roma minority – and focuses less on other issues, such as religion and gender (Interview SK19). This may also be the result of the emphasis given to this subject by the European Court of Human Rights and the UN's Committee on the Elimination of Racial Discrimination (CERD).

The Anti-discrimination Act states its scope in Paragraph 1 as applying the 'principle of equal treatment'. The principle is described as prohibiting 'discrimination on any grounds, in the exercise of rights and responsibilities in compliance with good morals, and insofar as the adoption of such measures is necessary in view of specific circumstances and possibilities of the person who has an obligation to comply with [this] principle' (Paragraph 2 (1) Anti-discrimination Act). The text continues to list the definitions of the various forms of discrimination (Paragraph 2 (2) – (9) Anti-discrimination Act), in accordance with the directives (Article 2 Employment Equality Directive and Article 2 Equal Treatment Directive).

The Anti-discrimination Act shall not apply to the treatment of aliens, which are provided for in separate provisions. Also exempted are members of armed forces, armed security services, armed services, National Security Office, Slovak Intelligence Service and Fire and Rescue Service (Paragraph 4 Anti-discrimination Act), who are covered by other legislation.

---

3   In October 2005, the Constitutional Court in a close vote struck down the affirmative action clause (Balogova 2005). It is noteworthy that the judge's opinions were in a tie and the court's president thus made the decision. The ruling does not elaborate the concepts of 'positive discrimination' or 'affirmative action' and states that only underage youths, women and persons with disabilities are entitled to special constitutional protection. 'The decision of the Constitutional Court abolishing the affirmative action clause was formally correct because the wording proposed by the deputies in parliament was not good. They failed to formulate a provision that would have been compatible with the Constitution' (Interview SK12). A more carefully worded clause would have likely prevailed.

The 'principle of equal treatment in employment and other similar relations' is enshrined in Paragraph 6 Anti-discrimination Act; it includes 'sexual orientation' as a ground of discrimination. It also contains a provision on "reasonable accommodation" for persons with disabilities (Paragraph 7). It is noteworthy that the definition of disabilities follows the medical rather than the social model (Paragraph 6 (3) d) Anti-discrimination Act) in that the emphasis is placed on the physical manifestation of the impairment rather than the barriers that persons with disabilities have to surmount; however, this is not a breach of the directive's standards.

As already mentioned, gender issues are featured as one among various grounds, thus not reflecting that they originate in a separate EU directive devoted solely to this subject. The same applies to pregnancy and maternity, which are listed as grounds in Paragraph 6 (3) a) of the Anti-discrimination Act among the various other grounds. However, many of the gender-related provisions for the workplace are covered in the Labour Code.

Labour Code   Certain anti-discrimination provisions were already contained in the Slovak Labour Code, as amended in 2002. However, adaptations were made, particularly in Paragraph 13, which stipulates non-discrimination also in relation to gender provisions. The Slovak Constitution – in Article 41 – sets out the principle that 'special care, protection in labour relations, and adequate working conditions are guaranteed to women during the period of pregnancy' (Paragraph 2). It also states childcare and the upbringing of children as a parental right (Paragraph 4). Furthermore, 'parents caring for children are entitled to assistance from the state' (Paragraph 5). The details are to be stipulated in other legislation (Paragraph 6).

The Labour Code starts off with a set of Fundamental Principles. Article 6 thereof is an equal treatment clause: 'Women and men shall have the right to equal treatment with regard to access to employment, remuneration and promotion, vocational training, and also with regard to working conditions. Women shall be secured working conditions which enable them to partake in work with regard to their physiological capacity, and with regard to their social function of motherhood, and also women and men with regard to their family obligations in the upbringing and care of children.'[4] Paragraph 41 regulates 'pre-contractual relations' and states *inter alia* that the (future) employer may not seek any information pertaining to pregnancy, family relationships, integrity (save the information necessary to verify suitability for the job), political affiliation, trade union membership and religious affiliation.

Part Seven of the Labour Code covers the 'company's social policy' and 'working conditions for women and men caring for children' (Paragraphs 160 ff), 'maternity leave and parental leave' (Paragraphs 166 ff), as well as 'breaks for breast feeding' (Paragraph 170). The latter are calculated as working time (Paragraph 179 (3)) and are covered by social insurance payments, as is maternity

---

4   English translation of the Slovak Labour Code derived from the Ministry for Labour's website: http://www.employment.gov.sk (accessed 15 November 2006).

leave. Furthermore, the framework ensuring working conditions for women and men caring for children includes the obligation that employers 'establish, maintain and improve the level of social facilities' for women (Paragraph 161, see also Debreceniova and Ocenasova 2005).

The scope of the already existing equality body, namely the Slovak National Centre for Human Rights (*Slovenské stredisko pre l'udské práva*), was vastly expanded in the second part of the law by which the Anti-discrimination Act was adopted (Article II 365/2004 Coll.). The Centre is entrusted with 'tasks in the area of human rights and fundamental freedoms' (Paragraph 1 (2) Act establishing the Slovak National Centre for Human Rights). The Centre shall monitor compliance with human rights and the principle of equal treatment, collect and provide information on racism, xenophobia and anti-Semitism, and conduct research and surveys to provide data concerning human rights (Paragraph 1). Furthermore, it shall 'arrange legal aid to victims of discrimination and of expressions of intolerance' (e) and, very broadly, 'provide services in the area of human rights' (h). Also, the Centre was given the explicit right to 'represent parties in the proceedings concerning violations of the principle of equal treatment' (Paragraph 1 (3)).

Assessing the coming about and the impact of the Slovak Anti-discrimination Act, all interviewees concur that both the process and the adoption, respectively, are a major achievement. It is generally agreed that the Anti-discrimination Act was 'a necessity' (Interviews SK12 and SK15). It has also been described as 'a good basis for the gradual reduction of discrimination' (Interview SK12). Many assert that the 'pressure from Brussels' was 'good and necessary' (Interview SK15) and that the 'accession process was a big support' in facilitating the adoption of the Anti-discrimination Act (Interview SK14). One interviewee stated that it was more of a mixed bag in that it was a 'benefit and a burden' that the anti-discrimination legislation was the transposition of EU law (Interview SK19). The importance of the process as such is underlined by one Member of Parliament, who stated: 'The details of the Act are interesting but more important is the process – particularly its contribution to the ongoing restoration of democracy' (Interview SK14).

At the time of the interviews, the decision of the Constitutional Court concerning affirmation action was still pending. Reportedly, many shared the view that the Anti-discrimination Act was not yet fully enacted because the possible removal of a part of the Act was seen as a 'blockage' to accepting the law as a full-fledged part of the Slovak legislature (Interview SK14).

Application and Enforcement

Application Problems

Slovak society, in its struggle to change from a 'no rights, all obligations' regime to a full-fledged democracy displays a certain kind of schizophrenia: people are increasingly aware of their rights and gradually appreciate the benefits of diversity and tolerance. However, people seem to maintain an abstract knowledge of these ideas, which they find hard to apply or which they cannot transform into action at the individual or personal level. There are, for the time being, manifold obstacles to challenging infringements and many of these problems have a significant economic twist. However, those who do step up usually do so secretly: fighting for and receiving recognition for one's rights is not something to be shared in and with the public.

Contemporary Slovakia also presents a peculiar mixture of liberalism: it has embraced wide-ranging economic reforms, which would have been impossible in neighbouring states, without resistance. Also, people looked toward the European Union because they wanted to *belong* to the 'liberal' value realm – more specifically the recognition of 'diversity' and minorities – for which the EU stands in the perception of Slovak people. On the other hand, people are personally frustrated with the effects of the (economic) liberal reforms and are seemingly intolerant towards 'others' on an individual basis. For example, a recent poll suggested that 42 per cent of Slovaks would not want a Romani neighbour (Bútorová, Gyárfásová and Velsic 2005).

Part and parcel of the 'liberal' approach of the government (including the increase of 'flexibility') is that people now have to take charge of their rights individually and – for the time being – have little to no hope for backing by institutional mechanisms. The government maintains that it has fulfilled its share of obligations by transposing the directives and making the rights enshrined therein available for the general public.

This focus on the independence of the individual, however, coincides with a multitude of challenges that people have to face in light of the transformation of society at large as well as in the political and economic spheres. The political sphere, as has been outlined above, is an area of special concern. The most obvious and most cited cause for a heightened degree of succumbing to infringements of rights is unemployment. Literally every interviewee and almost all participants in the focus groups agreed that the situation was out of sync as long as the unemployment rate did not reach the 'usual' level in market economies: 7–8 per cent, as one interviewee suggested (Interview SK20). In March 2006, the seasonally adjusted unemployment rate of Slovakia was 14.2 per cent; together with Poland this was the highest unemployment rate among all European countries (Eurostat 2007). The reciprocity of increased vulnerability and high unemployment runs counter to efforts aimed at increasing a culture where people feel sufficiently safe to stand up against abusive employment conditions as well as forms of discrimination. Of course, there are – as will be shown below – various factors that add to this 'reluctance', such as ill-functioning court systems and others which are mainly due to scarcity of resources.

Another problem is that it is formally possible to conclude working contracts also under commercial law (Focus Group SK2). This legal 'escape' route is frequently taken, depriving employees of the protections of labour law (Barancová). Allegedly, some employers expect their employees to register as self-employed '*zivnostensky list*', so much so that job postings stipulate such a status as a precondition for employment. Consequently, employees are not automatically safeguarded by the provisions of the Labour Code and often seem to bear the brunt of what usually are the employer's risks and costs.

Working time   The regime change in the labour law, namely to place many issues at the individual level between the employee and the employer, has manifold consequences. Trade unions have traditionally been weak at the company level, so employees are left to themselves both in their individual dealings with employers as well as during negotiations for collective agreements. Emphasizing individual liberty, i.e. liberty of contract, at such levels in an atmosphere of transition, fragility and insecurity without any institutionalized support could have strong effects in the long run (Focus Group SK2).

To name one example: Overtime is a two-sided coin with a particular sparkle in a transitional economy. Not only people who feel left out and behind feel a 'need' – if not to say a 'necessity' – to make use of financial prospects. Thus, 'employees sign anything possible to make sure that they can work' (Focus Group SK2). Also, 'employees are more interested in working more rather than less' (Interview SK16). The latter statement appears to reflect the status quo.

It was reported that overtime regimes beyond the 150-hour margin set out in the Labour Code frequently exist and that the excess framework of 250 hours annually is often set out as a basic requirement in working contracts. The labour inspectorate – according to the trade union representatives – maintains that such arrangements are in conformity with the law (Focus Group SK2).

Employers welcome the degree of flexibility that the amendments provide, particularly the benefits of negotiating collective agreements at company level are praised (Interview SK20), but even they concede that it is detrimental that regular trainings of employees, which used to be commonplace until the mid 1990s, are no longer facilitated by trade unionists (Interview SK20).

Equality at the workplace   In a 2005 assessment on public opinion in Slovakia by the Institute for Public Affairs (IVO), the debate of the Anti-discrimination Act was described as follows: 'Most respondents endorsed the adoption of the Anti-discrimination Act, but they remained sceptical about its actual impact. When defining the most serious barriers to its practical implementation, they named: deeply rooted negative stereotypes and prejudices toward certain population groups, imbalance in the labour market, poor law enforceability, citizen's general passivity and lack of courage to stand up for their own rights' (Bútorová, Gyárfásová and Velsic 2005, 266).

Among the practical application problems, which also include court fees and lengthy procedures, is the insufficient clarity of the term 'petition' (Interview SK1). The Anti-discrimination Act stipulates: 'Proceedings concerning the violation of the principle of equal treatment shall be initiated by petition from a person who feels wronged by the violation of the principle of equal treatment (hereinafter the 'plaintiff'). In the petition, the plaintiff is obliged to identify the person that has allegedly violated the principle of equal treatment (hereinafter the 'defendant')' (Paragraph 11 (1)). There are additional ambiguities as to what 'discrimination' really means – an issue raised by potential victims, attorneys and judges alike.

Besides, there are many practical concerns as to how a case of discrimination can be established.

For example, the concept of reversed burden of proof was unknown to Slovak law until it was added to the Labour Code in 2001 (Debreceniova and Ocenasova 2005, 23). According to Paragraph 11 (2) Anti-discrimination Act, 'the defendant has the obligation to prove that there was no violation of the principle of equal treatment if the evidence submitted to court by the plaintiff gives rise to a reasonable assumption that such violation indeed occurred.' As will be explained below, few cases are filed in the realm of labour law; therefore, there has been very little exposure to the concept of reversed burden of proof for all potential stakeholders.

Gender issues are pushed from the mainstream agenda for a multitude of reasons. Among the most obvious are the long-standing 'tradition' of accepting hidden discrimination such as preference for men in job application procedures as well as the historic experience that reduced the issue to mere formality and economic constraints by enshrining quotas and same-income stipulations on paper. As a result, there is an insecurity or lack of knowledge, respectively, as to what gender issues are, what women's rights are, and subsequently where the line between 'women's issues' and 'family matters' should be drawn.

A by-product of the domestic violence campaign '*Piata Zena*' was the raising of gender awareness. However, despite the government taking credit for this and related actions in their Beijing Report, the issue of gender stereotypes was removed from a recent National Action Plan on domestic violence (Interview SK7, see also International Helsinki Federation 2006).

The dire state of the situation is reflected by the near complete lack of institutional support. The special department in the Ministry for Labour, Social Affairs and Family was for the most part based on the personal initiative of a few people (Interview SK15). Experts working for the 'Department of Equality and Anti-Discrimination', which was founded in 1999 as a subordinate to the Ministry of Labour, Social Affairs and Family, soon left due to the lack of support. For one, the departmental staff was dependent on the Minister's approval, i.e. had no power to stipulate enforceable decisions and could not take any decision independently (Debreceniova and Ocenasova 2005, 34). However, Minister Ludovic Kanik of the Slovak Christian and Democratic Union (SKDU), who only stepped down in autumn 2005, had a personal dislike for anti-discrimination issues generally and gender issues more specifically. Reportedly, this went so far as the Minister sending the head of the department to all EU meetings – including the ministerial level – even after the expert had left the Ministry (Interview SK15).

As a consequence, the Department of Equality and Anti-Discrimination endured a high degree of fluctuation of frustrated experts, who felt that they were not able to make an impact because they lacked resources. Not surprisingly, the Department was subsequently led by persons who lacked both expertise and experience (Interviews SK15, SK7). As has already been noted above, the Ministry recently underwent an institutional reform, in the course of which the said Department for Equality and Anti-Discrimination was disbanded and replaced by the 'Department for Family and Gender Policy' (International Helsinki

Federation 2006). Within the National Council, there is a 'Committee for Human Rights, Minorities and the Status of Women', which set up a special 'Commission for Equal Opportunities and Status of Women in the Society' as an advisory body in March 2003. The Commission comments on proposed legislation that concerns issues of gender and women. While it is suggested that the comments and suggestions that the Commission makes – it has only advisory status – be passed on to Parliament, this has not happened very often (Debreceniova and Ocenasova 2005, 39).

A side aspect to the lack of institutional support was reflected in a number of interviews, which referred to the difficulties encountered in editing schoolbooks to reflect modern role models (Interview SK1).

With regard to gender-based discrimination, in particular sexual harassment, there appears to be a split in the perception of the problem: younger, more affluent women are very aware and also outspoken about gender-based discrimination. Women who were educated during Socialism and/or whose work experience dates back to Socialist times usually deny the existence of such discrimination. They tend to label it as a 'luxury problem' or a 'caviar concern' and insist that there are more pressing issues (Interview SK17). An interesting aspect is the complete dislike for 'quota systems', which is due to the connotation they earned during Socialist times: quota equates to fulfilling formal requirements without matching personal qualification.

Labour Courts

A further crucial precondition for ensuring that labour law is being applied properly is the existence of a well-functioning judiciary. The Slovak court system does not foresee any specialized labour courts. Labour disputes are to be settled in specialized civil courts and, generally, it appears that legal action in this field of law is taken very rarely.

Labour inspectors are regarded as the trouble-shooters for workplace related disagreements. Courts play into this realm by way of a possibility to appeal a decision of the national labour inspectorate (see below).

As regards working time issues, the hot spot is the adequate payment for overtime. The reluctance to stand up against the lack of such compensation appears to be grounded in the stance that a little increase of the wage (which is usually provided) is already an advancement. Besides, there is a fear of being dismissed – for a variety of reasons other than suing the employer – in case of court action.

In general, 'poor availability of competent legal assistance dissuades most citizens from filing complaints' (Fialová 2005, 152). Very little use is made of the existing provisions; therefore, there are very few attorneys who can take on such cases without having to work their way into the nuts and bolts of labour law. Also, the possible financial gain in such cases is comparatively small given the effort involved. The economic constraints are underscored by court fees of at least 5 per cent of the disputed amount, something of particular concern at both ends of the economic spectrum. People outside Bratislava simply do not have the means to go to court given their income, while people close or inside the capital city may appear to be earning enough but are confronted with disproportionately high costs for living.

The reluctance of employees is also grounded in the lack of foreseeability in such cases: firstly, the courts have a backlog that results in overly lengthy court procedures; secondly, the absence of case law makes it hard to assess what the likely outcome will be; and thirdly, the judges are seemingly overwhelmed by frequent changes in the respective laws.

All these aspects are also relevant for cases of discrimination, and, by tendency, the severity of the problems is multiplied: by and large, there is a lack of exposure to the specific problems of discrimination, also among judges. There is a near complete absence of good practice and case law, respectively. It is noteworthy that Slovakia has no established system of publishing court rulings other than those of the Constitutional Court (Interview SK1). It was reported that as of early 2006 some decisions from regional and district courts were being published online. While judges might have fairly good knowledge of regulations that were firmly established before the numerous reforms – such as the regime for working time – they are hardly familiar with EU-derived law and specialized laws such as anti-discrimination provisions. Efforts to raise the awareness and knowledge of judges are underway.

Other obstacles are seen in the lack of experience with the shifted burden of proof (Interview SK1) and the non-usage of immediate injunctions through which cases could theoretically be decided on a provisional basis within 24 hours (Focus Group SK2).

So far, there is one publicly known court case regarding discrimination in the workplace; it was decided in 2003 and concerned a female plaintiff who was removed from a project she had planned and designed herself. She was substituted by a male colleague with lower qualifications and less experience. According to non-governmental organizations, the judge applied the reversed burden of proof correctly and ruled that the change of assignment was void (Debreceniova and Ocenasova 2005, 73). 'There are no other cases known either on access to employment, working conditions, or unfair dismissal connected to unequal treatment based on sex, gender or family status,' states a thorough 2005 report (Debreceniova and Ocenasova 2005, 73). As was also confirmed in interviews, no cases of sexual harassment were reported.

Labour Inspectorate

The Slovak Labour Inspectorate (*Národný inšpektorát práce*) recently underwent a wide-ranging institutional reform, which, amongst others, resulted in a relocation of its headquarters outside Bratislava. The reform was used as a justification for reducing the number of labour inspectors, which was at about 200–250 in 2005 (Interview SK5). This figure is supposedly already about two or three times lower than that in other countries. However, it was stated that there were plans to further reduce this number by about 10 per cent (Interview SK9).

In our focus group, the labour inspectorate was described as 'malfunctioning', 'completely worthless' and 'not worth being contacted' (Focus Group SK2). It was held that though 'in principle it would seem a good idea to approach the labour inspectorate, given its lack of quality there is no point in doing so' (Focus Group SK2). In particular, the fact that 'technical experts decide over issues of working time' was criticized (Focus Group SK2).

If the labour inspectorate acts, it usually does so on issues of health and safety in the workplace, which appear to be its strong domain. Regularly, however, the inspectorate still comes too late and rushes to the scene of a severe accident or possibly fatality (Interview SK5). Recently, the labour inspectorate has been particularly preoccupied with the issue of illegal work, a governmental priority also reflected in a new law on such matters (Interviews SK5 and SK9). Other areas of particular concern are the transport sector and the problems pertaining to seasonal work, especially agriculture. Various sides maintained that the changes in the Labour Code had resulted in manifold questions and issues in relation to working time, particularly the reference period, but stated that these had been addressed and solved (Interview SK8). The labour inspectorate acknowledged one problem, the above mentioned loophole through which one person can – theoretically – work multiple full-time contracts at the same time. At the time of the interview, it was not yet possible for the labour inspectorate to access social insurance data, which should reveal cases of multiple contracts (Interview SK9).

For the most part, labour inspectors can barely keep up with the workload: while theoretically they may be asked to follow up on violations, including working time and discrimination, they are usually preoccupied with other issues. As can be derived from some of the statements, there appears to be a huge lack of adequately trained staff, in particular lawyers familiar with working time regulations but also persons with an understanding of the nature of discrimination cases. One labour inspector stated that while there had been 'some claims' on issues of discrimination, the labour inspectorates' findings did not confirm these allegations (Interview SK9). The 2003 Annual Report did not show any queries relating to equal treatment at all, and neither did the 2004 Report (Interview SK5, see also Debreceniova and Ocenasova 2005, 48).

The labour inspectorate was also described as having extremely close relations with the employers and thus not being neutral in monitoring 'fair play' at the workplace. It was asserted that the government had given its 'silent approval' to this development (in Slovak a *tichý súhlas*). If and when the labour inspectorate holds an employer responsible, it is possible to challenge the decision of a regional labour inspectorate at the national level of the inspectorate. Thereafter, it is also possible to appeal to a civil court, which decides on the validity of the merits and sends the issue back to the labour inspectorate. Among the labour inspectorate's powers is the possibility to impose fines; however, the amounts seem to be balanced carefully, given that the folding of the business – fees can reach 1,000,000 SK or €25,000 – should be avoided. However, the labour inspectorate can close a business if necessary, e.g. after infringements of health and security related provisions (Interview SK5).

The labour inspectors were not aware of any cases of religious discrimination (Interview SK9). Religious minorities supported this view, stating that most issues, such as the observance of religious holidays that are not Catholic holidays, could be resolved on an individual basis (Interview SK13).

In terms of gender discrimination, the labour inspectors reflected public perception and other interviews by maintaining that the pay gap was a huge problem (Interviews SK5 and SK9). In 2003, on request of the Ministry for Labour, Social Affairs and Family, the labour inspectorate took concerted action on the issue of equal pay and systematically controlled 63 entities; only two proved to be discriminating based on payment (Debreceniova and Ocenasova 2005, 46). In the same vein, specific controls on the observance of general equal treatment provisions protecting women as well as parents caring for young children were conducted in 55 entities; the result: 'The controlled employers are in principle observing the equal treatment principle, as entrenched in the Labour Code. In this field, neither any complaints nor any other submissions were recorded' (Debreceniova and Ocenasova 2005, 47).

Another aspect of discrimination that the labour inspectorate perceives as a major problem is discrimination based on age, particularly among teachers (Interview SK9). This problem was echoed by civil society representatives. As elsewhere, age discrimination is prevalent in the corporate field more generally.

Equal Treatment Bodies

The government's intention in creating the Slovak Centre for Human Rights was to minimize court proceedings, as it is meant, to function as an intermediary. However, as was outlined above, this is only one of the manifold tasks that the Slovak National Centre for Human Rights is in charge of.

Originally established in 1994, the Centre received a wide range of responsibilities by way of an amendment of the Act governing its establishment, passed by adoption of the Anti-discrimination Act (Article II 365/2004 Coll.). The Centre's competences were set out in the transposition section.

The Centre's mandate is very broad; its task is to 'provide services in the area of human rights', and it has to tackle an array of issues including the equality between men and women, since a specialized body has not been created. The Centre deals with gender as a crosscutting issue, as various departments deal with gender and equality issues on an inter-sectional basis (Debreceniova and Ocenasova 2005, 40).

The amount of cases and applications the Centre receives is increasing steadily, and it is gradually more involved in settling workplace-related disputes. The Centre strongly holds that achieving out-of-court settlements is its first goal, thus minimising court proceedings. Another main objective is the raising of awareness; thus campaigns on anti-discrimination issues form a core part of their work (Interview SK15). There are serious financial constraints for various levels of the Centre's work, but particularly in terms of establishing regional centres. To ensure low-level accessibility, the Plan of Activities for 2004 stipulates: 'It is inevitable to create contact places in every region of Slovakia' (cited in Debreceniova and Ocenasova 2005, 90).

In 2004, the Centre had a staff of 12 full-time workers and a budget, which it received straight from the Ministry of Finance, of 8,280,000 SK or €207,000 (Debreceniova and Ocenasova 2005, 19).

In 2001, Slovakia created an ombudsperson to observe 'human rights in general' in relation to public institutions, including state administration, regional self-administration, and legal and natural persons. While, on paper, the ombudsperson has the right to inquire the observance of the equal treatment principle – as part of human rights – in practice, s/he is limited by the means of investigating accorded to this office. The ombudsperson also does not have any power whatsoever to impose sanctions for human rights breaches (Debreceniova and Ocenasova 2005, 42).

Other Aspects of Enforcement

All sides lament the lack of good practice and exposure to cases dealing, in particular, with anti-discrimination. There appear to be two major forces at work: for one, there is a reluctance to expose the fact that one has unveiled and successfully claimed discriminatory behaviour; plaintiffs tend to conceal their involvement in such cases (Interview SK1). Also, if the media covers such cases, they tend not to discuss the merits or the issue of discrimination, respectively; they focus on the damages awarded (Fialová 2005, 152). In a similar vein, it has been stated that judges need to increase their communication with the media (Open Society Institute 2002a, 404). Subsequently, there is little to no coverage of such issues in the legal realm, resulting in a lack of exposure for the general public, potential plaintiffs but also judges and attorneys. The lack of available case law, both in terms of actual suits filed and non-circulation of decisions, also plays into this aspect of enforcement.

A number of lawyers involved in discrimination issues at various levels voiced their hope that cases would be brought to the European Court of Human Rights (ECHR). However, none could state that they had heard that an application had been filed. Given the backlog of the ECHR, it will take a few years until the Court processes such an application.

The economic and social effects of globalization can also be sensed and felt by people in Slovakia. As for experiencing 'other' side effects such as diversity, interviewees held that Slovaks have had very little exposure. Multicultural issues are still comparatively rare in the Slovak workforce. However, some interviewees were content that the increase of foreign workers (notably in big multi-national companies) would bring about a change of perception and the introduction of role models, which could provide examples of good practice. Such hopes have to be cautioned given that 91 per cent of Slovak businesses employ an average of three employees, and only 9 per cent of such businesses employ more than 500 (Interview SK11). One personnel manager was familiar with the term 'diversity management' but admitted that he was a bit lost as to what exactly it means, and acknowledged that there was hardly any possibility to make use of such measures even in a multi-national company because the workforce is still by and large very homogenous (Interview SK20).

For the time being, the discrimination debate in public perception is directly linked to racial discrimination, which is primarily discrimination of Romani people. The derogatory remarks of some interviewees and the complete unwillingness to appreciate the structural forces undermining various efforts to address the manifold challenges for the Romani community bear witness to the depth and severity of this issue.

Conclusions and Improvement Strategies

As this Chapter has demonstrated, Slovakia has largely succeeded in aligning its laws with the terms of the three EU directives. Except for a few loopholes, Slovakia has a clean transposition record. This positive assessment stands in stark contrast to the multitude of 'economic, structural and cultural obstacles' (Interview SK7) that has, as yet, prevented these legal provisions from becoming fully effective in everyday practice.

Several levels of – especially institutional – support need to be strengthened: for one, the general population's knowledge of rights could be improved through awareness campaigns. A crucial factor is the transformation of 'abstract awareness' of work related rights to the level of personal and individual applicability, both as a means for situations in which persons are subject to abuse but also as a way of improving general awareness of causes and effects of discrimination and other infringements of rights.

Such efforts need to be sustained by institutional support from within the government, civil society and public institutions. Therefore, the government's competence in the area of anti-discrimination has to be built up by way of making this issue part of the agenda, and by establishing a competent office within its organizational structure. Moreover, civil society should be further strengthened, also by providing support to trade unions as a way of making the 'checks and balances' stronger and as a contribution to a culture of awareness and empowerment. Existing institutions, such as the Slovak National Centre for Human Rights, should be supported in their efforts to take their work on awareness raising and support for victims to the regional level. This is obviously most of all an issue of financial resources.

Supranational political players, such as the European Union, should possibly reassess the framework for their awareness raising programmes: It appears that the duration of the programmes that are provided and often partially funded by the European Union cannot be adequately rooted in institutions because the maximum duration of four years – including a significant amount of administration – is perceived to be too short to achieve more than a 'dent' (Interview SK7).

A key factor is the public discussion of anti-discrimination issues and efforts towards improving societal attitudes to diversity, solidarity, empowerment and related issues. A major force of public discourse is the media. Looking at the hostile attitude – and its impact – of the public TV's director on an awareness raising campaign related to the Anti-discrimination Act (discussed above), it seems safe to say that improvements in the awareness of media are necessary.

While the judiciary obviously requires vast improvements, it seems inappropriate to make detailed suggestions for court proceedings, i.e. adversarial trials. In any case, the goal of any action taken after the infringement of rules pertaining to the workplace ought to be the continued employment of the employee who feels that her/his rights have been infringed. Therefore, it is usually counterproductive to have the parties engage in a dispute in the full glare of publicity. Even if court proceedings were speedy, even if the unemployment rate were down, an adversarial trial would potentially still cause a loss of face or leave behind bad feelings. To improve the culture at the workplace and foster an atmosphere of inclusion and respect, it could therefore be beneficial to use out-of-court proceedings to reconcile cases of work related rights violations. An arbitration panel of some sort, which could consist of a professional judge and two lay judges representing the employee and employer side, respectively, based on a distinctively mediatory model, could possibly contribute faster and more effectively to achieving the goals of the Working Time Directive, Employment Equality Directive and Equal Treatment Directive than conventional court proceedings (see also Chapter 6).

An important point is that a great deal of resources will have to be added to the realm of enforcement, if improvements are to be achieved. When this idea was put to an interviewee, the response was that such ideas were very much in line with considerations taken by the Slovak Centre for Human Rights.[5]

As one interviewee put it, the Anti-Discrimination Act is a 'tool that requires exposure' (Interview SK3). Exposure in this context connotes that the individual's awareness has to be increased to allow for a significant enhancement of potential cases, particularly for the Slovak National Centre for Human Rights but also court proceedings.

Similar to other countries, however, the business structure of Slovakia has to be kept in mind, considering that approximately 91 per cent of businesses employ an average of three employees. This would be one major factor explaining the predominance of fear of unemployment and victimization, particularly in rural areas.

Significant institutional support is necessary, in particular, to strengthen and sustain gender equality. Various aspects have to be vastly adapted: involvement of women in politics, awareness raising about gender equality, equal pay for equal work, establishment of adequate child care facilities, possibilities for both parents to work part time in their jobs and return to full time employment thereafter, etc.

The labour inspectorate should be strengthened with an increase of resources, which should include a raise in staff, particularly personnel that have expertise in

---

5   Reference was made to a programme initiated by the Ministry for Justice testing a minimally adversarial procedure based on mediation principles. It was not possible to verify this information of April 2007 further.

monitoring issues of working time and anti-discrimination. In addition, training of current staff needs to be facilitated.

As trade union membership has plummeted, it is crucial to provide far reaching institutional support for a partial restructuring of trade unions to enable their engagement at various levels including tripartism and businesses amongst others.

All stakeholders require a deeper understanding of EU legislation, particularly the fact that it provides a framework that has to be applied accordingly in each nation state. Finally, stakeholders should be made aware that establishing a hierarchy of 'rights' such as labelling certain aspects of anti-discrimination as 'Western' or 'luxurious', has a negative impact on the enforceability of the entire range of these rights.

To sum up, this chapter has shown that Slovakia managed to transpose the three selected EU directives in a rather compliant manner, albeit after some political struggles. What finds its way into the statute books, however, does not necessarily become effective 'on the ground'. Owing to severe deficiencies of the labour inspectorate and the judiciary, combined with little litigation activity and weakly organized civil society actors, many of the provisions laid down in European legislation have so far remained 'dead letters'. This mirrors the procedural patterns found in the Czech Republic and Hungary.

It remains to be seen in the next chapter if similar processes may be observed in Slovenia. The concluding chapter will then compare the results of the four country studies and discuss whether the observed patterns may be integrated into the existing typology of three 'worlds of compliance', or whether we need an additional fourth world to capture the challenges faced by the new member states from Central and Eastern Europe.

Chapter 5

Slovenia

Petra Furtlehner

Background Information

Political System

Approximately 1,400 years ago, the ethnic ancestors of the Slovenians first arrived on the territory; and yet, given the country's recent fifteenth anniversary in June 2006, it is still a comparatively young state. The entire period between the first Slovenian state of the seventeenth century, called Karantanija (Prunk 1994, 25), and present-day Slovenia was characterized by 'subordination ... to larger state formations in the region' (Prunk 1994, 12), e.g. during the Habsburg Empire, later the Austro-Hungarian Monarchy, as part of the Kingdom of Serbs, Croats, and Slovenians or the Kingdom of Yugoslavia, during the Italian, German and Hungarian occupation of the Second World War or as part of the former Socialist Federal Republic of Yugoslavia (hereinafter Former Yugoslavia). In the eyes of Fink Hafner and Lajh (2003, 28), Slovenia's declaration of independence on 25 June 1991 'was the last step in a long process of nation-building'.

National emancipation of the Slovenians was driven by civil society groups, who demanded that the single-party Communist regime be changed into a competitive democratic order (Fink Hafner 2000, 13–15). Their efforts culminated in the first free multi-party elections in 1990. In the same year, a convincing majority of more than 88 per cent of the electorate voted for an independent Slovenia. The Serb-dominated Yugoslav army tried to oppose the secession of one of its federal units,[1] but had to withdraw from Slovenia after a ten-day war. The cease-fire was followed by negotiations: With the help of the EU as a mediator, the so-called Brioni Agreement between the Federation and Slovenia was reached. Slovenia had to accept a three-month period in which it stalled the further implementation of its independence. After the end of the moratorium, in October 1991, Slovenia finally started to act as a fully sovereign country, introducing its own currency, establishing control of its borders and adopting a new Constitution.

The 1991 Constitution enshrines a democratic state with a centralized structure that lacks regional organization. But the Slovenian Constitution assigns a specific

---

1   The former Yugoslavia was made up of six republics (Bosnia and Herzegovina, Croatia, Macedonia, Montenegro, Serbia and Slovenia) and two autonomous regions (Vojvodina and Kosovo).

relevance to local self-governance (Part V). 193 municipalities (*občine*, singular: *občina*) are the territorial units in charge of local matters.

Although Slovenia's constitution-makers created a parliamentary structure with two chambers, strictly speaking it is not a bicameral system: Whereas the first chamber, the National Assembly (*Državni zbor*), acts as the supreme lawmaking power, the second, the National Council (*Državni svet*), has an advisory role only. Therefore, the Slovenian legislature has been called a 'unicameral system with a second chamber' (Borak and Borak 2004, 56), a 'one and a half chamber system' (Fink Hafner 2000, 21) or an 'incomplete bicameral parliament' (Lukšic 2001, 18). The National Assembly consists of 90 deputies and is elected every four years, 88 of the members are elected in a system of proportional representation. The country's autochthonous minorities – Italians and Hungarians – choose the remaining two members (Constitution, Article 80). In the last National Assembly election, held on 3 October 2004, seven parties were able to overcome the 4 per cent threshold necessary for representation.[2] The ideological range between them is fairly modest, covering the centre-left to the centre-right. Extremist parties of both the left and right existed in the early years of Slovenian independence, but were unable to sustain long-term support (Bebler 2002, 134).

The National Council consists of 40 members representing interest groups, who are elected indirectly by electoral bodies for a term of five years. 18 seats are set aside for representatives of employers, employees, farmers, crafts, trades, independent professions and non-economic activities.[3] The remaining 22 seats are apportioned according to local interests (Constitution, Article 96).When creating the new Constitution, Slovenia considered the advantages of not only a pure parliamentary but also a presidential system (Lukšic 2001, 12); as a result the Constitution comprises elements of both. The Slovenian political system can be described as essentially parliamentary with the addition of a State President (Borak and Borak 2004, 59). The president represents the Republic of Slovenia and is the supreme commander of its military forces (Article 102). Although the president's real power is comparatively weak, the process of direct elections endows her/him with an important integrative role in the state. The current president, Janez Drnovšek, of the left-wing LDS was elected in December 2002.

No single party has ever been strong enough to form a government on its own in Slovenia (see Table 5.1). The first government in the country's democratic history led by Lojze Peterle (SKD) collapsed soon after the main purpose of attaining independence had been achieved. Since then, the left-wing LDS has been in power almost continuously. The only exception was in 2000, when a centre-right government ruled for six months. However, in the last parliamentary elections people opted for change. The current government, formed in December 2004, is a centre-right coalition made up of the SDS, NSi, SLS and the DeSUS, headed

---

2   The 90 seats in the National Assembly are divided as follows: right-wing SDS 29 seats; left-wing LDS 23 seats; left-wing ZLSD ten seats; right-wing NSi nine seats; right-wing SLS seven seats; nationalist SNS 6 seats; left-wing DeSUS four seats.

3   The specific interests of employers and employees are additionally institutionalized within a social partnership system; see Section on the socio-economic background below.

by Prime Minister Janez Janša. The two members representing the Hungarian and Italian minorities support the coalition. The shift to the right can be seen as a sign of voters being frustrated with the LDS after more than a decade of virtually uninterrupted rule (Interviews SI20, SI21). The LDS took its defeat as an indication that the electorate wanted to see it in opposition. But it – as well as the other opposition parties – vowed to cooperate with the government on projects of national interest (Gaube 2004).

Table 5.1   Governments of Slovenia (1990–2006)

Period	Government	Other parties	Political orientation
May 1990– May 1992	Lojze Peterle (SKD)	SKZ, ZS, SDSS, SDZ, LS	Centre-right
May 1992– Jan. 1993	Janez Drnovšek I (LDS)	SDSS, ZS, SSS, DS	Centre-left
Jan. 1993– Feb. 1997	Janez Drnovšek II (LDS)	SKD, ZLSD, SDSS[1]	Centre-left
Feb. 1997– June 2000	Janez Drnovšek III (LDS)	SLS, DeSUS	Centre-left
June 2000– Nov. 2000	Andrej Bajuk (SLS + SKD)	SDS	Centre-right
Nov. 2000– Dec. 2002	Janez Drnovšek IV (LDS)	ZLSD, SLS + SKD, DeSUS	Centre-left
Dec. 2002– Dec. 2004	Anton Rop (LDS)	ZLSD, SLS, DeSUS	Centre-left
Dec. 2004–	Janez Janša (SDS)	NSi, SLS, DeSUS	Centre-right

Source: Government Public Relations and Media Office (2000); Government of the Republic of Slovenia (2005).

Consensus on major topics is a core value of Slovenian politics, a remnant of the Communist past (Bertelsmann Stiftung 2003, 14) where ordinary people experienced limited but real decision-making powers in the subsystem of grassroots-level self-management (*samoupravljanje*), especially in the workplace (Bebler 2002, 130). This meant that employees were also the owners of companies as well as the means of production and were thus employers at the same time. Therefore, the Slovenian system was referred to as 'social' and not 'state' ownership as in other Socialist countries (Skledar 2002). The change of the Slovenian system, which required the creation of a new state in addition to political and economic transformation, was characterized by consensual politics. This is also true for EU integration (Bucar and Brinar 2005, 120–21), as this process has always been regarded as a means of strengthening the transition process. The promise of greater external security, legal harmonization, and stability; of involvement in the European decision-making processes, and of access to a single European market of 450 million consumers helped to overcome initial concerns regarding the loss of national sovereignty (Inotai and Stanovnik 2004). However, since 1991, when

92 per cent of respondents were in favour of EU/EC membership, the attitude towards the EU has drastically drifted apart between political elites and voters (Bucar and Brinar 2005, 120–24). A recent survey showed that in 2006 only 40 per cent of Slovenian citizens trusted the EU (Österreichische Gesellschaft für Europapolitik 2006, 10).

According to the same source, the President of the Republic is the political institution that Slovenian citizens trust most (57 per cent). The Prime Minister, the government and the parliament are far behind with 32 per cent, 19 per cent, and 18 per cent respectively (Österreichische Gesellschaft für Europapolitik 2006, 10). A drop in voter turnout since the first general election in 1992 raises concerns, too. The turnout of voters in the 2004 elections (60.5 per cent) was substantially lower than the 70.1 per cent turnout in the previous general elections in 2000. As an attempt to restore the public's shattered opinion in politics, the new Prime Minister, Janez Janša, did not only promise that he and his government are serious about transparency and accountability but also made his ministers sign a special code of ethics (Gaube 2004).

Legal System

The foundations of the legal system are laid out in the Slovenian Constitution. Judicial power is implemented by courts with general responsibilities and specialized courts, which deal with matters relating to specific legal areas. Separately, the Constitution provides for a Constitutional Court (Part VIII). The State Prosecutor's offices (Articles 135, 136), the Attorney General (Article 137 [1]), the Notariat (Article 137 [2]), and – as an additional means of extrajudicial protection – the Human Rights Ombudsperson (*Varuh človekovih pravic*) also form part of the Slovenian legal system.[4]

Apart from provisions in the Constitution, the judicial branch is organized by two major laws and several other regulations. The Law on Courts institutes all the courts in Slovenia with the exception of the Constitutional Court. The Law on Judicial Service determines the status of judges. Among the other regulations is the Law on Labour and Social Courts, which establishes the procedure in specialized labour and social courts. In its report on 'Judicial Independence' in Slovenia, the Open Society Institute (2001, 437) confirms that the 'Constitution and the major legislation create a framework incorporating all the important elements necessary to ensure judges a high degree of individual and institutional independence'.

Except for the nine constitutional judges, who are proposed by the State President and then elected by the National Assembly for one term of nine years (Constitution, Articles 163, 165), judges are elected by the National Assembly on the proposal of the Judicial Council (Constitution, Article 130). Their office is permanent (Constitution, Article 129 [1]). The Law on Judicial Service prescribes a mandatory retirement age of 70 years (Open Society Institute 2001,

---

4   A list of judicial bodies is presented by the Ministry of Justice: http://www. mp.gov.si/en/judicial_bodies/ (accessed 20 October 2006).

463). The function of a judge is incompatible with other functions in state organs (Constitution, Article 133).

The 11-member Judicial Council, which is composed of law professors, lawyers, and judges, does not only enjoy specific rights regarding the procedure of appointing judges but also supervises the work of judges and can make proposals for improving their performance (Open Society Institute 2001, 451). In spite of its important role, however, the Judicial Council is not the formal representative of the judiciary. This role is performed by the Supreme Court, the highest court in the state (Open Society Institute 2001, 446).

Altogether, there are four judicial instances with general responsibilities: Besides the Supreme Court, there are four courts of appeal, 11 regional courts of first instance, and 44 district courts of first instance. In addition to the general courts, there are specialized courts with competence in labour and social security disputes. Another specialized court, the Administrative Court, supervises the legality of documents and the operations of administrative bodies of the state. Furthermore, the Constitutional Court protects the constitutionality, legality, and compliance with human rights and fundamental freedoms of legislation. Lukšič (2001, 65) reports that the Constitutional Court functioned in an 'explicitly political way' during its first judicial mandate. It interfered in individual policy decisions by using provisions that essentially dictated how the National Assembly should react in certain cases and what the contents of laws should be. During the new judicial mandate, the Constitutional Court has become less activist and more removed from day-to-day politics.

Specialized courts for labour and social security disputes – the old self-management courts or Courts of Associated Labour, which reviewed cases relating to self-management at work only – were first established in 1974 and started operating a year later. The reasons for founding such special courts were numerous. According to Janez Novak, Judge of the Supreme Court of the Republic of Slovenia, the most important were: the specific nature of labour and social security relations, the independence of the judicial branch in labour law and social security matters, the specific knowledge required of judges working in the area of labour and social security law, the specific nature of the legal basis for decision-making (e.g. collective agreements), and the necessity of special legal protection for workers as the weaker party in labour and social security relations (Novak 2004). The fundamental political, legislative and economic changes of the period of post-independence transition, however, did not stop at self-management courts. As a response, parliament enacted a new legal basis for their functioning in 1993. The 1993 Labour and Social Courts Act adapted the way of resolving labour disputes to the new circumstances, which were characterized by the abolition of social ownership and a new framework for labour relations. The old self-management courts were replaced by the current system of labour and social courts (see below, section on labour courts). In 2003, the law on labour and social courts was again reformed. The 2003 Labour and Social Courts Act was designed to speed up and improve court procedures as well as harmonize practice with recent substantive changes in labour law, e.g. the new 2002 Employment Relationships Act, social security law, and procedural regulations (Kanjuo Mrcela

2004). Hence, the new legislation can be described as 'a fundamental reform of the judicial avenues' (Tóth and Neumann 2003), even if it maintained the system, competencies and organization of labour and social courts. The new Labour and Social Courts Act entered into force on 1 January 2005 (Novak 2004).

As already mentioned, the Slovenian Constitution also provides for the position of a Human Rights Ombudsperson (Article 159). Its role is to protect the human rights and fundamental freedoms of individuals in relation to the state and state-related bodies. The Human Rights Ombudsperson is elected by the National Assembly by qualified majority. S/he serves a six-year term and can be reappointed once. According to the law, all individuals have the right to initiate a procedure through this institution. The Ombudsperson may also initiate procedures *ex officio*. S/he reports annually to the National Assembly on her/his work (Lukšic 2001, 65–6).

The involvement of the judiciary in the accession negotiations was only marginal. However, the competent delegation of the European Commission and the Supreme Court have had several meetings in order to make a joint assessment of progress with regard to judicial issues raised in the reports of the Commission (Open Society Institute 2001, 411).

The European Commission has mostly expressed concern about the huge backlog of pending cases and the slowness of court proceedings (European Commission 2004b). That is why, in May 2002, the Slovenian government adopted an Action Plan, which provides for the increased use of out-of-court dispute settlements, the introduction of paralegals[5], and the transfer of judges to overburdened courts. Since the time frame of the plan is ten years (European Commission 2002b, 22), it is of course too early to assess the impact and effectiveness of the measures. However, up until now it seems that they have not changed the situation much. In its latest report, the Human Rights Ombudsperson (2004, 10) refers to 'repeated complaints' about violations of the right to adjudication within a reasonable time frame as an 'annual constant'. In 2004, 893 cases regarding judicial and police procedures[6] were dealt with among 2,992 total cases (or 29.8 per cent), making this the area with the largest number of cases being handled (Human Rights Ombudsman 2004, 21).[7] The report also states that the majority of complaints lodged with the European Court of Human Rights concern adjudication within a reasonable time frame. Finally, it warns of the serious consequences of delayed court rulings, especially in social and labour disputes, which may further increase the already serious existential problems of the plaintiff (Human Rights Ombudsman 2004, 10).

Still, there are about 600,000 pending cases; the average length of court procedures is two to three years (Austrian Federal Economic Chamber 2006).

---

5   Paralegals, also known as legal assistants, are persons qualified by education, training or work experience who assist lawyers in the delivery of legal services.

6   792 cases were opened in 2004, 85 cases were carried over from 2003, and 16 cases were reopened.

7   The Ombudsperson's office uses the term 'Human Rights Ombudsman' in its English documents.

Most labour disputes take longer than a year to be resolved (Kanjuo Mrcela 2004).

The Open Society Institute (2001, 439) appears to be correct in its assessment that an inefficient judiciary is closely linked with a lack of public trust in the judiciary. In 2006, only about one fifth of Slovenian citizens (21 per cent) trusted courts (Österreichische Gesellschaft für Europapolitik 2006, 10), whereas the common legal understanding is shaped by a strong belief in the effectiveness of legal norms (Bertelsmann Stiftung 2003, 13).

Socio-economic Background

Slovenia has often been described as one of the economic front-runners among the transition countries. In its 1997 Opinion on Slovenia's application for EU Membership, the European Commission stated that the country 'can be regarded as a functioning market economy ... [and] should be able to cope with competitive pressure and market forces within the Union' (European Commission 1997). This finding was subsequently confirmed in all periodic reports on Slovenia's preparation for EU accession by the European Commission (2004b). Silva-Jáuregui (2004, 117), however, recalls that the early days of transition from socialism to capitalism were 'not painless'. The loss of the market of the former Yugoslavia, large external debt and the transformation of the economic structures led to a recession, which in turn resulted in a considerable decline in the country's GDP. Given the decrease of economic activity, the number of unemployed nearly quadrupled in three years and the number of pensioners doubled in the same period (Mencinger 2001, 163).

While other transition countries chose the 'big bang approach', Slovenia has – to the irritation of several commentators – adopted a 'gradualist approach' (Mencinger 2004) to changing its socio-economic system. On the one hand, it thereby avoided shocks prompted by the transformation elsewhere (Mrak, Rojec and Silva-Jáuregui 2004, xxii–xxiii). On the other hand, the pace of privatization remained slow and the social security system suffered huge losses.

Table 5.2   Basic economic developments in Slovenia (1993–2004)

	1993	1994	1995	1996	1997	1998	1999	2000	2001	2002	2003	2004
Real GDP growth (%)	2.8	5.3	4.1	3.7	4.8	3.9	5.4	4.1	2.7	3.5	2.7	4.4
Unemployment rate (%)	9.1	9.0	7.4	7.3	7.4	7.9	7.6	7.0	6.4	6.4	6.7	6.3
Inflation rate (%)	32.3	19.8	12.6	9.7	9.1	7.9	6.1	8.9	8.4	7.5	5.6	3.6
General government balance (% of GDP)	0.3	–0.2	0.0	0.3	–1.2	–0.8	–0.6	–3.9	–4.3	–2.5	–2.8	–2.3

Source: Statistical Office of the Republic of Slovenia; Mrak, Rojec and Silva-Jáuregui (2004).

Thanks to a macroeconomic recovery programme, characterized by trade liberalization and the synchronization of monetary and fiscal policy, Slovenia managed to stop the downward trend, the turnaround becoming visible as of 1993. Since then, the economy has been growing steadily – averaging 4 per cent annually. Already in 1996, output had risen to levels above those before transition (Silva-Jáuregui 2004). In 2005, the GDP per capita reached €13,807 (Statistical Office of the Republic of Slovenia 2005), which is about 70 per cent of the EU average (European Commission 2004b) and the highest of the transition economies in the region. On 1 January 2007, Slovenia joined the Euro area, replacing its currency, Tolar, with the common European currency.

In line with the gradualist reform approach, Slovenia has also undertaken cautious labour market reforms. It has maintained a costly unemployment benefit system. To stimulate reemployment, it has spent considerable resources on active labour market policies. Also a heavy tax burden has been imposed on labour, and the minimum wages have been kept relatively high. In addition, despite further changes introduced by the 2002 Employment Relationships Act, it has retained rather strict employment protection legislation (Vodopivec 2004, 294–6). Similarly to the economic output, after an intense but short-lived reduction in the early transition period, both employment and wages began to increase, and recovery started in 1993–1995. In 2001, employment and wages exceeded their 1991 and 1990 levels, respectively, and unemployment stabilized at a low level (Vodopivec 2004, 296–7).

Social stability has remained an important characteristic during the change of the socio-economic system. Article 2 of the Constitution enshrines that Slovenia is a social state, bound to make arrangements for compulsory health, pension, disability and other social insurance schemes, and to see that they function properly (Article 50). At the same time, the country is obliged to protect persons with disabilities, the family, motherhood, fatherhood, children and young people (Articles 52–56). The compulsory insurance scheme that was created with the aim of implementing the constitutional provisions generally deserves good marks for its coverage and adequacy of benefits. However, due to the high standard of workers' protection, Slovenia's social security system is comparably expensive. In order to ensure the system's financial viability at least in the medium term, partial amendments were inevitable. The reforms were designed in such a way as to reduce benefits within the public system, but, concomitantly, a greater role was envisaged for private schemes, which was to compensate for the decrease of public benefits (Avolio 2004; Stanovnik 2004). Stanovnik (2004, 331) and other experts, however, expect that public finance realities will necessitate further reforms in the future.

In this context, it is important to mention an institution that has contributed substantially to the successful implementation of basic economic and social reforms and the process of transition: the Economic and Social Council, the country's central body for tripartite cooperation. It consists of five government representatives, five representatives of trade unions and five representatives of employers. Its importance has increased steadily since its establishment in 1994. Since 1995, social partners have regularly drafted a social agreement which outlines the obligations of each relevant entity regarding economic, social and wage policies (Lukšic 2001, 56). Trade unions, however, regret that since the recent change of government in December 2004, when a centre-right coalition came to power, the Economic and Social Council has degenerated to a mere 'debate club'. Problems are discussed but the new government shows no commitment to act on results from this forum (Focus Group SI2, Interviews SI3, SI16). In order to revive the Economic and Social Council, trade unions are of the opinion that the institution, which is neither foreseen in the Constitution nor by law, should have a legal framework (Focus Group SI2). Trade unions are comparatively strong in Slovenia. In 2004, the unionization rate stood at 44 per cent (European Commission 2006g, 25; see also Stanojevic 2005, 341 for a similar figure).

Relevant Aspects of Societal Order

Particularly with a view to EU standards in the field of minority protection, it should be mentioned that Slovenia has a pluralistic society, based on its history as part of larger political entities. There are members of various ethnic groups that moved to the respective territory throughout the decades, some of them also representing distinct religious communities. According to the latest census in 2002, Slovenia has a population of 1,964,036, of which 83.06 per cent are Slovenians, 0.11 per cent Italians, 0.32 per cent Hungarians, and 0.17 per cent Roma. Another 1.98 per cent are Serbs, 1.81 per cent Croats, 1.1 per cent Bosnians, and other ethnic minorities from the Former Yugoslavia. According to the same source, 69.1 per cent of the population are Roman Catholic, 1.1 per cent Protestant, 0.6 per cent Orthodox, 0.6 per cent Islamic, 5.3 per cent Atheist, and 2.5 per cent state no religious affiliation. As no one is obliged to declare their religious or other belief (Constitution, Article 41), the religious affiliation of about 20 per cent of the population is unknown (Statistical Office of the Republic of Slovenia 2002).Life in such a pluralistic society is not without tensions. The nature of Slovenian society, however, cannot be blamed for such conflicts alone. In the eyes of some commentators, one reason also lies in the fact that the traditionally conservative cultures of transition countries are not always aligned with the rapid democratization that their governments have executed to become an EU member. In Slovenia, especially the attitude towards immigrants, Roma, homosexuals, and a still very patriarchal attitude towards women is perceived as problematic (Interview SI5, Focus Group SI1).

The country's commitment to respect for diversity and equality is reflected in the Constitution as well as in different laws and regulations. Article 14 of the Constitution guarantees equal human rights and fundamental freedoms irrespective of national origin, race, sex, language, religion, political or other conviction, financial situation, birth, education, social status or any other personal circumstances.

Three national minorities enjoy special legal protection: Hungarians, Italians, and, to some extent, Roma. Members of the Italian and Hungarian ethnic minorities are autochthonous minorities (Constitution, Article 64); as such, they are granted extensive rights (Kristan 1999, 163–6). For example, they always choose one parliamentary representative each (Constitution, Article 80). Also, Roma are guaranteed special protection by the Constitution (Article 65) and beyond (Kristan 1999, 172–3). However, the high level of protection of Italians, Hungarians and Roma stands in sharp contrast to other ethnic groups, which have no collective minority rights. At the forefront in this context is the issue of the so-called 'erased', about 20,000 people from the Former Yugoslavia who did not change their Yugoslav citizenship to Slovenian in time. As a result, they were degraded to 'non-citizens' and therefore have trouble obtaining work, receiving pensions, and accessing medical care.

Article 7 of the Constitution enshrines that the 'state and religious communities shall be separated. Religious communities shall enjoy equal rights under the law and shall be guaranteed freedom of activity'. There are 41 religious communities, spiritual groups, societies and associations registered by the Governmental Office for Religious Communities, which coexist without any major problems (Interview SI14). Among the oldest is the Protestant Church, which has its roots in the Reformation (Prunk 1994, 31). But, as the results of the latest population census show, most Slovenians are Catholic (see above). The Roman Catholic Church is not only the biggest but also the most active religious group. Smaller religious communities view the activities of the Catholic Church – above all its close cooperation with the state – rather critically. Especially in the process of drafting a new Religious Communities Act, which is to substitute for the 1976 Law on the Legal Status of Religious Communities, it seems that religious groups were not equally involved (Interview SI19). One religious minority also faces public opposition: the Muslims' plan to build a mosque in Ljubljana has been a bone of contention for years.

Equal to ethnic minorities and religious groups, legislation theoretically promotes and protects women's equality. Women's good legal status is partly due to the legislation dating from the Yugoslav period (Bahovec, Vodopivec and Salecl 2002, 299–301); but also because Slovenia, as a young state, wants to prove to the international community that it is a competent member of international organizations, and the EU (Office for Equal Opportunities 2004).

Among the first successes of several women's groups that were established during national emancipation at the end of the 1980s was the defence of women's constitutional right to make choices concerning reproductive rights, including the free choice of contraception and abortion, which were already enshrined in the 1974 Yugoslav Constitution. The article regarding the human right to decide 'whether to bear children' (Constitution, Article 55) was the last point of disagreement in the general constitutional debate in Slovenia following independence (Bahovec, Vodopivec and Salecl 2002).

In spite of legal promotion and protection, women in Slovenian society are far from being equal to men. MP Majda Širca describes the prevalent mentality as one that 'perceives women as housewives' (Kotnik 2003). Consequently, women have to bear the double burden of paid and unpaid work (Interview SI16), just like in many other countries of the world, although to varying degrees. As Table 5.2 shows, the rate of employed women, which was already high during Socialist times (Bahovec, Vodopivec and Salecl 2002, 301), is still comparatively high: 61.3

per cent. Moreover, women's unemployment rate is lower than that of the other EU member states studied in this project (7.4 per cent). However, stereotyped as the unpredictable segment of the labour force due to their family responsibilities, women have to face considerable disadvantages in the labour market, resulting in gender segregation and a persistent wage gap. Gender segregation is apparent both horizontally and vertically. Horizontal segregation puts women and men in different areas of activity. Typical female jobs are in the service sector. Vertical segregation puts women in positions of lower status and provides them with fewer promotion opportunities. Regardless of women's higher education, men still dominate the managerial positions (Interview SI16, see also Bahovec, Vodopivec and Salecl 2002, 327–9). Also in the political domain, women are still a minority, particularly in high-ranking positions (Potrata 2005, 19–26). To tackle the persistent under-representation of women in political decision-making, the Constitution and the Act on Elections to the European Parliament were changed in 2004. While the latter ensures a minimum of 40 per cent of each gender for European Parliament candidates, the amendment to Article 43 of the Constitution encourages the adoption of positive measures for equal opportunities of women and men in running in national elections (Office for Equal Opportunities 2004, 17–18). Efforts to introduce legally binding quotas for political parties have so far failed (Bahovec, Vodopivec and Salecl 2002, 306–7).

Sexual orientation is not explicitly mentioned among the grounds on which the Constitution's general equality clause (Article 14) prohibits discrimination but is seen as being included in the savings clause 'any other personal circumstances'. In July 2006, a law on same-sex partnerships, which gives lesbians and gays the right to register their unions and covers property issues along with inheritance rights, was passed by the parliament. Even so, a representative of LGBT persons – as lesbians, gays, bisexuals, and transsexuals call themselves – declared that they are not satisfied with their legal status, since the new law does not grant any other rights associated with marriage including social security or adoption rights. An earlier, more comprehensive version of the current law was rejected after a second reading in parliament in 2005 (Focus Group SI1).

However, discrimination of LGBT persons takes on different forms. Greif (cited in Bahovec, Vodopivec and Salecl 2002, 303) observes a 'persistently high level of social intolerance towards homosexuality' fuelled by statements opposed to sexual minorities by leading representatives of the Catholic Church as well as the media. According to a survey called 'Sexual Orientation Discrimination in Slovenia' published in 2001 by SKUC-LL,[8] half of the respondents had experienced violence or harassment because of their sexual orientation. 60 per cent were attacked/harassed more than once (SKUC-LL 2001). But the survey still does not provide the real picture since many homosexuals hide their sexual orientation. Thus, the actual situation might be even worse.

---

8   NGO promoting non-discrimination regarding sexual orientation.

For Slovenia, the accession to the EU[9] was 'a confirmation that it has managed to achieve its goal of becoming a democratic, legal and social state with an open market economy' (Pavlic Možina 2005, 49–50). Slovenia completed its negotiations on accession after almost five years in 2002. In 1997, the Ministry of Foreign Affairs established the Government Office for European Affairs in order to ensure that Slovenia's legislation complies with the *acquis*, to revise the National Programme for the Adoption of the *acquis*, to report monthly to the government on the implementation of the National Programme, etc. The office's staff includes many specialists in European affairs who gained experience in Slovenia's accession process. Slovenia requested and was granted a very limited number of transitional periods during the negotiations (Bucar and Brinar 2005, 105–17). 'This proves', states the European Commission (2004b), 'that Slovenia is already well prepared for implementing the *acquis*'.

Transposition of EU Directives

Working Time

Like many other EU social and labour law directives in Slovenia, the provisions of the Working Time Directive were transposed in the Employment Relationships Act (*Zakon o delovnih razmerjih*) (hereinafter ERA), adopted on 24 April 2002. Until the ERA came into force on 1 January 2003, Slovenia still enforced the previous dating from the Yugoslav period, which consisted of two pieces of legislation: the 1989 Federal Law on Basic Rights of the Labour Relationship[10] and the 1990 Slovenian Law on Labour Relationships. The federal act introduced – as its name already indicates – basic rights and obligations relating to labour relations. The Slovenian Law on Labour Relationships regulated these rights and obligations in more detail and therefore had stronger validity than the federal act (Skledar 2003). Both laws included provisions on the organization of working time.[11]

It is often said that – due to the nature of ownership in those days – the regulation of working time was not of big importance during Socialism. Since labour relations under the previous self-management system were marked by mutual dependence, reciprocity, and solidarity between employees (Konèar 1999, 2), nobody worked excessive hours and thus had no motive to force anybody else to do so (Interviews SI2, SI10, SI21). Consequently, it is rather surprising that the working time provisions stipulated in the old labour law and collective agreements respectively were quite elaborated and also favourable for Slovenian workers. Indeed, the Working Time Directive did not require a high degree of

---

9   A referendum on EU accession was held on 23 March 2003. Eighty-six per cent of the electorate voted in favour of accession to the EU, the turnout was 60 per cent.

10   Short: Federal Law on Basic Labour Rights.

11   The Federal Law on Basic Labour Rights, for example, contained the regulation of Working Hours (Articles 24–27) and Breaks and Absence (Articles 28–35) in its Part III Worker Rights, Obligations and Responsibilities.

change within the country's new ERA, which substituted the Federal Law on Basic Labour Rights and the Slovenian Law on Labour Relationships.

This can easily be explained by the fact that the working time provisions valid until the entering into force of the ERA had been established in a period of constitutional and legislative transition in the former Yugoslavia – following the system of self-management at work with its inherent view on working time. The Federal Law on Basic Labour Rights was one of several laws that were adopted in order to introduce a market economy and a new socio-economic system. For the first time, it put labour relations on a contractual basis (Skledar 2003).

As for the main changes required to meet the EU's standards in the area of working time, only a few points have to be mentioned. Firstly, both the Federal Law on Basic Labour Rights and the Slovenian Law on Labour Relationships provided for a 42-hour working week. Concerning overtime work, the federal act stated that an employee's working time was not supposed to exceed additional ten hours per week (Article 24 [5]). The Slovenian Law on Labour Relationships, however, definitely limited overtime work to eight hours per week. The maximum weekly working time, including overtime, was thus 50 hours. Since the Working Time Directive stipulates a weekly limit of 48 hours (Article 6), the maximum working week had to be shortened by two hours. Secondly, also in both laws, paid annual leave was not counted in weeks but in days and comprised at least 18 workdays. To bring the country in line with the standards of the Working Time Directive, employees had to be entitled to at least four weeks paid annual leave. Thirdly and fourthly, night work limits and a definition of working time had to be added to the new labour law because both were not included in the Federal Law on Basic Labour Rights and the Slovenian Law on Labour Relationships, respectively.

Following various interruptions, including three changes of government, the draft of the ERA was finally submitted to the Council after seven years of negotiations. Three rounds of consultation with trade unions and employers' associations were held (Interview SI9). Finally, the draft was discussed in the tripartite Economic and Social Council. The protracted discussions on the new labour law between the social partners caused a delay in Slovenia's national timetable for the transposition of EU legislation. While the ERA was scheduled for parliamentary approval by 31 December 1999 (Government Office for European Affairs 1999), the new labour law was actually enacted no sooner than on 24 April 2002. Nevertheless, the postponement of the adoption of the ERA did not interfere with the Commission's Agenda for Slovenia's accession to the EU.

Also, the preparation of the chapters that regulate working time in the Slovenian workplace[12] caused lively debates – above all between employers' associations and trade unions. Among the last articles that were harmonized out

---

12   Chapters 4: Working Time (Articles 141–148); 5: Night Work (Articles 149–153); 6: Breaks and Rests (Articles 154–156); 7: Particularities of Arrangements of Working Time, Night Work, Breaks and Rests (Articles 157–158); 8: Annual Leave (159–166); included in Part III Rights, Obligations and Responsibilities arising from Employment Relationship of the ERA.

of altogether 246 ERA-articles was the restriction of the annual maximum for overtime work (*Slovenia Business Week*, 5 November 2001), which was limited to 180 hours per year in the old labour law. However, it should be stressed that the controversies over the organization of working time were not related to the EU's requirements as such – be it to specific provisions of the Working Time Directive or to the transposition mode – but to cases where, as in the above-mentioned example, the minimum standards in the directive were lower than the pre-existing ones (Interview SI3). The country was well aware that the transposition of the Working Time Directive (just like all the other EU directives) was a necessity in order to become a member of the EU. So, the involved parties 'did not question much' (Interview SI9) whether they should incorporate the EU working time provisions or not.

In this spirit, the employers' side did not oppose the inclusion of provisions foreseen by the Working Time Directive, either, even if originally they would have preferred to have more flexible arrangements (Interview SI7). However, as the directive only lays down minimum requirements (Working Time Directive, Article 1 [1]), employers' associations tried at least to change practices and triggered discussions of lowering national standards. One of their goals was to do away with the long standing 30-minute daily break, which was counted as working time and thus had to be paid by the employer. The 30-minute daily break has a long tradition in the country. Employers' associations claimed that 'nobody has that in the EU' (Interview SI3). Trade unions of course protested and in the end none of the pre-existing higher working time standards was lowered. As a result, the ERA retained older provisions that go beyond the EU's requirements.

Firstly, the ERA extends the Working Time Directive's daily rest period of at least 11 uninterrupted hours per 24-hour period to at least 12 such uninterrupted hours. Secondly, while the Working Time Directive entitles a worker to a rest break for a working day longer than six hours, in Slovenia this right is granted to a worker who works at least four hours a day. Thirdly, while the Working Time Directive restricts overtime work to eight hours per week on an average, Slovenia has a stronger limitation in its law: overtime work may not exceed eight hours a week, 20 hours a month and 180 hours a year as an average over a period of six months (ERA, Article 143 [3]) or 12 months on the basis of branch collective agreements (ERA, Article 158 [5]). Fourthly, the ERA foresees a 30-minute daily break that is counted as working time and paid by the employer for every worker who works full-time (ERA, Article 154 [1]). That is why employers say that, although the new law introduced 40 hours (normal) weekly working time, the actual working time is 37.5 hours in Slovenia (Interview SI7).

The fact that Slovenia kept some of the higher working time standards of the previous labour law shows that trade unions successfully defended existing workers' rights. Nevertheless, to finally reach consensus with the employers' side in the Economic and Social Council, trade unions also had to make concessions in the drafting process. With the government acting as a mediator, a compromise was finally found and 'both sides won something: on the one side the rights of the workers were strengthened and on the other side employers got more flexibility' (Interview SI7).

Flexibility, the big novelty, was increased by easing the process of dismissal for employers (*Slovenia News*, 28 January 2003). Whereas the old labour law only gave the employee the right to an ordinary termination of the employment contract by notice of leave, according to the ERA the employer now also has the right to do that (ERA, Article 80 [1]). The only difference is that whereas the worker can ordinarily terminate employment without explanation, the employer's respective decision must be based on substantiated reasons (ERA, Article 81 [1], [2]).

In the area of working time, the following provisions of the ERA allow for a relatively high degree of flexibility: Slovenia derogated from the Working Time Directive's four-month reference period for the calculation of the maximum weekly working time and provided for a statutory six-month reference period instead (ERA, Article 143 [3]). Additionally, branch collective agreements may extend this reference period to 12 months when required by objective or technical reasons or reasons concerning the organization of work (ERA, Article 158 [5]). Further derogations from the provisions of the Working Time Directive are applicable to certain categories of workers, like managers and family workers (ERA, Article 157), and to certain activities, e.g. activities requiring permanent presence (ERA, Article 158). Slovenia also made use of the individual opt-out from the 48-hour week, which is provided for by Article 22, Paragraph 1 of the Working Time Directive; but only in the public health care sector – because of a shortage of doctors in particular. Consequently, this possibility was not directly included in the ERA and is thus generally not applicable.

So, all in all, it seems that the transposition of the Working Time Directive into the new ERA turned out well. Based on the quite advanced labour law dating from the Yugoslav period, the crucial question was how to accommodate the existing higher working time standards. With a mix of provisions, which exceed the EU's requirements on the one hand and derogations from the directive on the other hand, a solution could be found that finally satisfied the social partners.

Two points, however, are problematic: firstly, interest groups which are not official members of the Economic and Social Council were almost completely excluded from the process of transposing the Working Time Directive (or of preparing the new Slovenian labour law as a whole) under the auspices of the Ministry of Labour, Family and Social Affairs. Although the Ministry organized events to hear the input of these groups, their involvement was not assessed as satisfactory, as they could hardly exert any influence on the outcome (Interview SI7). Secondly, working time in the Slovenian workplace as regulated in the ERA does not fully comply with the EU's requirements in this area. The Working Time Directive provides for a basic reference period of four months (Article 16b), which can be extended to six months in certain sectors (Article 17 [3]) and to 12 months on the basis of collective agreements (Article 19). Yet in Slovenia, the reference period for averaging out the 48-hour week was generally set at six instead of four months.

Equality in the Workplace

Slovenia first regulated anti-discrimination in the workplace in the new ERA (*Zakon o delovnih razmerjih*). Protection against gender discrimination in employment is also provided in the *Act* on Equal Opportunities for Women and Men (*Zakon o enakih možnostih žensk in moških*). Only since the adoption of the Act Implementing the Principle of Equal Treatment (*Zakon o uresničevanju načela enakega obravnavanja*), however, have all provisions of the Equal Treatment Directive and the Employment Equality Directive been covered adequately. As a transposition method, Slovenia thus chose a combination of a multi-ground anti-discrimination act, a single-ground act and labour law (European Commission 2005a, 13).

Before the above-mentioned laws entered into force, a ban on discrimination in the field of work only resulted from the principle of equality enshrined in the Constitution and ratified international agreements. Article 14 of the Constitution prohibits discrimination on the grounds of national origin, race, sex, language, religion, political or other conviction, financial situation, birth, education, social status or any other personal circumstances. Sexual orientation is not expressly stated among the various grounds but is included in the savings clause 'any other personal circumstances'. In addition to Article 14, the general equality clause, there are articles in the Constitution that stress equality in relation to different areas of life. Article 49, for example, provides that 'everyone shall have access under equal conditions to any position of employment'. Anti-discrimination provisions are also found in international treaties such as the International Covenant on Civil and Political rights, the International Convention on the Elimination of all forms of Racial Discrimination, and relevant International Labour Organization conventions to which Slovenia is party. Slovenia has signed Protocol 12 to the Convention for the Protection of Human Rights and Fundamental Freedoms which covers discrimination, but still has to ratify it (European Commission 2003c, 112).

Although some claim that the legislative measures to transpose the Equal Treatment Directive and the Employment Equality Directive where just taken 'to make the EU happy', since the content of both directives is covered by the Constitution anyway (Interview SI2), Slovenia's legislators were convinced fairly easily by the EU *acquis* that the existing legal framework was insufficient to provide adequately for the principles of equal opportunities and equal treatment, irrespective of people's specific personal circumstances (Javornik 2004). Amongst others, clear definitions of the forms of unlawful discrimination and backing institutional mechanisms had to be provided for, thereby also making the principle of equality less abstract. The new ERA, which came into force on 1 January 2003, presented a number of provisions on equal opportunities and equal treatment in the workplace. The most important is Article 6, included in Part I, General Provisions, which prohibits direct and indirect discrimination based on various grounds, including sex, religious conviction and sexual orientation. This ban applies to recruitment, the conditions of employment, as well as the termination of an employment contract, in both the public and the private sector. Article 6 is a novelty in Slovenian labour legislation. Its introduction into the ERA can be viewed as a direct result of the EU's requirements, since previous labour legislation did not contain any such explicit provision on prohibition of discriminatory treatment in the workplace.

Many other provisions included in the ERA apply the general prohibition of discrimination in employment as set out in Article 6. Some of the main examples are: Article 25 provides equal opportunities and equal treatment for women and men as regards the conclusion of employment contracts. The employer is not allowed to advertise jobs only for one sex or give priority to one sex. According to Article 26, the employer may not demand information on the family and/or marital status, a possible pregnancy, family planning or other information, unless this information is directly related to the employment relations (Paragraph 2). Moreover, the employer may not subject the conclusion of an employment contract to the condition of providing such information (Paragraph 3). Article 27 states that job applicants are not obliged to answer questions that are not directly related to employment. Article 45 prohibits sexual harassment. Article 89 makes the termination of an employment contract based on some of the personal circumstances listed in Article 6 invalid (Javornik and Skledar 2004).

Even if the ERA's regulation of anti-discrimination is definitely 'a step forward in the protection of the most vulnerable groups' (European Commission 2003c, 112) in the workplace, its provisions do not completely transpose the Equal Treatment Directive and the Employment Equality Directive. It does, for example, not contain definitions of direct discrimination, harassment or instruction to discriminate. Also, the prohibition of direct discrimination is not explicitly mentioned. Further efforts in the legislative area were thus needed. Many provisions foreseen by the Equal Treatment Directive were transposed in the *A*ct on Equal Opportunities for Women and Men, which was adopted on 21 June 2002. On 6 May 2004, however, the Slovenian Parliament passed a general systemic law prohibiting discrimination – the Act Implementing the Principle of Equal Treatment. Since then, the country's law has been in full compliance with the said directives. Accordingly, the correct transposition of the Equal Treatment Directive and the Employment Equality Directive was not achieved when Slovenia joined the EU on 1 May 2004. Given the minimal delay of only a few days, it does not come as much of a surprise that the European Commission did not take any informal or formal measures such as a letter of formal notice or a reasoned opinion (Interview SI6).

The Act Implementing the Principle of Equal Treatment can be described as the centrepiece of Slovenian anti-discrimination legislation. As a general systemic law, it ensures equal treatment and equal opportunities based on any personal circumstances, in all areas of social life (Article 1). The act is harmonized with the previously adopted *A*ct on Equal Opportunities for Women and Men, which means that the two acts are consistent regarding terms, institutions and procedures. The Act Implementing the Principle of Equal Treatment contains all the provisions prescribed in the Equal Treatment Directive and the Employment Equality Directive that were missing until its adoption.

The two Slovenian anti-discrimination acts, the Act Implementing the Principle of Equal Treatment and the Act on Equal Opportunities for Women and Men, were drafted by the Governmental Office for Equal Opportunities together with experts from various ministries and other governmental offices. In the process of preparing the legislation, the Office for Equal Opportunities cooperated with social partners. In addition, consultations with NGOs took place, but at a slower pace. One NGO complained that they were consulted only after the drafts had already been completed and that their suggestions were not considered (Interview SI4). Before the proposals were sent to the government and finally to the parliament for adoption, the tripartite Economic and Social Council gave its opinion.

The transposition of the Equal Treatment Directive and the Employment Equality Directive created no problems and therefore caused no conflicts among the actors involved. Both trade unions and employers' associations supported the process of preparing anti-discrimination legislation. To put it in the words of a representative of an employers' association, the introduction of Article 6 into the ERA '... did not touch us so much. It is just one article. There were more than 200 other articles. Some of them were very important for the price of the labour force. Equal treatment does not raise the price of the labour force. So, it was nothing to be negotiated' (Interview SI2). The Equal Treatment Directive and the Employment Equality Directive were significantly over-implemented in Slovenia. The Slovenian legislation transposed the equality principle to include any personal circumstances and any area of social life. Yet, Slovenia used the derogations concerning difference of treatment based on genuine occupational requirements, concerning religion and belief, and the positive action derogation.[13]

By passing first the ERA, then the *Act on Equal Opportunities for Women and Men* and finally the Act Implementing the Principle of Equal Treatment, Slovenia harmonized its legal framework in the area of equal opportunities and equal treatment (in the labour market and beyond) with EU standards. The degree of changes required by the Equal Treatment Directive and the Employment Equality Directive can be classified as high because Slovenia previously did not have explicit provisions on prohibition of discrimination in employment. Anti-discrimination provisions had to be enshrined in three different legal acts, until

---

13   Applicants for jobs in the army, in the police, and in courts, for example, may be treated differently in the process of recruitment. In order to get a position in the above-mentioned institutions, one has to meet genuine occupational requirements determined by a special law (Tratar et al. 2005). The derogation concerning difference of treatment based on religion and belief makes it possible for religious communities to establish religious schools for training priests. Religious communities manage those schools autonomously, determine their curricula, and select their teachers (Law on the Legal Status of Religious Communities). However, the new Religious Freedom Act, which is currently (in April 2006) still in the process of adoption (second reading), no longer contains this provision (Interview SI19). The positive action derogation has for example been used in the ERA to grant special protection for some categories of employees such as (pregnant) women, parents, juveniles, disabled, elderly workers (Part IV Protection of Certain Categories of Workers). Juveniles *inter alia* are prohibited from working at night and performing certain jobs and are entitled to longer annual leave (Articles 194–198).

the provisions of the Equal Treatment Directive and the Employment Equality Directive were finally covered adequately. Nevertheless, according to employers' representatives, the changes required by the directives did not cost a lot of money (Interview SI2). Only the government had to provide money for the establishment of two new bodies which should put the principle of equality into effect: the Advocate of the Principle of Equality, and the Council of the Government for the Implementation of the Principle of Equal Treatment.

Application and Enforcement

Application Problems

The proper application of the Working Time Directive, the Equal Treatment Directive, and the Employment Equality Directive requires some commitment from the employers' as well as from the employees' side. Both employers and employees have to know their rights and obligations stemming from EU legislation in order to be able to apply them correctly. Employers, in addition, must be willing to comply with the law. Employees, by contrast, must be ready to defend their rights and entitlements if necessary. In Slovenia, some problems can be observed that raise concerns. A lack of information, a lack of trust in public institutions, the fear of suffering negative consequences, and the potential opposition of employers are major factors.

Application problems in general   In theory, the knowledge of labour law should not be problematic at all because Article 26, Paragraph 7 of the ERA states: Before concluding an employment contract, the employer must inform the employee about the working conditions and the rights and obligations related to the position in question. In practice, however, the situation is different. It is questionable whether companies including larger entities follow this rule (Interview SI18), not to mention small ones. As a result, employees but also employers are generally not as informed about their rights and responsibilities as they should be.

Especially the awareness of anti-discrimination provisions is considered low, although the Governmental Office for Equal Opportunities, social partners and NGOs have initiated campaigns to make equality laws better known. Sometimes employers do not even realize that discrimination is prohibited and can be penalized with a fine. The same can be said for employees (Interview SI1). Equally, it appears that the Advocate of the Principle of Equality, who assists victims of discrimination, is not very well known.

By comparison, the knowledge of working time provisions seems to be better. This is due to the fact that Slovenia's working time provisions were already quite developed prior to the transposition of the Working Time Directive into national legislation. Consequently, the changes in this area were much smaller than the changes required by the two anti-discrimination directives. It might thus be the case that the reluctance of employees to defend their rights stemming from working time provisions is rather explained by the lack of trust in public institutions and/ or the fear of suffering negative consequences.

Even if employees are informed about their rights and entitlements and about the bodies which are responsible for putting them into effect, it is not certain that they will take action when it comes to breaches of the law. Many people do not trust public institutions; the enforcement bodies of labour law are no exception. They are perceived as either weak or inefficient or being more on the employers' side (see below, section on the labour inspectorate). Therefore, people do not approach them as they know it costs money and/or time, and decisions on legal claims are not necessarily made correctly.

One more cause prevents workers from fighting for their employment rights: the fear of suffering negative consequences or rather the fear of being victimized by the employer. Although there are judicial and out-of-court safeguards against breaches of employment rights, there is no practical safeguard against mobbing or psychological stress following the lodging of a complaint with the enforcement bodies of labour law (Interview SI15). Above all, of course, people are afraid of losing their job and of the associated economic hardship. The experience that a job is not necessarily secure is relatively new for Slovenian employees. In Socialist times, it was not at all unusual that people retained one employment position their whole life (Vodopivec 2004). With the transition to a market economy, however, which brought a clear division of employers' and employees' interests, working conditions have changed significantly. These changes resulted in the adoption of the new ERA, which made dismissals easier. People have adapted to this new situation and are typically ready to abide by their employer's wishes in order to maintain employment. The reluctance of workers to defend their rights is even greater in regions where unemployment is especially high, i.e. in rural areas. Only if the job is lost is an employee likely to seek legal action in court. Accordingly, court cases dealing with termination of employment are the most frequent after disputes over wages/benefits (Kanjuo Mrcela 2004).

Finally, the correct application of the national norms stemming from the Working Time Directive, the Equal Treatment Directive, and the Employment Equality Directive is threatened by opposition of employers. When employees are not well informed about their rights, do not trust in the enforcement of their rights, and are also afraid to complain, it is often cheaper for employers not to abide by the laws (Interview SI5).

Partially as a result of application problems in general, violations of the rights and obligations as foreseen by the Working Time Directive, the Equal Treatment Directive, and the Employment Equality Directive are reportedly easily found in everyday working life. A selection of application problems specific to the area of working time and equality, respectively, is presented below.

Application problems specific to the Working Time Directive   As already mentioned, Slovenia provides for an individual opt-out from the 48-hour week pursuant to Article 22, Paragraph 1 of the Working Time Directive in the public health care sector. Furthermore, the ERA virtually extends the possibility to voluntarily work longer than an average of 48 hours per week to every Slovenian employee. In its Article 146, the ERA states that in exceptional cases another employment contract for a maximum of eight hours a week may be concluded by a worker who already works full time. Nevertheless, in practice, there are many Slovenian employees who work more than 48 hours per week on average without the use of either the formal opt-out procedure (Working Time Directive, Article 22 [1]) or the possibility of supplementary work (ERA, Article 146). In case of an inspection, employers are not hesitant to show falsified working time records (Interview SI3), which is not only a breach of working time provisions as prescribed in the ERA but also a violation of the Law on Work Records (1996) (Interview SI18).

Some employees cannot make use of their rest break during working time, e.g. when they are working with machines which can neither be left unattended nor stopped. As a consequence, those employees have to eat as they work (Focus Group SI2). The Working Time Directive takes this reality into consideration by offering the possibility to derogate from the right to a rest break during working time, but only if equivalent rest periods are granted (Articles 17 [2], [3]; 18). In Slovenia, for example, the energy sector made use of this option and entitled workers to 13 days additional leave per year. But in other branches, like in the paper industry, negotiations over some kind of compensation for the lost break failed (Focus Group SI2).

Additionally, there is an application problem – well-known from the other EU member states – that is linked to the definition of working time. As the ERA does not explicitly include on-call duties in its definition of working time, the interpretation of on-call varies from sector to sector. The respective practice is regulated in collective or individual agreements. Mainly, employees receive 30 per cent of their normal pay for time spent on-call at the workplace, for time spent on-call at home they receive 10 per cent. In the health care sector, on-call duties are not considered working time at all. This is a clear breach of the ECJ's jurisprudence in the *SIMAP* and *Jaeger* cases. However, trade unions active in this sector have not gone to court so far because collective agreement negotiations are underway (Focus Group SI2).

Application problems specific to the Equal Treatment Directive and the Employment Equality Directive The provisions enshrined in the directives prohibit, amongst others, discrimination against women, members of religious groups, as well as lesbians and gays in the workplace. Nevertheless, each of these individual groups within society experiences breaches of this prohibition in day-to-day working life, even though the directives have been transposed correctly into national legislation.

Women mostly face discriminatory treatment by employers in the context of possible or actual pregnancy and motherhood, as they are often denied jobs because they already have children or because the employer assumes that they will become pregnant. A 'particular phenomenon' in this regard is the 'blank notice of termination of employment'. Before employing a female job applicant, the employer demands that she signs an undated document giving notice of termination of her employment contract. If the woman becomes pregnant, the date is inserted in the pre-signed document and the woman loses her job (Javornik and Skledar 2004). Yet this is not the only way employers avoid retaining a woman's position during maternity leave. In many cases, employers do not prolong fixed-term employment contracts, if they find out that a woman is pregnant. Sometimes, employers even exert pressure on women by threatening to dismiss them if they are absent from work to care for a sick child (Focus Group SI1, see also Javornik and Skledar 2004). Furthermore, the gap between female and male wages is 6.9 per cent for work of the same value (Carley 2005). And although sexual harassment cases are rarely reported, they do occur. However, it can be assumed that most of the victims do not want to go public.

Members of religious groups as well as lesbians and gays mostly choose not to speak as openly as women about their discrimination. Accordingly, there is not a lot of information available about discrimination in the workplace experienced on the grounds of religion and sexual orientation. Still, the following can be discerned: Muslim women who wear headscarves are not accepted in certain positions (Focus Group SI1). Members of the Adventist Church often have difficulties to take leave on Saturdays, although they offer alternatives, e.g. to work longer on other days or to work on Sunday instead (Interview SI19). According to a NGO representative, many lesbians and gays have lost their jobs because of their sexual orientation (Interview SI4). In 2001, SKUC-LL, an NGO promoting non-discrimination based on sexual orientation, conducted a nationwide survey.[14] According to this study, a relatively low proportion (2.9 per cent) of the respondents stated that they had been dismissed from a job because of their sexual orientation, while a further 2.3 per cent suspected that they had been dismissed for this reason. What is alarming, however, is the fact that 37.8 per cent of all respondents reported that they conceal their sexual orientation at work. In that sense, the workplace frequently turns out to be an insecure place for lesbians and gays: those definitely dismissed or who suspected dismissal represent almost 10 per cent of those whose sexual orientation was definitely known or suspected to be known (SKUC-LL 2001).

Employees who want to tackle their application problems pertaining to working time or equality rights have the following possibilities. If the breach of law is related to an act or deed of state authorities, local self-government authorities or bearers of public authorities, the concerned person is best advised to approach the Human Rights Ombudsperson. In case of a violation of the ban on discrimination in the workplace by a private employer, the victim can file a petition with the Advocate of the Principle of Equality, who is employed by the Governmental Office for Equal Opportunities. Persons whose working time or equality rights have been breached can also turn to the labour inspectorate, as this is the body responsible for the supervision of the implementation of the ERA (Article 227 [1]). A violation of the law is punished by payment of a fine. Finally, the employee can initiate a civil proceeding in labour court in order to

---

14   The survey addressed issues of violence/harassment and discrimination in employment, health care services, housing and military service. It was completed by 172 persons and conducted from January until March 2001.

secure her/his right to damages. NGOs have the right to take part in judicial and administrative proceedings initiated by victims of discrimination (Act Implementing the Principle of Equal Treatment, Article 23). However, it was reported that the formulation 'right to take part' causes problems in practice since it does not clearly determine what the role of NGOs – especially in court proceedings – really is (Interview SI22). In any case, a representative of a trade union can represent an employee in a proceeding before court, if s/he holds a law degree (Labour and Social Courts Act, Article 16).

Labour Courts

Labour courts in Slovenia have jurisdiction over individual labour cases (disputes arising over the rights and obligations in the relationship between an employer and an employee, disputes relating to property rights stemming from such relations), collective labour cases (disputes in which one of the involved parties is usually a trade union or other institutional form of employee representation), cases relating to the legality of strikes, and cases relating to employees' rights to co-determination (employee participation in company management) (European Judicial Network in Civil and Commercial Matters 2006). Thus, all employees – and others, such as candidates for a job – may report a violation of, amongst others, their working time or equality rights to the competent court of first instance. In addition to three regional labour courts of first instance with headquarters in Celje, Koper, and Maribor, there is the Labour and Social Court in Ljubljana with jurisdiction for the whole of Slovenia. Appeals against judgements by courts of first instance in labour – and social security – disputes can be filed at the Superior Labour and Social Court in Ljubljana. The Labour and Social Department of the Supreme Court of the Republic of Slovenia is the highest-level court in this area.

As an alternative to court proceeding, the ERA foresees that parties involved in individual labour disputes can agree on alternative conflict resolution via arbitration (ERA, Article 205) or mediation by a labour inspector (ERA, Article 228). Some experts are convinced that problems in the workplace could be solved faster and much more efficiently in this manner, but, according to them, there is a lack of awareness about such alternative methods of dispute settlement. Consequently, the procedures of arbitration and mediation are not very well known by people at large and have not been used frequently since the entry into force of the new labour law (Interview SI7, see also Kanjuo Mrcela 2004).

Prior to the commencement of a labour dispute at court, the employee who believes that the employer is not fulfilling her/his obligations arising from the employment relationship or is violating any of her/his rights may demand the cessation of the undesired situation in writing (ERA, Article 204 [1]). If s/he does not receive an answer from the employer within eight working days, the employee has the right to take action within 30 days (ERA, Article 204 [2]). An unsuccessful applicant who thinks that the prohibition of discrimination has been violated in the selection process may request judicial protection within 30 days of the receipt of the employer's notification (ERA, Article 204 [5]). Decisions of labour courts of first instance are passed by senates made up of professional and lay judges from the employers' and the employees' side. The role of lay judges – as specialists in the field – is to contribute to a better understanding of the problems before a court (Novak 2001); lay judges are nominated by the social partners and elected by parliament for a five-year term (Kanjuo Mrcela 2004).

According to the 2003 Labour and Social Courts Act, first instance courts – as a rule – pass judgements in individual and collective labour disputes in senates made up of a professional judge, who presides over the senate, and one lay judge from either side of industry. This composition of senates in first instance courts is one of the novelties that were introduced in order to reduce the length of court procedures. Earlier, only individual labour disputes were resolved this way. Judgements in collective labour disputes in contrast were decided in senates comprising of a professional judge and two lay judges from each side of industry. Moreover, the new Labour and Social Courts Act greatly broadened the competencies of the president of the senate in individual labour disputes. The president is thus able to pass decisions on matters such as suspending an employment contract, on trial periods, on absences from work, on obligations to perform other work due to exceptional circumstances, on disciplinary sanctions, on removal from work, on temporary transfers, and also on overtime (Novak 2004).

As already mentioned, the Superior Labour and Social Court in Ljubljana is the court of second instance in labour and social security disputes. A judgement passed by a first instance court may be challenged at the Superior Labour and Social Court on any grounds for appeal (e.g. a considerable violation of the procedural rules) and without limitations (such as the value of the subject of dispute). Decisions on appeals against judgements by first instance courts are passed by a senate consisting of three professional judges: the president of the senate, a reporting judge and a deciding judge (Novak 2004).

At third instance, judgements are passed by a senate of five professional judges at the Labour and Social Department of the Supreme Court of the Republic of Slovenia. Lodging an appeal with the Labour and Social Department of the Supreme Court of the Republic of Slovenia, however, is only possible in exceptional cases, specified by law (Novak 2004).

Even if serious efforts have been made to improve the operation of labour courts (e.g. with the adoption of the new Social and Labour Courts Act in 2003, see above), Slovenians still do not perceive them as being efficient (Focus Groups SI1, SI2, SI3). Firstly, it is argued that court procedures are too slow and 'it takes years until you get the final decision' (Interview SI4). In fact, most cases at labour courts still take longer than a year to be resolved, due to a huge backlog of proceedings (Kanjuo Mrcela 2004). Secondly, Slovenians perceive going before a court as a rather expensive exercise (Focus Groups SI1, SI2, SI3), although Kanjuo Mrcela (2004) claims that 'the costs of the court procedures should in principle not be a burden of workers'. This argument is sustained by trade unions' provision of free legal assistance for their members. To employees who are not unionized and who lack the financial means necessary legal services are provided for free. A court may decide that the employer should pay the costs of a case even if the employee did not succeed fully in winning the dispute. Moreover, a court may exempt the employee from paying the court fee.

A third cause that prevents victims from filing court proceedings is the awareness that court decisions are not necessarily made correctly. It is reported that different courts come to different conclusions in similar cases (Focus Group SI2). This is also due to the fact that EU legislation is still not considered a part of Slovenian legislation by judges and lawyers but perceived as being imposed from outside. Their knowledge about rights and obligations stemming from EU directives is thus not very high (Interviews SI3, SI11). Judges' permanence of office seems to be interpreted in a way that makes it difficult to force them to study European law (Focus Group SI1).

The described situation is reflected in the number and subject matters of cases in Slovenian labour courts. The current labour court system was instituted by the 1993 Labour and Social Courts Act and started to operate one year later. Among the individual labour disputes referred to the courts of first instance in Celje, Koper, Maribor, and Ljubljana since then, cases dealing with wages, benefits and termination of employment were the most frequent (Kanjuo Mrcela 2004). No data is available on how many disputes on working time provisions or discrimination based on sex, religion or sexual orientation in the workplace have been referred to court to date. Certainly, there was no proceeding dealing with the provisions derived from the Working Time Directive, the Equal Treatment Directive, or the Employment Equality Directive so far. Lengthy procedures and legal insecurity at labour courts are obviously only accepted when it is worth it, and a breach of working time or equality provisions seems hardly ever to qualify.

Labour Inspectorate

Both the enforcement of working time provisions as well as of anti-discrimination provisions aimed at ensuring equality in the workplace fall under the competencies of the labour inspectorate. The labour inspectorate's responsibility as regards the latter does not only stem from its duty to supervise the implementation of the ERA (Article 227). The Act Implementing the Principle of Equal Treatment also foresees the labour inspectorate as one of the bodies in charge of putting the equality principle – at least in the field of employment and labour relations – into effect (Articles 20, 21).

The labour inspectorate, established in 1994, is an administrative body within the Ministry of Labour, Family and Social Affairs. Its duties are specified in two acts, the 1994 Labour Inspectorate Act, and the 2002 Inspection Act. The labour inspectorate thus controls the implementation of laws, other regulations, collective agreements and general acts that govern labour relations, pay and other receipts from employment, the employment of workers at home and abroad, worker participation in management, strikes and occupational safety, unless otherwise provided by law. The labour inspectorate also supervises the implementation of regulations that expressly determine this (Slovenian Labour Inspectorate 2006), like, for example, the above-mentioned Act Implementing the Principle of Equal Treatment.

Headed by a Chief Labour Inspector, the labour inspectorate is organized in three sections. The first section carries out inspections in the area of labour relations, the second is responsible for safety and health at work, and the third section is active in the area of social security, where it oversees – amongst other things – the work of social security institutions. The work in these sections centres on the following three laws: the ERA, the Occupational Safety and Health Act, and the Social Assistance Act. Besides the head office of the labour inspectorate in Ljubljana, there are 13 regional units (Slovenian Labour Inspectorate 2006).

Supervisions by the labour inspectorate are carried out in response to complaints but also *ex officio*. When the new ERA entered into force in January 2003, the inspectors responsible for labour relations based 80 per cent of their work on complaints. Only 20 per cent of the inspections in this area were carried out proactively. Today, the ratio is about 60/40. Following the amendment of the Act inspectors often found employers who did not even know that a new labour law existed and thus worked on the basis of the old labour law (Interview SI10). The increased level of information about the ERA can also be credited to the labour inspectorate because its tasks include the provision of expert assistance for the elaboration of and information about law within its area of competence (Slovenian Labour Inspectorate 2006). Hence it took part in the drafting of the new labour law under the auspices of the Ministry of Labour, Family and Social Affairs (Interview SI10) and in the working group which prepared Slovenia's negotiating position on 'Chapter 13: Social Policy and Employment' (Government Office for European Affairs 1999).

The adherence to working time provisions is covered by both the area of safety and health at work and the field of labour relations. Since there are 40 inspectors active in each area, altogether 80 inspectors are responsible for the proper enforcement of working time provisions. The supervision of the respect of anti-discrimination provisions, however, is reserved to the area of labour relations. Nevertheless, there are still 40 inspectors in charge of putting the equality principle in the workplace into effect (Interview SI10).

If a breach of working time provisions or a violation of the ban on discrimination in the labour relationship is detected, the labour inspectorate has the following sanctions at hand (Interview SI10): providing advice (in case the employer does not know the law), issuing an improvement note to the employer, and fining the employer. According to the ERA (Articles 229–231), fines may range from a minimum of 50,000 to a maximum of 1 million SIT (equivalent to €208 and €4,167, respectively). The penal provisions foreseen by the Act Implementing the Principle of Equal Treatment for an employer (legal person or natural person) who violates the equality principle are even higher (Article 24 [3]): S/he may be sanctioned with a fine between 500,000 and 10 million SIT (equivalent to €2,080 and €41,670, respectively).

Although the labour inspectorate in principle is also in charge of violations of equal treatment legislation, this area is only of marginal importance in its everyday practice. In 2004, the labour inspectorate only dealt with four cases of discrimination in the workplace, the same as in 2003 (Slovenian Labour Inspectorate 2005).

Slovenians are rather critical in the evaluation of the performance of the labour inspectorate (Focus Groups SI1, SI2, SI3). The frequency of inspections depends on a company's size and is regulated by law (Interview SI10). However, in practice the labour inspectorate apparently has its own principles as regards the frequency of inspections: allegedly particularly successful employers have to face continuous inspections, while ailing companies may be spared (Interview SI21). Furthermore, apparently there have been cases when employers who obviously breach employees' rights and entitlements do not have to fear any consequences. The reasons for this may be that Socialist habits are still alive, 16 years after the introduction of capitalism, or that labour inspectors are afraid of 'repercussions' because they have amicable relations with employers (Focus Groups SI1, SI2). More likely, though, is that given the competitive pressure and the market forces within the EU that Slovenia has to cope with, labour inspectors do not want to be blamed for a company's difficulties. Finally, it was argued that the labour inspectorate does not have enough personnel in order to carry out inspections systematically (Interview SI20).

Equal Treatment Bodies

According to Article 8a of the Equal Treatment Directive, member states have to designate a body or bodies for the promotion, analysis, monitoring and support of equal treatment of all persons. These bodies should facilitate the application of the principle of equal treatment by providing independent assistance to victims of discrimination in pursuing their complaints; conducting independent surveys concerning discrimination; and publishing independent reports and making recommendations on any issue relating to such discrimination. The Employment Equality Directive, which aims at combating discrimination on the grounds of religion or belief, disability, age or sexual orientation in the workplace does not include such a requirement. However, reasons like the possibility of a more effective utilization of limited resources suggest the establishment of equality bodies that deal with all of the grounds of discrimination included in the equality directives (Equinet 2006, 11).

In Slovenia, a single body covering all the tasks listed in Article 8a of the Equal Treatment Directive with respect to all of the grounds of discrimination included in the equality directives does not exist. Although, with the institution of the Advocate of the Principle of Equality, who assists victims of discrimination based on any personal circumstance by dealing with cases of unequal treatment (Act Implementing the Principle of Equal Treatment, Article 1 [2]), this idea has at least partly been realized. The Advocate of the Principle of Equality may take up the case of an alleged breach of the prohibition of discrimination following a written or verbal complaint. Such a submission may also be done anonymously; the procedure is informal and free of charge. The discriminated person is entitled to assistance irrespective of whether all legal remedies have been exhausted. At the end of the hearing, the advocate writes an assessment of the circumstances. If discrimination is established, the advocate points out the irregularities and makes recommendations for possible remedies (Act Implementing the Principle of Equal

Treatment, Articles 12-18). In case the established irregularities are not remedied as recommended within a certain period of time, the advocate hands the case to the competent inspection body, which, in the area of labour law, is the labour inspectorate (Act Implementing the Principle of Equal Treatment, Article 20).

The Act Implementing the Principle of Equal Treatment foresees in its Article 11 that another Advocate of the Principle of Equality may be established 'if the number of cases, their complexity or particularities with regard to a specific circumstance should so require'. The incumbent advocate has already worked for two years as an Advocate for Equal Opportunities for Women and Men, when she started to assist victims of discrimination based on any personal circumstance on 1 January 2005. In 2003 and 2004, she dealt with 19 cases of discrimination on the ground of sex. Between January and September 2005, she dealt with 40 cases based on different circumstances. Very few of them were connected to discrimination in the workplace. In light of these facts, the Advocate of the Principle of Equality herself thinks that there is no need to create a second advocate now because – even with an increase in cases – the workload is still limited (Interview SI1).

The comparatively low amount of submissions received by the Advocate of the Principle of Equality since its installation in 2003 can be interpreted in two different ways. Firstly, the body, which is still rather new, is not very well known. Secondly, the informal procedure carried out by the advocate is not deemed very helpful, as the body is perceived as weak if the established irregularities are not remedied in accordance with its recommendations. Its only sanction is to inform the responsible inspectorate where the victim can turn to anyway.

In addition to the Advocate of the Principle of Equality, the Act Implementing the Principle of Equal Treatment introduces a second special body responsible for putting the principle of equality into effect: the Council of the Government for the Implementation of the Principle of Equal Treatment. Composed of ministers, directors of governmental offices, representatives of professional organizations, national minorities and non-governmental organizations it has – according to the law – the following duties: to provide for the implementation of the provisions of the Act Implementing the Principle of Equal Treatment; to monitor, ascertain and assess the position of minority groups within society; to submit to the government proposals, initiatives and recommendations for the adoption of directives and measures that are necessary for the implementation of the principle of equal treatment; to submit proposals for the promotion of education, awareness-raising and research in the field of equal treatment; and to perform other duties, determined by the decree establishing it (Act Implementing the Principle of Equal Treatment, Article 9). As the 30 members of the Council of the Government for the Implementation of the Principle of Equal Treatment only held their inaugural session in 2005, there is not enough information available about the performance of this body yet.

However, neither the Advocate of the Principle of Equality nor the Council of the Government for the Implementation of the Principle of Equal Treatment would be able to fulfil their duties foreseen by law without the existence of a third equal treatment body, the Governmental Office for Equal Opportunities. The Advocate of the Principle of Equality was instituted to function within this office.

The Council of the Government for the Implementation of the Principle of Equal Treatment may take advantage of its technical and administrative support.

The Governmental Office for Equal Opportunities was founded in 1992; at that time it was called Office for Women's Policy. It was established as a professional service responsible for the realization of the rights of women guaranteed by the Constitution, other legislation and international treaties. Thereby, the government committed itself to integrate the principle of gender equality in government policy and to eliminate inequality between women and men in all areas of life. The change of name to Office for Equal Opportunities took place in 2001. Although the office is a governmental body, it is independent in its work. The office's main focus is still on equality between women and men. It thus fulfils all the tasks of an equality body pursuant to Article 8a of the Equal Treatment Directive; save the assistance of victims of discrimination for all other grounds of discrimination prohibited by the Act Implementing the Principle of Equal Treatment, it only serves as a coordinating body. The most significant achievements of the Governmental Office for Equal Opportunities include: the drafting of the *A*ct on Equal Opportunities for Women and Men, the drafting of the Act Implementing the Principle of Equal Treatment, the employment of the Advocate for Equal Opportunities for Women and Men/of the Principle of Equality, as well as several actions and projects regarding sexual harassment, domestic violence, employment rights of women.

Human Rights Ombudsperson

Unlike labour courts, the labour inspectorate and the Advocate of the Principle of Equality, the Human Rights Ombudsperson (*Varuh človekovih pravic*) is not an enforcement body in the classical understanding (Interview SI11). Even so, s/he belongs to the bodies which see to it that the provisions prescribed in the Working Time Directive and the two anti-discrimination directives are put into effect. The Human Rights Ombudsperson is an additional means of protection of the rights of the individual. The institution of the Ombudsperson was founded to function as a watchdog vis-à-vis state and state-related bodies' use of authority.[15] In this spirit, the Ombudsperson can challenge the work of labour inspectors, the Advocate of the Principle of Equality and in exceptional cases if necessary also the work of labour courts. For employees – and all other individuals – who believe that their rights and entitlements have been infringed, it is another body to which they can turn.

Within the Ombudsperson's office, three deputy ombudspersons work in their respective field of expertise. Complaints regarding working time fall under the realm of the deputy ombudsperson who covers employment and legal matters. In the event of a breach of the ban on discrimination – even in the workplace – complaints can be lodged with the deputy ombudsman who deals with discrimination. It is true that the Human Rights Ombudsperson can only start a proceeding if the violation of rights of an individual is related to an act or

---

15   The Ombudsperson's office uses the term 'Human Rights Ombudsman' in its English documents.

deed of state authorities, local self-government authorities or bearers of public authority. Contrary to its broad competencies in relation to employers within the public sphere, its powers in relation to employers outside the public sphere are limited. Nevertheless, in cases where the Ombudsperson cannot become active herself/himself, s/he provides explanations, advice and information about possible alternatives.

A petition to the Ombudsperson's office can be submitted orally or in writing, including the personal data of the petitioner. The procedure is informal and free of charge. However, it can only be initiated if – amongst other conditions – all available legal remedies have already been exhausted. The Human Rights Ombudsperson can also institute proceedings on her/his own initiative. All state bodies or other bodies holding public authority are obliged to help the Ombudsperson to clarify the case. Once all the necessary information has been collected, the Ombudsperson gives an assessment of the circumstances. If the rights of the plaintiff have been violated, remedies are recommended. If the established irregularities are not remedied as recommended within a certain period of time, the Ombudsperson may directly inform the offender's superior body or respective ministry, or submit a special report to the parliament, or publicize the facts (Human Rights Ombudsman Act, Articles 26–40).

The Human Rights Ombudsperson does not receive many cases concerning employment relations. In 2004, 199 labour law cases[16] were dealt with among a total of 2,992 cases (share of 6.7 per cent) (Human Rights Ombudsman 2004, 21). However, this figure also includes cases related to unemployment and scholarships, which means that initiatives concerning actual problems in the sphere of labour relations in a more narrow sense account for only half of the total number. Cases dealing with working time or equality in the workplace are even fewer. The Ombudsperson's office handled a few cases regarding working time but as they referred either to the poorly regulated ordering or the payment of overtime work, they are not related to provisions foreseen by the Working Time Directive. As regards discrimination in the workplace, the Ombudsperson received a few cases dealing with employers' ignorance of the special needs of mothers with young children, one case regarding sexual harassment at work and the case of a member of the Adventist's Church who could not take leave on Saturdays (Interview SI17).

The work of the Ombudsperson's office is highly regarded by Slovenian people. Also, the institution's international reputation seems to be quite high, since a number of international organizations dedicated to the protection of human rights have made reference to the annual reports of the Human Rights Ombudsperson (Lukšic 2001, 66). The reason for the small number of employees that turn to the Ombudsperson's office concerning problems within labour relations, though, may be that people are familiar by now with the lack of powers of the body in relation to employers outside the public sphere (Interview SI17).

---

16   One hundred and seventy-five cases were opened in 2004, 20 cases were carried over from 2003 and four cases were reopened.

Conclusions and Improvement Strategies

As the above analysis has demonstrated, Slovenia has a fairly clean slate in terms of legal compliance with our three sample directives. Apart from a few minor shortcomings, Slovenia has managed to incorporate the European provisions into domestic legislation. However, there is a considerable gap between what is written in the statute books and what ordinary employees actually experience in the workplace. A raft of societal and institutional problems hampers the application of the laws in practice.

When Slovenian experts were asked what they would do to remedy the implementation gaps of the Equal Treatment Directive, the Employment Equality Directive and the Working Time Directive if they could rule Slovenia for one day, they immediately answered that they would create more jobs, increase salaries and provide a healthy economy (Focus Group SI2). Undoubtedly, such measures would make the life of employees but also of employers much easier and many difficulties creating implementation obstacles in the workplace would be prevented. Subsequently, in the event of a violation of labour law, the injured person would not have to be afraid of suffering negative consequences if s/he takes any action. Nevertheless, on closer examination, many improvement strategies can be formulated that tackle the problems in implementing the three directives studied much more directly and are also easier to realize (Focus Groups SI1, SI2, SI3).

The information deficit, particularly in the area of equality law, can best be tackled if all relevant actors in the field make a contribution: the government by providing resources, NGOs and experts by providing their know-how, and trade unions by mobilising their members. In addition to short-term strategies such as information campaigns, there should also be long-term strategies aimed at changing the attitude of society vis-à-vis diversity. Therefore, equal treatment should become established in school and university curricula. As regards the elaboration of an approach on how to teach human rights, teachers could cooperate with the Governmental Office for Equal Opportunities and the Ombudsperson's office.

Representatives of civil society highly recommend a joining of forces of social actors and common interests. As regards public information campaigns, for example, it seems to be more useful to produce one comprehensive brochure rather than each organization compiling a separate one. But there are a lot of other possibilities, like common fund raising or lobbying, where goal-oriented collaboration among NGOs, trade unions and other social actors is expected to yield positive results.

Many suggestions were made by the experts assembled during our project that are suitable to boost the trust in and the performance of enforcement bodies of labour law. As far as labour courts are concerned, a thorough analysis should be made of why there are – after all the recent reforms – still so many pending cases. Some experts further considered abolishing judges' permanence of office in order to open the system for younger people. This proposal has to be judged with great caution, however, as such a move could have a detrimental effect on judicial independence. To ease the workload of courts, the use of alternative dispute settlement – especially arbitration and mediation – could be promoted. As for the labour inspectorate, the suggestion was made to establish a control mechanism for the work of inspectors. One possibility of such checks and balances would be the introduction of a senior level of inspectors. Moreover, an employers' representative even suggested that the competencies of labour inspectors could be extended to include the possibility to close down a company in case of extremely serious violations of labour law (Interview SI21). Also, the powers of the Advocate of the Principle of Equality could be extended to foresee the right to bring individual complaints to court or the right to impose sanctions. Training on EU legislation should play an important role for people working in enforcement bodies of labour law.

Since every EU member state is challenged to implement the Equal Treatment Directive, the Employment Equality Directive and the Working Time Directive properly, Slovenia is not alone in searching for improvement strategies. It is thus advisable to see how problems are solved elsewhere and to follow best practices from other EU countries (see Chapter 6). What is important to note, however, is that all the suggestions aiming at a better implementation of the Equal Treatment Directive, the Employment Equality Directive and the Working Time Directive as well as other rights and obligations stemming from labour law, only have a chance of success if politicians acknowledge the problems in practice and initiate changes.

In short, this chapter has shown that the implementation problems found in Slovenia arise less from the transposition processes. These were marked by considerable political contestation, especially in the case of working time, but nevertheless could be concluded relatively successfully. Instead, serious shortcomings in the Slovenian enforcement system are responsible for the significant gulf between the law in the books and its actual application. This mirrors the procedural patterns found in the other three countries.

After having summarized the main empirical findings of the four country studies, the following chapter will now present the 'world of dead letters', a concept that is intended to grasp the implementation styles observed in this book.

Chapter 6

Conclusions: The State of EU Social Standards in Central and Eastern European Practice

Oliver Treib and Gerda Falkner

Implementation Processes and Outcomes: Findings in Comparative Perspective

This section summarizes the main findings of our case studies and discusses their theoretical implications.[1] What did the three selected directives mean for the four CEE countries studied in terms of required policy adaptations? How did the countries perform with regard to the legal incorporation of the EU policies as well as to the enforcement and application of the transposed legislation in everyday practice? Finally, how can we explain the observed implementation patterns and what does this mean for the wider theoretical debate on the implementation of EU legislation?

More than Meets the Lawyer's Eye: Formal and Actual Reform Requirements

How much change did the three directives necessitate in the Czech Republic, Hungary, Slovakia and Slovenia? A sound answer to this question made it necessary to operationalize the concept of 'reform requirements' or, as it has often been called, of 'misfit'. In order to determine the misfit created by a given directive in a particular country, we need to carefully establish, first, the status quo ante, i.e. where the country started its process of adaptation, and, second, compare this status quo ante with the demands embedded in the European directive. In our earlier work (Falkner, Treib, Hartlapp and Leiber 2005, ch. 2), we have argued that this comparison needs to take into account both the level of *legal misfit*, which denotes the gap between European standards and existing legislation at the domestic level, and the *practical significance* of these legal reform requirements in terms of the actual implications for the norm addressees. In combination, this results in the total *policy misfit* of a particular directive in a given member state. Further to this substantive dimension, directives may also touch upon aspects

---

1   A shorter version of this chapter, which focused more narrowly on the worlds of compliance argument, was published in the *Journal of Common Market Studies* (Falkner and Treib 2008).

of the *politics and/or polity dimension* of the status quo ante. For example, they may interfere with the traditional pattern of public–private interaction, or they may require the creation of specific supervisory or supportive administrative bodies. Finally, the *economic costs* for employers and the public budget need to be taken into account.

In order to *aggregate all dimensions of misfit* we apply the following system: we rate high degrees of misfit in any one dimension as a high degree of total misfit created by a particular directive in a particular country. This results from the idea that no dimension of misfit can eradicate or soften adaptational pressure in another dimension. A high degree of misfit in terms of domestic state–society relations (or, alternatively, in terms of a specific new right granted to workers) cannot be outweighed by the fact that the costs, for instance, may be low. In turn, significant costs seem an important factor regardless of the abstract importance of the changes in terms of substance or politics. Consequently, our values for total misfit consist of the highest parameter values found in the three subcategories.

With regard to *legal misfit*, the Working Time Directive required surprisingly few legal adaptations in the four selected CEE countries. All of them could use older provisions on maximum weekly working hours, rest periods, breaks and annual leave as a basis. Nevertheless, the existing legislation had to be updated and specified in order to fulfil the detailed requirements of the EU's working time regime. For example, Slovenia had to reduce maximum statutory weekly working hours (including overtime) from 50 to 48 hours, increase annual leave entitlements by two days and introduce specific night work regulations. The other three countries required similar gradual reforms of their existing legal frameworks governing working time. By contrast, the Equal Treatment Directive and the Employment Equality Directive implied much more legal reforms. Although all four countries had relatively broad constitutional provisions on anti-discrimination, these provisions generally did not pertain to private employment relationships, or their horizontal effect beyond the public sphere was at least legally highly disputed. The Czech Republic and Slovenia needed much more specification to fulfil the detailed requirements of the directives. In Slovakia, it was especially homosexuals and other sexual minorities who lacked protection from work-related discrimination, while Hungary was only required to implement a number of slight improvements of its already high legal standard.

However, it seems that the *practical significance of these legal reform requirements* (assuming that these rules would actually be put into practice) was significantly higher in all cases since much of the pre-existing legislation had remained 'dead letter'.[2] This means that many people actually worked longer or

---

2   In fact, our impression is that the previous legal standards were disregarded to such a large extent that this is not equalled by the situation in any of the older member states. However, this would need an own study and systematic empirical comparison to be confirmed as reliable information. In the absence of such knowledge, we had to opt for a viable system of categorizing misfit. After long debates, we decided to account for the rather systematical non-application of the prior standards in our new project. It should be mentioned that this is a slight departure from the system used in our previous book

with less rest periods or breaks than prescribed by the pre-existing legislation, and that the extent of actual discrimination of women, sexual minorities etc. was considerably higher than the previous legal provisions suggested. Therefore, we assessed the degree of overall policy misfit as being one category higher than the degree of legal misfit (see Table 6.1).

As to the *politics or polity dimension*, none of the directives interfered with domestic state-society relations. Unlike in some Nordic countries (Falkner, Treib, Hartlapp and Leiber 2005, Chapter 12; Leiber 2005), state intervention in the field of employment conditions, as required by the directives, was a customary feature in all four CEE countries. However, some administrative reforms were called for in order to comply with one of the three directives, the Equal Treatment Directive, which required the creation of an independent equal treatment body intended to support discriminated women in the pursuit of their rights.

In terms of *economic costs*, the Working Time Directive clearly stands out as the relatively more 'expensive' of the three directives (see Table 6.1).[3] Effectively cutting the hours to be worked per employee raises an employer's labour costs, as s/he has to hire additional employees or has to pay extra premium for overtime working. The directive also implies costs for improved health protection, e.g. for medical checks of night workers. Changing shift systems to accommodate the directive's system of maximum daily working time and minimum daily and weekly rest periods, moreover, also implies certain organizational expenses. The economic costs of implementing the Working Time Directive were thus medium in all four countries. The two equality directives, in contrast, were less costly to comply with regarding gender, sexual orientation and religion.[4] Although putting an end to discriminatory practices in employment theoretically may involve significant costs for employers, especially in the area of equal pay, which is not directly covered by our two directives, much of the existing discrimination in our four countries pertained to less cost-related forms of unequal treatment, for example when employers avoided hiring employees who belong to a certain group or when employers or other employees harassed a colleague or a member of a sexual or religious minority. Yet, ensuring equal treatment in the field of promotion or training may involve certain costs for employers. In addition, the state also had to bear the expenses of creating and maintaining the equal treatment body prescribed by the Equal Treatment Directive.

(Falkner, Treib, Hartlapp and Leiber 2005). It affects six cases in which the degree of overall misfit would have been one category lower if we had not applied the new system. We feel that this is justifiable for we do not directly compare the misfit levels across the two projects and, most importantly, the worlds of compliance typology is not affected by this. We would still like to highlight this practice just in case any scholars would like to work with our measurement system of misfit in the future.

3   This debate should not, however, outshine the fact that discrimination is doubtlessly also expensive, at least for society as a whole.

4   The costs of complying with the Employment Equality Directive, and the overall misfit, might have been considerably higher if we had included discrimination on grounds of age and disability in our study. As the directive allows an extended deadline until the end of 2006 for these areas, however, we excluded them from our empirical analysis.

Table 6.1 Reform requirements of three directives in four CEE countries

Country	Directive	Degree of legal misfit	Practical significance	Degree of policy misfit	Degree of politics/ polity misfit	Economic costs	Degree of overall misfit
Czech Republic	Working Time	Low	Higher	Medium	–	Medium	Medium
	Equal Treatment	Medium	Higher	High	Medium	Low	High
	Employment Equality	Medium	Higher	High	–	Low	High
Hungary	Working Time	Low	Higher	Medium	–	Medium	Medium
	Equal Treatment	Low	Higher	Medium	Medium	Low	Medium
	Employment Equality	Low	Higher	Medium	–	Low	Medium
Slovakia	Working Time	Low	Higher	Medium	–	Medium	Medium
	Equal Treatment	Low	Higher	Medium	Medium	Low	Medium
	Employment Equality	Medium	Higher	High	–	Low	High
Slovenia	Working Time	Low	Higher	Medium	–	Medium	Medium
	Equal Treatment	Medium	Higher	High	Medium	Low	High
	Employment Equality	Medium	Higher	High	–	Low	High

The three directives thus created medium levels of *overall misfit* in seven cases, whereas the degree of total misfit can be considered high in five cases. The Employment Equality Directive involved the highest degrees of overall changes in our four countries, followed by the Equal Treatment Directive and, finally, the Working Time Directive which, however, still implied medium levels of overall misfit in all four countries.

In sum, therefore, the three directives in our sample actually made a difference in our four CEECs in terms of reform requirements. They called for quite a number of significant improvements for employees, although none of the three pieces of EU legislation had a 'revolutionary' impact. From this viewpoint, the new member states do not differ too much from the EU15 (Falkner, Treib, Hartlapp and Leiber 2005, 345–8). Our research on the CEECs proves yet again that EU social policy is more than just symbolic politics without significant impact in the member states (for discussions of the substantive quality of EU social policy, see e.g. Goetschy 1994; Ross 1994; 1995; Streeck 1994; 1995).

Transposition: Political Contestation in the Shadow of Accession Conditionality

In overall terms, the four CEE countries fared comparatively well in transposing the three directives into domestic legislation. With regard to the Working Time Directive, all four countries managed to complete the transposition process in an essentially correct manner before they joined the EU (see Table 6.2). The only important issue that they have not yet fulfilled is the ECJ's case law in *Simap* and *Jaeger* with regard to on-call duties, but this is true for almost all other member states as well. It has been linked politically to the ongoing EU-level debates about a revision of the directive, the understanding being that the member states would wait until the adoption of the revised directive before they would take action in this respect. As some drafts discussed so far provided for an amended definition of working time to the effect that inactive periods spent on call would no longer have to be treated as working time, the revision of the directive would mean that member states would no longer have to take action with regard to on-call working. After the governments repeatedly failed to agree on the updated version of the directive, however, the Commission has announced that it will initiate infringement proceedings against 23 member states that do not comply with the ECJ's case law (Council of the European Union 2006; Weiler 2006).

The transposition outcomes of the two equality directives are somewhat more mixed (see Table 6.3). While Hungary completed transposition well before the deadline, Slovenia and Slovakia managed to adopt their respective anti-discrimination acts only a few days (Slovenia) or weeks (Slovakia) after their actual accession to the European Union. Given that the delays were very short (less than six months), we treat these cases as having been completed largely on time. The Czech Republic, however, has so far failed to transpose the two directives in an essentially correct manner. Although reforms were enacted to incorporate the provisions of both directives in a multitude of existing legislation governing various aspects of the employment relationship, this diffusive approach to transposition failed to fulfil all essential parts of both directives. In spring 2006,

Table 6.2   Transposition outcomes (1): The Working Time Directive

Country	Transposition completed essentially correctly and largely on time?	Transposition steps taken after accession?	Essential provisions of Directive fulfilled (as of 30/11/06)?	Compliance with ECJ case law on on-call duties (as of 30/11/06)?
Czech Republic	Yes	No	Yes	No
Hungary	Yes	No	Yes	No
Slovakia	Yes	No	Yes	No
Slovenia	Yes	No	Yes	No

efforts to enact a general anti-discrimination act, which would have closed the remaining gaps, foundered on the lack of support for this broad reform among the members of the government coalition (see Chapter 2 for more details).

Despite the two cases of transposition failure in the Czech Republic, the overall record of our four countries in terms of legal compliance is good. Ten out of 12 cases (more than 80 per cent) were completed largely on time and in an essentially correct manner. This may come as a surprise, especially in comparison with the EU15 performance in transposing six similar labour-law directives, where 'not even one third of all cases was transposed "almost on time" and "essentially correctly"' (Falkner, Treib, Hartlapp and Leiber 2005, 267).

The good transposition record is all the more remarkable since most reform processes were politically highly contested. With regard to working time, the bone of contention between political parties, trade unions and employers' associations was the extent of flexibility. The political leaning of the respective governments clearly left its stamp on the substantive outcomes. The right-wing Slovak government under Prime Minister Dzurinda, for example, made full use of the flexibility offered by the directive, thus incorporating a minimalist version of the directive into domestic law. In the Czech Republic, by contrast, the centre-left Zeman government rejected the employers' calls for more flexibility. In the end, therefore, transposition of the Working Time Directive in the Czech Republic turned out to be relatively supportive of employee protection.

Similar patterns of political contestation could be observed in the transposition of the two equality directives. The partisan orientation of governments again played a crucial role in these processes. The transposition of the two directives in Hungary and Slovenia could be completed relatively swiftly, primarily due to the determination of the two centre-left governments to push these reforms, backed by trade unions and civil society organizations. The resulting anti-discrimination acts even went far beyond the European minimum requirements. They both covered many more grounds of discrimination than laid down in European legislation, and they extended the scope of the non-discrimination principle beyond the area of employment. In the Czech Republic and Slovakia, by contrast, Christian-democratic government parties dragged their heels on the

Table 6.3 Transposition outcomes (2): the equality Directives

Country	Directive	Transposition completed essentially correctly and largely on time?	Transposition steps taken after accession?	Essential provisions of Directive fulfilled (as of 30/11/06)?
Czech Republic	Equal Treatment	No	Some smaller adaptations plus (failed) attempts to enact general anti-discrimination act	No: equal treatment body has not been established; a number of other shortcomings of the multitude of transposition laws
	Employment Equality	No	Some smaller adaptations plus (failed) attempts to enact general anti-discrimination act	No: a number of shortcomings of the multitude of transposition laws
Hungary	Equal Treatment	Yes	Efforts[1] to improve the law with regard to sexual harassment	Yes
	Employment Equality	Yes	No	Yes
Slovakia	Equal Treatment	Yes	Adoption of transposition law three weeks after accession	Yes
	Employment Equality	Yes	Adoption of transposition law three weeks after accession	Yes
Slovenia	Equal Treatment	Yes	No	Yes
	Employment Equality	Yes	No	Yes

[1] Approved by Parliament but referred back by President for modifications.

creation of encompassing anti-discrimination legislation. In Slovakia, members of parliament and ministers of the Christian democratic KDH openly opposed the creation of legal provisions to guarantee the equal treatment of homosexuals. This resistance could only be overcome after members of the opposition parties agreed to vote with the other coalition partners in order to get the transposition bill adopted without the votes of the Christian democrats. In the Czech Republic, it was primarily the Christian-democratic coalition partner KDU-CSL whose lack of support for the enactment of comprehensive equal treatment legislation finally led to the failure of the anti-discrimination bill in spring 2006.

Given the relatively high level of political controversy that characterized most of the transposition processes we looked at, how can we explain the good overall transposition performance of our four countries? In our view, the answer is accession conditionality (Schimmelfennig, Engert and Heiko 2005; Schimmelfennig and Sedelmeier 2004). Although some of the provisions in our sample had to be complied with after accession only, most of them were subject to the Commission's pre-accession pressure. The prospect of being criticized for not fulfilling the *acquis communautaire*, and thus probably endangering smooth accession to the EU, served as a strong incentive for the political actors in our four countries to solve their disputes over how to transpose the directives within the given time limits and in essential conformity with the legal requirements.

At the same time, this does not imply that implementation efforts significantly decreased once accession had been accomplished. There is thus no pattern of 'revenge' for the high pressure exerted by the Commission in the pre-accession phase (for hints in this direction, see e.g. Ágh 2003; Goetz 2005). In Slovakia, the Anti-Discrimination law was adopted three weeks after EU accession. After becoming a member of the EU, moreover, the Hungarian parliament passed a piece of legislation intended to tighten the prohibition of sexual harassment. In the Czech Republic, at least some minor adaptations were accomplished after joining the EU. All this indicates that there was certainly no systematic end to transposition activity immediately after the end of pre-accession supervision, although the fact that the Czech anti-discrimination bill was not adopted in spring 2006 and that the country thus continues to breach the legal requirements of the two equality directives might give the impression that the importance of complying with EU rules has lost steam now that the country does no longer have to fear not being admitted to the 'club'.

In any case, it should be mentioned here that official data by the European Commission show that the transposition rates of our four new member states have steadily increased – rather than decreased – since accession. The Czech Republic, for example, improved its transposition rate from 89.88 per cent in August 2004 to 99.63 per cent in August 2006. For Slovakia, the figures are 92.21 and 99.67, respectively. The other two countries show similar developments, although starting from a somewhat higher level.[5] For sure, official transposition rates do not allow any insights on the completeness or correctness of the measures communicated to the Commission. Therefore, systematic empirical studies at a later point in time than ours are still needed to judge the post-accession transposition performance of the new member states in an authoritative manner.

Enforcement and Application: The Gulf between Law and Action

The favourable picture changes significantly if we look at the enforcement and application stage. As a result of the societal and institutional difficulties associated with the transition from Socialist rule, the Czech Republic, Hungary, Slovakia and Slovenia are all plagued by a multitude of problems that have so far largely prevented the legislation from being realized in practice.

In the field of *working time*, many employees voluntarily work longer hours than allowed by the law because they need the extra pay. This is a phenomenon that has already been observed in other (former) low-wage countries such as, e.g., Ireland (Falkner, Treib, Hartlapp and Leiber 2005, 114–15). Among the sectors where working excessive overtime is particularly widespread is health-care, where shift systems and on-call duties result in working hours that by far exceed the limits laid down in the European directive. Major problems with overtime working were also reported from building, transport, agriculture, tourism and seasonal work, commerce, the food industry and catering.

With regard to *equality in the workplace*, discriminatory practices, especially to the detriment of women and homosexuals, are still a widespread phenomenon in the four countries. There is a tendency among employers not to hire younger women because of possible pregnancies. Additionally, women are often discriminated with regard to promotion, which is highlighted by the low share of women in leadership positions. In general, female employment is concentrated in low-paid sectors where part-time, fixed-term and other forms of precarious employment are widespread. Moreover, many women are confronted with sexual harassment by their male colleagues or superiors. Homosexuals often do not disclose their sexual orientation vis-à-vis their employers or colleagues for fear of being discriminated. The way in which high-ranking Christian democratic politicians in Slovakia openly agitated against the employment of homosexuals in schools, although certainly representing an extreme example, shows that these fears are not entirely unfounded. Religious minorities seem to encounter less discrimination in our four countries, although we also found examples of discriminatory practices against religious groups.

The bulk of these application problems may be explained by societal and institutional shortcomings in the countries' enforcement systems. It is important to highlight, therefore, that the wide gulf between transposition and practical implementation is not due to deliberate efforts of cheating by CEE governments. Rather than amounting to purposeful 'tick the boxes implementation' (Richardson 1996, 282), these shortcomings thus reflect genuine capacity problems in the CEECs. To shed more light on these capacity problems, it is useful to distinguish two parallel enforcement tracks that are important for the areas covered by our three directives. The two equal treatment directives are mainly based on individual enforcement, which requires effective and easily accessible courts and well-informed and courageous employees willing to pursue their rights. Enforcement of working time rules also encompasses this bottom-up mechanism. As an indispensable supplement (see Chapter 1), however, it involves monitoring compliance by public authorities. In order for this to be effective, labour inspectorates must be equipped with sufficient resources, must be organized effectively and must have effective sanctions at their disposal to punish non-compliers. We will first discuss problems related to individual litigation (1–4) and then turn to the limits of monitoring activities by labour inspectorates (5).

1) *A lack of individual litigation from below.* The first major obstacle for employment legislation to become reality in the workplaces of the four countries is the lack of active litigation by employees. This has a number of reasons. As the introduction of the new laws was not accompanied by effective information campaigns either by the governments, by lower-level public authorities or by civil-society actors, *employees often do not know their rights.* This is particularly true for the field of equal treatment. In the area of working time, employees are traditionally better informed, mostly through their trade union organizations. Moreover, many employees do not dare to file complaints against their employer because they are *afraid of losing their jobs.* Although the equality directives explicitly rule out such retaliatory action by employers, our information on everyday practice in the four CEE countries suggests that this provision has not been effective in overcoming litigation reluctance. The problem seems to be particularly severe in post-socialist countries such as our four CEECs, where many employees were used to life-long job security. It is aggravated in regions and branches with high unemployment rates and, therefore, low chances of finding a new job. As a result of the socialist heritage, finally, individual court actions have been introduced as an alien element of enforcement after 1989. Therefore, there is *no litigation culture among the citizens* of the four countries. In other words, the four CEECs cannot build on long-standing traditions of invoking one's rights in court, as is the case in many 'old' member states.

2) *A lack of support by civil society actors.* Trade unions and other civil society actors are too weak to effectively support employees in pursuing their rights. Trade unions, which are confronted with widespread distrust among the populations of our four countries, as they are associated with the former socialist regimes, struggle with steadily declining membership rates. In 2004, these had dropped to 17 per cent of all employees in Hungary, 22 per cent in the Czech Republic (2003 figure), and 31 per cent in Slovakia. Slovenia, in contrast, stands out with a relatively high unionization rate of 44 per cent (European Commission 2006g, 25). Even there, however, less than half of all employees are organized in a trade union. Compared to countries like Denmark or Sweden, with unionization rates of around 80 per cent (European Commission 2006g, 25), this still seems rather modest. Other civil society organizations, such as organizations of gays and lesbians, have only developed rather recently and struggle with a shortage of resources. Employees who may want to invoke

their rights have thus *too little support from societal organizations*. Similarly, employers' federations often find themselves in an equally precarious state of organization and unification.[6] Moreover, *procedures for involving societal organizations in judicial proceedings* have remained at a rather minimalist level in most countries. In general, interest associations may only support individual employees in legal proceedings relating to discrimination, as called for by the equality directives. It is only in Hungary that societal groups may initiate, under certain conditions, discrimination-related proceedings themselves, without an individual being involved. In other areas and in the other three countries, however, the possibility of *actio-popularis* claims as a replacement for individual litigation does not exist.

3) *Equal treatment bodies: promising babies with some teething problems.* Another way of supporting individuals in pursuing their rights is the creation of independent public bodies that offer advice and assistance to individuals who feel that their rights have been violated. It has to be highlighted that those countries that have so far created equal treatment bodies surpassed the European minimum requirements and extended their sphere of competence beyond the area of race and gender. The equal treatment bodies of Hungary, Slovakia and Slovenia are also responsible for assisting discrimination claims related to sexual orientation or religion. Moreover, these bodies do not only assist individuals in legal proceedings but they also act as easily accessible contact points that offer mediation and out-of-court settlements in discrimination-related disputes. In this sense, they are certainly a valuable instrument for giving effect to the principle of equality in practice. However, all of these bodies are plagued by a lack of visibility, institutional standing and resources so that their actual performance has so far lagged behind their formal competences. Due to the political problems surrounding the transposition of the equality directives, finally, the Czech Republic has not yet managed to create a proper equal treatment body.

4) *Shortcomings in the organization of the judiciary.* Lacking resources in the court systems make for lengthy court proceedings in some of our countries. According to our information, the usual period until a first-instance ruling is achieved in the field of labour law ranges from about one year in Slovenia, fourteen months in Slovakia, between one and two years in Hungary, and up to three years in the Czech Republic. Unfortunately, we lack comparable data for the EU15. In any case, durations of two or three years definitely bring about a negative effect on people's willingness to go to court in the first place. The fact that it can take several years until a ruling is handed down thus acts as a serious impediment to individual litigation. Moreover, there seems to be a lack of attention for rulings by other courts, resulting in a situation where

---

6   Stronger employers' organizations could be useful partners in tripartite or bipartite systems of labour law enforcement, just like, for example, in the Nordic countries, and they could help clarify potential ambiguities in court cases, for they have an interest in clarification and even application of labour standards (thanks to Miriam Hartlapp for pointing out this aspect).

similar cases are often decided differently by different courts. This problem
was reported to be particularly prevalent in the Czech Republic.
5) *A lack of skilled inspectors and determination strains the work of labour
inspectorates.* The problem in our four countries seems to be less the absolute
number of inspectors in charge of monitoring compliance with labour law
provisions or a lack of competences to act directly against cases of non-
compliance. Although more personnel could certainly improve the situation,
the rate of inspectors per 100,000 employees is not significantly below Western
European standards. Moreover, they all have powers to act *ex officio* and
are empowered to impose certain sanctions directly, without prior court
proceedings. Instead, there are three other reasons to explain why many
observers criticize the labour inspectorates for being ineffective in ensuring
compliance with working time and equal treatment law.

First, the labour inspectorates in the four countries focus heavily on issues
of occupational safety and health, such as preventing work-related accidents,[7]
and on combating undeclared work. As most resources are deployed on these
topics, not much is left for monitoring working time or equality issues. Second
and related to this, inspectors often have a technical background and therefore
lack expertise in the fields of our directives. This is especially true for the relatively
new equality laws. Third, there were reports from employee representatives,
especially in Slovakia and Slovenia, accusing the labour inspectorates of having
too close relations to employers and deliberately sparing companies that are in
an economically tense situation. It thus seems that many employees do not see
the labour inspectorates as a neutral partner to turn to if there is a problem in the
workplace. Despite these problems, it has to be noted that there have been recent
efforts to improve the organizational structures and the capacities of the labour
inspectorates in Hungary and the Czech Republic. In these countries, there thus
seems to be political willingness to improve the performance of the respective
inspection services. In Slovakia, by contrast, recent reforms by the centre-right
government rather yielded toward the opposite direction, involving a reduction
of, rather than an increase in, the number of inspectors.

In sum, there are many problems in the enforcement systems of the four
countries we studied. As a consequence, many of the legal provisions that entered
the statute books in order to fulfil the EU's social policy *acquis* have so far largely
remained 'dead letters'. The first major research desideratum identified in the
introduction – the need to pay closer attention to the phase of application and
enforcement – has thus proven to be very fruitful. Had we followed the example
of many current studies on compliance with EU legislation and only looked at
transposition, our conclusions would have been much more positive. In contrast,
following a broader approach by scrutinizing how transposition laws are being
put into practice in the four CEECs has revealed a much gloomier picture. Just
like Puchala's (1972) blind men who try to discover the nature of an elephant by
touching its ears or its trunk, our findings thus suggest that scholars who focus

---

7   It should be mentioned that this is also the case in many old member states.

exclusively on the legal side of implementing EU legislation will fail to grasp the true nature of the whole implementation process.

Our transdisciplinary approach, too, has proven very fruitful. The political science tradition of looking beyond the legal sphere and also paying attention to the political, socio-economic, and societal systems has served us well. Indeed, our study highlights that it is, above all, due to structural issues that such a multitude of compliance problems is to be found in the CEECs. We could not have come to this conclusion without starting from an encompassing and transdisciplinary approach, and neither could we have proceeded to suggest meaningful improvement strategies (see below).

Finally, a word on the reliability of our findings. We trust that our data are as good as they could possibly be in a field where trustworthy 'hard' data are in short supply.[8] Hence, qualitative field work 'on the ground' was indispensable. To make this a feasible task, we decided to base our study on expert information. Interviewing individual citizens in all regions of the various countries, in all sectors of the economy and from all the potentially affected minorities (for the Equal Treatment Directive) exceeds any research team's practical capacities. Therefore, we tried to profit from expert knowledge as much as possible. Additionally, going beyond interviewing experts one after the other was crucial, as an additional methodological means. Conducting focus groups proved an extremely valuable tool, as did the strategy development conference we organized towards the end of the empirical work of our project. These group encounters allowed us to have new information counter-checked and – where necessary – supplemented or corrected immediately by other experts present. This resulted in a much more variegated picture and in more reliable data than any series of individual expert interviews could have yielded with a similar amount of time and travelling. While we cannot offer truly quantifiable data, we trust that our assembly of qualitative working methods can live up to the standards prevalent in this field of empirical enquiry and may legitimately claim to be one of the few high-quality sources of information on the crucial features of non-compliance (including non-application and non-enforcement) with EU standards in the enlarged European Union.

Theoretical Implications: Towards a World of Dead Letters

What are the implications of our findings for the wider field of EU implementation research? In particular, how do the patterns observed in the four CEECs fit into the typology of 'worlds of compliance' developed by Falkner, Treib, Hartlapp and Leiber (2005; see also Falkner, Hartlapp and Treib 2007)? In order to answer these questions, we should first recapitulate the main features of the (hitherto three) worlds of compliance. On this basis, we will then be able to discuss our findings on the four CEECs against the background of this typology.

---

8   On the shortcomings of available EU statistics, which are frequently but mistakenly assumed to mirror actual compliance with EU law, see Hartlapp/Falkner (2008). In fact, these are mostly data on the EU level actors' – often strategic – reactions to the small part of all compliance problems which is, at all, visible to them.

Our earlier study of 90 implementation cases in the field of EU labour law in the EU15 indicated that there is neither a single overriding factor, nor a general set of factors, that could explain the countries' variegated implementation performances (Falkner, Treib, Hartlapp and Leiber 2005, 317). Even two of the best-established hypotheses, the misfit or veto player arguments, had at best very weak explanatory power if applied across all EU member states. Even more crucially, a closer look at our qualitative case studies revealed that even their basic rationale did not hold in some clusters of countries (Falkner, Hartlapp and Treib 2007). The solution to this puzzle was a typology of three worlds of compliance within the EU15, each of which is characterized by an ideal-typical implementation style.

In the *world of law observance*, the compliance goal typically overrides domestic concerns. Even if there are conflicting national policy styles, interests or ideologies, transposition of EU directives is usually both in time and correct. This is supported by a 'compliance culture' in the sense of an issue-specific 'shared interpretive scheme' (Douglas 2001, 3149), a 'set of cognitive rules and recipes' (Berger and Luckmann 1967; quoted in Swidler 2001, 3064). Application and enforcement of the national implementation laws is also characteristically successful, as the transposition laws tend to be well considered and well adapted to the specific circumstances, and enforcement agencies as well as court systems are generally well-organized and equipped with sufficient resources to fulfil their tasks. Non-compliance, by contrast, typically occurs only rarely and not without fundamental domestic traditions or basic regulatory philosophies being at stake. In addition, instances of non-compliance tend to be remedied rather quickly. The three Nordic member states (Denmark, Finland and Sweden) belong to this country cluster.

Obeying EU rules is at best one goal among many in the *world of domestic politics*. Domestic concerns frequently prevail if there is a conflict of interests, and each single act of transposing an EU directive tends to happen on the basis of a fresh cost-benefit analysis. Transposition is likely to be timely and correct where no domestic concerns dominate over the fragile aspiration to comply. In cases of a manifest clash between EU requirements and domestic interest politics, non-compliance is the likely outcome. While in the countries belonging to the world of law observance breaking EU law would not be a socially acceptable state of affairs, it is much less of a problem in one of the countries in this second category. At times, their politicians or major interest groups even openly call for disobedience with European duties – an appeal that is not met with much serious condemnation in these countries. Since administrations and judiciaries generally work effectively, application and enforcement of transposition laws are not a major problem in this world – the main obstacle to compliance is political resistance at the transposition stage. Austria, Belgium, Germany, the Netherlands, Spain and the UK belong to this type.

In the countries forming the *world of transposition neglect*, compliance with EU law is not a goal in itself. Those domestic actors who call for more obedience thus have even less of a sound cultural basis for doing so than in the world of domestic politics. At least as long as there is no powerful action by supranational actors, transposition obligations are often not recognized at all in these 'neglecting' countries. A posture of 'national arrogance' (in the sense that indigenous standards are typically expected to be superior) may support this, as may administrative inefficiency. In these cases, the typical reaction to an EU-related implementation duty is inactivity. After an intervention by the European Commission, the transposition process may finally be initiated and may even proceed rather swiftly. The result, however, is often correct only at the surface. Where literal translation of EU directives takes place at the expense of careful adaptation to domestic conditions, for example, shortcomings in enforcement and application are a frequent phenomenon. Potential deficiencies of this type, however, do not belong to the defining characteristics of the world of transposition neglect. Instead, negligence at the transposition stage is the crucial factor in this cluster of countries, which includes France, Greece, Luxembourg and Portugal.

The typology can be used as a filter that decides which explanatory factors are relevant for different countries and what the direction of their influence is. In this sense, crucial theoretical propositions in EU implementation research, including the misfit and the veto player approaches, are only 'sometimes-true theories' (Falkner, Hartlapp and Treib 2007). The point is that implementation processes tend to depend on different factors within each of the various worlds. Cultural dispositions towards respecting the rule of law should be crucial in explaining implementation processes in the world of law observance. Political variables such as party ideologies, veto players and interest group pressure should have a major impact in the world of domestic politics. Finally, administrative factors should be particularly important in the world of transposition neglect.

As the above summary of this book's case studies shows, we observed the following pattern in our four CEE countries:

1) political contestation at the transposition stage which, mainly due to the considerable pressure exerted by accession conditionality, resulted in relatively timely and correct transposition outcomes;
2) the good transposition record is clouded by serious application problems that reflect systematic shortcomings of the countries' enforcement systems.

In procedural terms, this pattern is quite similar to two of the countries in the EU15, Ireland and Italy. Both feature procedures characterized by domestic politics considerations when it comes to transposition and have problematic enforcement systems. Therefore, we originally classified these two countries as belonging to what we then referred to as the world of transposition neglect if the focus is placed on the implementation process as a whole, and not only on transposition (Falkner, Treib, Hartlapp and Leiber 2005, ch. 15). With our new cases at hand, however, and with a view to ensuring a systematic and comprehensible typology, it seems preferable to conceptualize an additional world of compliance to grasp the new combination of typical patterns in the different phases. Consequently, we now subsume Ireland and Italy, along with the Czech Republic, Hungary, Slovakia and Slovenia, under a separate world of compliance.

To capture this combination of politicized transposition and systematic shortcomings in enforcement and application, we suggest a fourth category: the *world of dead letters*. Countries belonging to this cluster of our typology may transpose EU directives in a compliant manner, depending on the prevalent political constellation among domestic actors, but then there is non-compliance at the later stage of monitoring and enforcement. In this group of countries, what is written on the statute books simply does not become effective in practice. Shortcomings in the court systems, the labour inspections and finally also in civil society systems are among the detrimental factors accounting for this.

The typical process patterns of our extended typology of four worlds of compliance, and the countries belonging to each cluster, are summarized in Table 6.4.

Table 6.4   Four worlds of compliance

	World of law observance	World of domestic politics	World of dead letters	World of transposition neglect
Process pattern at stage of transposition	+	o	o	–
Process pattern at stage of practical implementation	+	+	–	+/–
Countries	Denmark, Finland, Sweden (3)	Austria, Belgium Germany, Netherlands, Spain, UK (6)	Ireland, Italy, Czech Republic, Hungary, Slovakia, Slovenia (6)	France, Greece, Luxembourg, Portugal (4)

+ = respect of rule of law; o = political pick-and-choose; – = neglect

Three issues deserve special highlighting: First, our typology refers to typical process patterns, not to implementation outcomes.[9] It is thus not tantamount to groups of good, mediocre or bad performers.[10] Therefore, the typology can

---

9   If the typology were geared towards different implementation outcomes itself, this would be tautological.

10   Only if we look at a large number of cases that cover many different (favourable and unfavourable) constellations of government, etc., can we expect the transposition performance of the world of domestic politics to fall in between the two other worlds – with the world of law observance typically producing better results than the world of transposition neglect. Although the official statistics are far from trustworthy, we could show that the three clusters of our original typology performed as expected when comparing the average annual transposition rates of the fifteen member states covered by our prior compliance project (Falkner, Hartlapp and Treib 2007).

fruitfully serve as a filter deciding which theoretical factors explain implementation processes in which country settings.

Second, each world refers to a combination of typical process patterns in the two major phases of implementing EU directives: transposition and application/enforcement. Sometimes, the same pattern applies to both phases (e.g. dutiful transposition and effective practical implementation in the world of law observance), and sometimes each phase shows a peculiar pattern (e.g. politicized transposition and major shortcomings in enforcement and application in the world of dead letters). This implies that many more worlds would be theoretically possible than those we specify. Our decision was to create useful labels for those constellations we actually found empirically rather than cataloguing potential forms.

Third, the titles of our worlds refer to the most significant characteristic of each cluster. This characteristic is not necessarily present in both stages of the implementation process. This was a compromise solution for the sake of offering 'telling' labels that are easy to capture and to memorize. At least at first glance, the label 'world of dead letters' is closer to the outcome than a process pattern. However, we understand it as saying: first, there is transposition into rather good domestic laws, with domestic politics being crucial, but then these countries lack proper institutions and processes for turning these laws into action.

With a view to generalising these findings, we should close with a word of caution. This book has discussed the findings of a research project on the implementation of three directives from the fields of working time and equality in four CEE countries. It is true that the expert knowledge shared with us in interviews, focus groups, and in our strategy conference, indeed often times exceeded the narrow realm of our enquiry. We learned much about the general features of life and the law in these countries, hence our insights cover more than 'just' three directives, strictly speaking. Nonetheless, it goes without saying that more case and country studies would be useful in order to judge the overall compliance record, and the typical implementation patterns more generally, in Central and Eastern Europe.

There are, in any case, signs that the pattern of relatively successful transposition but flawed enforcement and application, which is typical for the world of dead letters, may also be found in further CEECs, such as Poland (Leiber 2007). And the fact that many of the problems revealed in terms of control and enforcement arise from shortcomings in the bureaucracies and the court systems, or from the weakness of civil society and interest groups, suggests that the pattern will most probably not be restricted to a few policy areas.

Promising Strategies for Improving the State of Affairs

Our country chapters and the comparative section immediately above have indicated that in day-to-day practice, women, homosexuals and religious minorities are, *inter alia*, still subject to discrimination in the workplace. At the same time, violations of the legislation on working time are still rather common in the four countries we studied. Closer scrutiny reveals that most of these shortcomings are due to enforcement deficiencies, not to transposition failures. In most of the cases we researched, there hence are 'good letters' that, however, need more support in order to thrive and prosper. Crucial hurdles for making a practical success of EU social rights are typically a lack of resources generally, particularly for labour courts and equal treatment bodies; education and information shortcomings; and weakness of civil society representation. Improvements in these fields would certainly enhance not only compliance with EU law but also with national legislation.

Our recommendations for *improving the status quo* are based on the analysis of numerous shortcomings, as summarized above.[11] They fall into two groups: firstly, strategies that directly target the processes or institutions supervising rule enforcement (1 below); and secondly, improvement strategies that seek to enhance social rights by strengthening actors that may support those fighting for their rights (2 below). Such measures could hence indirectly work towards better implementation of EU social rights, at least in the longer term. A final group of strategic recommendations will at the end of this chapter specifically target the European level (3 below).

1) In this sense, let us first discuss the more *direct* ways to foster good practice in the member states. Legislative or at least administrative action will typically be indispensable for strengthening the relevant institutions or their working modes. Member state governments and parliaments should therefore be convinced to improve the respective conditions by, for example (see below in detail), increasing resources, simplifying labour laws, establishing specialized departments for equal opportunity policy, strengthening equal treatment bodies and labour inspectorates, and finally improving the court systems.

    Adequate resources: the problem of scarce means applies to all enforcement and litigation bodies more or less alike, particularly labour inspectorates, courts and equal treatment bodies. In most cases they require a significant increase of funding to provide more personnel and advanced training for staff to ensure higher effectiveness and turn around, a better quality of decisions and general awareness of anti-discrimination but also working time issues, thus also enabling the development of good practice.

    Simplification of labour laws: labour law provisions tend to be phrased in a highly complex fashion, making it difficult to impossible for individuals to derive their rights directly from the text of the law. This adds to the burden of having to explain the rights and obligations of all involved, which is already comparably high given the manifold recent changes made in this area of law in the CEECs.

---

11   Most of the proposals discussed above originate from a trans-national 'strategy workshop' convened at the Institute for Advanced Studies in Vienna (IHS) to discuss the status quo and possible improvements. Legal and administrative experts as well as expert practitioners from all four states studied and from Austria as a comparator met for a full day of mutual exchange.

Specialized ministerial department for equal opportunity policy: governments may want to consider institutionalising a sufficiently equipped department with experts on such issues, also to ensure the mainstreaming of equal treatment in all policy areas. Our study revealed that to date, there are frequent changes to specialized departments within the governments of the CEECs, which is detrimental to a coherent equal opportunity policy. Often there are 'Units' within several ministries that are responsible for the enforcement of a gender equality policy within the respective ministry. However, these units are underdeveloped and since they are subordinated administrative units they typically cannot produce any effective impact.

Equal treatment bodies: most countries have established equal treatment bodies, however, some have only granted the very minimum powers and resources to such institutions, thus making effective work and advancement of equality issues very difficult. There appear to be a number of possibilities to enhance compliance with anti-discrimination standards and principles:

- equal treatment bodies should have a legally enshrined right to bring individual complaints to court;
- best practice shows that *ex officio* powers and the possibility of imposing administrative sanctions are a very effective way to improve equality practices and policies;
- given that equal treatment bodies are generally designed – and also perceived – as watchdogs and advocates for individuals, it appears necessary to entrust the overarching issues of awareness raising and information sharing in a different way. One way forward could be the creation of a separate communication department within the entity, which receives additional financial resources for these important tasks;
- equal treatment bodies need visibility. If the people concerned do not know about the existence of these institutions, it is not possible for them to seek assistance. A separate web site, on which all the relevant information is available and European and national case law is published, would be an important step supporting the development in the right direction;
- sharing best practice has proven time and again to be beneficial to all parties, thus the experts concur that an increase of transnational cooperation among the bodies, also cooperation with NGOs, will strengthen the effectiveness of equal treatment practices;
- to increase accessibility of equal treatment bodies it is necessary to decentralize them. Bringing them to the local level ensures that individual action is not obstructed because the body is perceived as being too far away. Additionally, administrative and financial independence seems important.

Strengthening the labour inspectorates: labour inspectorates are well established monitoring agencies, however, they struggle in all member states to fulfil the manifold tasks put to them. Traditionally, these bodies focus on issues of illegal work as well as safety and health at work. The expertise on discrimination issues but also the sensitivity toward issues of working time therefore needs to be strengthened in most countries. In addition it appears that one way of improving their authority could be increasing the severity of sanctions and an increase of leverage for the individual inspectors on the most suitable sanction(s). Often the superior ministry gives guidelines for the labour inspectorates indicating that sanctions and especially fines should be the 'last resort', to be used only if and where consensual modes fail. In practice this appears to favour employers. Additionally, in order to enhance the adherence to anti-discrimination provisions it appears necessary to empower the labour inspectorates to take *ex officio* action in such cases. Legislation should be amended accordingly. Also, it may be useful for labour inspectorates to increase the existing cooperation at the binational, multinational and European levels to share best practice and to increase their efficiency. The most important task in the field of labour inspections, however, remains the expansion of their resources. As long as too few labour inspectors have to deal with too many tasks, effective and efficient supervision of the compliance of the employers with labour law provisions will remain difficult to achieve.

Court system improvements: under this heading, a number of relevant steps were discussed in our expert meetings:

- *specialized labour courts*: in some member states labour disputes are handled by civil courts, which may have specialized departments for industrial legal action. From the experience of countries with specialized labour courts it is safe to assume that separate labour courts benefit the quality of jurisprudence in this field. This also allows for judges to develop stronger expertise in labour law issues. Therefore, employers and employees can take advantage of decisions that are better tailored to their needs. Furthermore, lay judges with relevant expertise taking part in procedures handled by specialized labour courts may add further to the degree of satisfaction with the outcome of labour disputes;

- *mediation*: court cases are often the result of bad communication, thus court action is not always the most suitable means of resolving such disputes. Less adversarial means of dispute resolution can be more effective and efficient in finding the best possible way forward. Mediation is a low cost, least formal way of addressing disputes on sensitive issues such as equality and working time issues. Contrary to other civil proceedings, the aim of any labour dispute is to return to a feasible working relationship and ensure that the employee – with her/his expertise – continues to work in that very workplace. However, issues of balancing the power between the employer and employee (trade union) may require special facilitation. Also, the closed-door fashion of such proceedings makes it difficult to share the outcome of mediation with the wider public and thereby raise awareness about labour disputes and add to the overall legal culture of society;

- *actio popularis*: in societies where the settlement of disputes over cases of alleged discrimination is not yet common, it may be beneficial to give individuals the opportunity to join in a collective action to ensure that the violation of their rights is addressed. This possibility could in particular be strengthened by giving representative organizations such as NGOs and trade unions the right to initiate such cases, opening the possibility for individuals to join in. Experiences from other countries – also in other fields like environmental policy – show that the *actio popularis* has potential as an effective method of asserting collective interests.[12] Also, because it solves the 'David versus Goliath' problem of one employee trying to fight against an employer who is perceived as far more powerful;

- *right of trade unions to represent individuals in court cases*: given the current constraints in the field of labour disputes individuals appear hesitant to take action against alleged violations of their labour rights. Therefore, it may be feasible to take advantage of established representative organizations, such as trade unions, to take action on behalf of such persons. Thereby, expert bodies could also take on a part of the watchdog function in this field. This also serves as a way of empowering such organizations. Legislation should be amended accordingly, to explicitly grant the right of individual representation to specialized organizations;

- *protection of victims and witnesses*: one of the minimum requirements to ensure that victims seek redress for violations while their concerns for privacy are safeguarded and their current employment is secured is the protection of victims and possible witnesses throughout the process;

- *support for court proceedings*: many victims do not seek redress for poor conduct because they fear the costs of such proceedings. Several member states provide support for persons who could otherwise not afford legal action. This can be done in a variety of ways: financial support or the institutionalization of an agreement with the Bar Association, which provides a roster of attorneys who work *pro bono*;

- *extending training possibilities*: lawyers in all transition countries have had to adjust to a rapidly changing legal landscape: many laws have been amended multiple times within a relatively short period. Most of them have not had sufficient time to update their knowledge in specialized fields as well as in general EU law. Furthermore, working time as well as anti-discrimination affairs are very complex matters. Working time laws contain a great many of derogations and exemptions, which can hardly be reviewed even by experts with long standing experience. Anti-discrimination affairs are permanently enhanced by the jurisdiction of the ECJ, which means that practitioners have to be familiar with several recent judgements of the Court. Thus, substantial additional training should be provided for attorneys, judges and specialists such as labour inspectors. Additionally, it could be helpful to include independent experts in new highly specialized fields such as anti-discrimination to ensure that training and application are state of the art;

---

12   On the role of litigation as an instrument for asserting public interests in environmental policy, see de Sadeleer, Roller and Dross (2005); Deimann and Dyssli (1995); Ebesson (2002); Schmidt, Zschiesche and Rosenbaum (2004).

- *developing case law*: in order to ensure effective awareness raising it would be beneficial to enhance the transparency of decisions. This can be done in a number of ways, e.g. by institutionalising the anonymous publication of decisions, possibly also through a website. Such efforts assist the process of finding mutually agreed solutions to cases of discrimination and working time. Practitioners could easier catch up on the recent legal developments, which is of crucial importance for a better application of the laws. Only practitioners who know the current legal position and judgements of the competent bodies can guarantee a complete application. Therefore it would also be necessary to translate the ECJ's important judgements of the past into the respective languages. A positive side effect of better-published court decisions is the increased public awareness, which adds to the knowledge about such issues and thus leads to better practices; it also encourages victims to seek redress for perceived violations of their rights.

  In most, if not all of these cases, many old EU member states could profit from relevant reforms, too. Even in the absence of authoritative comparative studies, however, it seems clear that crucial differences do exist – at least in terms of the severity of the problems encountered. The same is true for most fields mentioned below.

2) We now turn to the more *indirect* improvement strategies. They aim at strengthening civil society actors and at increasing media attention to social right implementation.

   Strengthening cooperative governance seems one promising project: the new EU member states have established some consultation and coordination patterns between public and private actors as part of their pre-accession adaptation to EU-level standard procedures. However, the culture of such 'tripartism' could be further strengthened in our four countries. While consultation among social partners takes place on a regular basis, the frequency and scope of these meetings could be increased in most countries. Higher frequency of meetings could assist efforts to rectify the impression that some bodies are merely formally established and are not yet working on a mutual and collaborative level.

   A further point stressed by a number of interest group representatives involved in our project is the need for better inclusion in drafting processes, particularly with regard to time provided for comments and statements on EU and national draft legislation. Given that the member states by now already have transposed the pre-accession *acquis* and thus should now have more time in preparing legislation, a rapid improvement of the status quo can be expected, at least on this level.

   It should also be noted that tripartism could be slowed down because of ineffective cooperation between and among employers' and employees' representatives ('bipartism', intra-group relations). Therefore, the CEEC's newly established employer organizations as well as trade unions, which had to adjust their agenda in the wake of transition, should find institutionalized ways of increasing their level of coordination and cooperation.

With regard to specific interests, the important role of trade unions in putting employees' rights and entitlements into effect could potentially be strengthened further. One possibility is that trade unions should have the right to bring a case to court on behalf of an individual or a group of employees. To increase the rights of trade unions is, however, just one side of the coin. Equally important is to ensure sufficient financial resources.[13] Close collaboration among NGOs, trade unions and other civil society actors could be useful for common fund raising and lobbying. Especially in the field of equal treatment and anti-discrimination the cooperation between trade unions and NGOs can be strengthened. Therefore, some of the classical role models – still represented in some conservative parts of the trade unions – should be renounced. The 'male breadwinner model' – in the past sometimes an implicit aim of trade unions – cannot be combined with modern equal treatment policy. Since in most CEECs supportive civil society actors are weak and/or small, closer cooperation could raise their visibility. Corresponding networks should be established at the national, trans-national and European level, or strengthened where they already exist.

In short, civil society actors, such as women's groups and trade unions, can contribute a lot to a better implementation of EU social law by raising awareness among individual citizens and by acting as watchdogs vis-à-vis their governments. However, cooperative governance potentials have certainly not yet been fully exploited in the CEECs.

Improving communicative action on social rights is another promising improvement strategy: labour law is highly complex, but only if the people concerned know their rights and entitlements, can they be motivated to go to court where they can enforce their claims through legal action. Broad dissemination of brochures on crucial laws, customized for a non-expert readership, could prove highly useful.

Otherwise, adequate coverage by the mass media is certainly crucial, particularly when it comes to efforts aimed at altering role models and overcoming stereotypes. Also, media are important for giving victims (e.g. of discrimination) a voice. On the other hand, the risk of going public is that media change the story (or misinterpret it). Journalism education should thus include sensitivity training on equal treatment issues. Furthermore, it is

---

13   Currently, those unions which are only funded through membership fees particularly have to cope not only with a constantly diminishing membership but also with the ensuing economic constraints. For trade unions (but other interest groups as well), a 'tax deduction system' may be able to improve the financial situation and make them more independent. In Slovakia, for example, every employee can donate two percent of his/her income tax to one of the NGOs that are on an official list. However, such a system has shortcomings: Firms may create their own 'NGOs' and demand more or less openly that their employees donate to this entity. Given that donators make their own choices, NGOs with less 'attractive' topics such as racism or domestic violence usually fare poorly in this system. Naturally, the degree of publicity also has an impact on the level of donations.

important to strike a balance between the publicity of cases and the protection of the victims' privacy.

Media coverage on equal treatment policies should be enhanced not only in quality, but also in frequency. Relevant authorities and bodies should try to provide journalists with 'tailored' information, since the latter often do not have the time to investigate on their own, in depth. Interest groups (e.g. trade unions and employer federations) with own newspapers could reserve a specialized section to EU-related information and the follow-up on national level. A further means to disseminate information on EU-related social rights could be Equal Treatment reports and articles on court proceedings, but only after being customized for public use. For example, reports by equal treatment bodies could highlight best practices instead of only mentioning lengthy lists of 'problems'. Efforts to alter the overall situation, particularly by overcoming stereotypes, can be supported by showing positive examples in conjunction with remaining problems.

Finally, scientific studies will sometimes be needed to shed light on complex questions (such as regarding reasons of the lack of efficiency of a court system, or of attitudes leading to discrimination). In Hungary, for example, a research project was successful in revealing stereotypes against Roma people within the police.[14] The publication of such results can be expected to influence the decision-making in courts and ministries. Customized versions for broad dissemination throughout civil society will further enhance the effectiveness of this strategy.

Raising awareness of equal treatment policies is also of great importance, in the CEECs and elsewhere. Stereotypes within society, such as expressed and diffused by school books depicting the husband reading the newspaper while the wife cooks, are not easily changed – above all if they are reproduced in mass media and advertisements. What is called for are education and training efforts on various levels. Besides addressing adults (e.g. via information at the company level), it is equally important to attract the attention of children and adolescents to this topic. Therefore, equal treatment should become established in school and university curricula and, more generally, mainstreamed in official publications. Teachers together with experts (from equal treatment bodies or ombudsperson's offices) could elaborate an approach on how to best teach human rights.

Lastly among the possibilities to (at least indirectly and in the long run) improve the situation of social rights in EU member states, it should be mentioned that language empowerment, in general, could help to improve effective implementation of EU law in practice. It is difficult to represent interests, follow EU decision-making processes and participate in debates at the EU level with lacking language proficiency in English, and the latter is not yet sufficiently common in the CEECs (such as in some other EU member states, for sure).

3) A third (and final) group of recommendations on 'how to make the letters live' target not the national but the *EU level*. Although implementation is a

---

14   Expert information shared during our strategy workshop.

rather de-centralized affair in European integration, the European Union is undoubtedly a crucial actor in the improvement of the respect of the rules it sets out in all its member states. The Community treaties require the European Commission to ensure that they are properly implemented (e.g. Article 211 ECT), together with any EU decision taken on the basis of the treaties (the 'secondary law').

The Commission fulfils its role as guardian of the treaties mainly through the 'failure to act' procedure under Article 226 ECT. If it considers that a member state has failed to fulfil an obligation under the treaty, it can initiate proceedings, potentially leading up to a ruling by the European Court of Justice and, if this is not complied with, finally even to financial sanctions to be imposed by the ECJ. The use of this so-called infringement procedure, which allows the Commission to take action against a member state that does not comply with EU law, is laid down in a number of internal documents. It consists of four different stages: the 'Letter of Formal Notice', the 'Reasoned Opinion', the 'Referral to the ECJ' and the 'Judgement by the ECJ' (see Falkner, Treib, Hartlapp and Leiber 2005, Chapter 11).

Although the Commission's enforcement policy has recently been further elaborated and somewhat intensified, as a response to increasing public awareness of compliance failures, it could be helpful if the European Commission would further systematize and increase its efforts. Regular monitoring reports have already proven to be both a useful and very successful way to ensure better quality implementation during the accession process of new member states. More systematic and regular Commission scrutiny, leading (for example) to annual publication of individual national reports on the implementation of the *acquis* – including new legislation – in all the member states would most probably lead to a better respect of EU rules at the national level. The overall monitoring function of the Commission would probably be enhanced if the interaction with NGOs and trade unions was further intensified (Hartlapp 2007). These sub-state actors often have valuable information concerning a member state's shortcomings in transposition, application and enforcement. Overall, the timing of the Commission's response to breaches – particularly to overt ones – should be speeded up whenever possible and more resources should be devoted to the enforcement of EU derived regulations.

It is true that the governments do not always support this, for they have an immediate self-interest in preserving autonomy, including in the field of policy implementation. However, they need to realize that this is rather short-sighted. Considering the extreme interdependence prevailing in the EU, systematically producing dead letters would in the end be detrimental to the goals set by the community, which presumably serve the interests of all member states.

In that sense, it is high time that all relevant political actors join forces to prevent the emergence of a potential vicious circle whereby the modes of deficient compliance with EU law described in this book might actually persist and, in the long run, endanger the future of European integration.

References

Ágh, A. (2003), *Anticipatory and Adaptive Europeanization in Hungary* (Budapest: Hungarian Centre for Democracy Studies).

Anderson, J., Bernstein, D. and Gray, C. (2005), *Judicial Systems in Transition Economies – Assessing the Past, Looking to the Future* (Washington, DC: The World Bank).

Anderson, J.H. and Gray, C.W. (2007), 'Transforming Judicial Systems in Europe and Central Asia', in F. Bourguignon and B. Pleskovic (eds), *Annual World Bank Conference on Development Economics, Regional: Beyond Transition* (Washington, DC: The World Bank Publications).

Asiedu, D. and Horakova, P. (2005), 'Court Rules St Vitus' Cathedral Belongs to Catholic Church' <http://www.radio.cz/en/article/72072>, accessed 11 May 2005.

Austrian Federal Economic Chamber (2006), Entschädigungen bei zu langen Gerichtsverfahren <http://portal.wko.at/wk/sn_detail.wk?AngID=1& DocID=526858&StID=254282>, accessed 25 May 2006.

Avolio, C. (2004), *Welfare in the Mediterranean Countries – Slovenia* (Acro Felice: Centre for Administrative Innovation in the Euro-Mediterranean Region) <http://unpan1.un.org/intradoc/groups/public/documents/CAIMED/ UNPAN018930.pdf>.

Baer, J. (2001), 'Boxing and Politics in Slovakia: "Meciarism" Roots, Theory and Practice', *Democratization* 8:2, 97.

Bahovec, E., Vodopivec, N. and Salecl, T. (2002), 'Slovenia', in G. Griffin (ed.), *Women's Employment, Women's Studies, and Equal Opportunities 1945–2001* (Hull: University of Hull), pp. 292–339.

Balogh, E. and Neumann, L. (2005), 'Trade Union Membership and Workplace Presence Continue to Shrink', *EIROnline Document HU0501103F* (Dublin: European Foundation for the Improvement of Living and Working Conditions) <http://www.eurofound.europa.eu/eiro/2005/01/feature/hu0501103f.htm>.

Balogova, B. (2003a), 'EC Inspires Confidence', *Slovak Spectator*, 10 November 2003 <http://www.spectator.sk/articles/view/14343>.

—— (2003b), 'KDH Opposes Campaign for Anti-discrimination Law', *Slovak Spectator*, 3 September 2003 <http://www.spectator.sk/articles/view/13758>.

—— (2003c), 'STV Director Halts Spots Featuring Homosexuals', *Slovak Spectator*, 30 September 2003 <http://www.spectator.sk/articles/view/13983>.

—— (2004), 'Anti-discrimination Bill Passed', *Slovak Spectator*, 16 February 2004 <http://www.spectator.sk/articles/view/15096>.

—— (2005), 'Court Rules Affirmative Action not in Line with Constitution', *Slovak Spectator*, 19 October 2005 <http://www.spectator.sk/articles/view/21306>.

Barancová, H. (2006), 'The Entry of the Slovak Republic into the European Union and Development of the Employment Legislation', unpublished manuscript (Trnava: Trnava University).

Barrett, S.M. (2004), 'Implementation Studies: Time for a Revival? Personal Reflections on 20 Years of Implementation Studies', *Public Administration* 82:2, 249–69.

Barry, B. (2001), *Culture and Equality: An Egalitarian Critique of Multiculturalism* (Cambridge, MA: Harvard University Press).

Batory, A. (2002), 'The Political Context of EU Accession in Hungary', *Briefing Paper* (London: The Royal Institute of International Affairs) <http://www.chathamhouse.org.uk/research/europe/papers/>.

BBC (2006), 'Czech MPs Approve Gay Rights Law' <http://news.bbc.co.uk/2/hi/europe/4811030.stm>, accessed 2 April 2007.

Beach, D. (2005), 'Why Governments Comply: An Integrative Compliance Model that Bridges the Gap Between Instrumental and Normative Models of Compliance', *Journal of European Public Policy* 12:1, 113–42.

Bebler, A. (2002), 'Slovenia's Smooth Transition', *Journal of Democracy* 13:1, 127–40.

Bell, M. (2002), *Anti-Discrimination Law and the European Union* (Oxford: Oxford University Press).

Berger, P.L. and Luckmann, T. (1967), *The Social Construction of Reality: A Treatise in the Sociology of Knowledge* (New York: Anchor).

Berglund, S., Gange, I. and van Waarden, F. (2006), 'Mass Production of Law: Routinization in the Transposition of European Directives: A Sociological-institutionalist Account', *Journal of European Public Policy* 13:5, 692–716.

Berki, E. and Neumann, L. (2006), 'Draft Laws on National and Sectoral Social Dialogue Submitted to Parliament', *EIROnline Document HU0602101F* (Dublin: European Foundation for the Improvement of Living and Working Conditions) <http://www.eurofound.europa.eu/eiro/2006/02/feature/hu0602101f.htm>.

Bertelsmann Stiftung (2003), *Bertelsmann Transformation Index 2003: Slovenia* (Gütersloh: Bertelsmann Stiftung) <http://www.bertelsmann-transformation-index.de/fileadmin/pdf/en/2003/EasternCentralAndSoutheasternEurope/Slovenia.pdf>.

Bitskey, B. and Gyulavári, T. (2005), 'Hungarian Anti-discrimination Act: A new Member State's Perspective', unpublished manuscript (Budapest: Office of the President of the Republic of Hungary).

Bitusikova, A. (2003), 'Women's Social Entitlements in Slovakia', conference paper, *NEWR Conference 'Women's Social Entitlements'*, October 2003, Athens <http://www.newr.bham.ac.uk/pdfs/Social/Slovakia%20report.pdf>.

Bodnár, L. and Neumann, L. (2005), 'Government Proposes Increased Powers for Labour Inspectors', *EIROnline Document HU0510102F* (Dublin: European Foundation for the Improvement of Living and Working Conditions) <http://www.eurofound.europa.eu/eiro/2005/10/feature/hu0510102f.htm>.

Borak, N. and Borak, B. (2004), 'Institutional Setting for the New Independent State', in M. Mrak, M. Rojec and C. Silva-Jáuregui (eds), *Slovenia: From*

Yugoslavia to the European Union (Washington, DC: The World Bank), pp. 53–66.

Borghetto, E., Franchino, F. and Giannetti, D. (2006), 'Complying with the Transposition Deadlines of EU Directives: Evidence from Italy', *Rivista Italiana di Politiche Pubbliche* 5:1, 7–38.

Börzel, T. A. (1999), 'Towards Convergence in Europe? Institutional Adaptation to Europeanization in Germany and Spain', *Journal of Common Market Studies* 37:4, 573–96.

—— (2000), 'Why There Is No "Southern Problem": On Environmental Leaders and Laggards in the European Union', *Journal of European Public Policy* 7:1, 141–62.

—— (2001), 'Non-Compliance in the European Union: Pathology or Statistical Artefact?', *Journal of European Public Policy* 8:5, 803–24.

—— (2003a), *Environmental Leaders and Laggards in Europe: Why there is (not) a 'Southern Problem'* (Aldershot: Ashgate).

—— (2003b), 'Guarding the Treaty: The Compliance Strategies of the European Commission', in R.A. Cichowski (ed.), *The State of the European Union*, vol. 6: *Law, Politics, and Society* (Oxford: Oxford University Press), pp. 197–220.

Börzel, T.A., Hofmann, T. and Sprungk, C. (2004), 'Why do States not Obey the Law? Non-Compliance in the European Union', conference paper, *Workshop on Transposition and Compliance in the European Union*, 11–12 June 2004, Leiden <http://userpage.fu-berlin.de/~europe/forschung/docs/ boerzel_hofmann_sprungk_2004.pdf>.

Börzel, T.A. and Risse, T. (2000), 'When Europe Hits Home: Europeanization and Domestic Change', *European Integration Online Papers* 4:15 <http://eiop. or.at/eiop/texte/2000–015a.htm>.

Bouckova, P. (2005), *Report on Measures to Combat Discrimination: Directives 2000/43/EC and 2000/78/EC: Country Report Czech Republic* (Brussels: European Commission) <http://ec.europa.eu/employment_social/ fundamental_rights/pdf/legnet/csrep07_en.pdf>.

Boulanger, C. (2003), 'Europeanisation through Judicial Activism? CEE Constitutional Courts' Legitimacy and the Return to Europe', conference paper, *European University Institute, Workshop on Implications of Enlargement for the Rule of Law and Constitutionalism in Post-Communist Legal Orders*, 28–29 November 2003, Florence.

Bucar, B. and Brinar, I. (2005), 'Slovenia – Political Transformation and European Integration', in A. Skuhra (ed.), *The Eastern Enlargement of the European Union: Efforts and Obstacles on the Way to Membership* (Innsbruck: Studienverlag), pp. 93–276.

Bureau of Democracy, Human Rights, and Labor (2006), *Slovak Republic – International Religious Freedom Report 2005* (Washington, DC: Bureau of Democracy Human Rights and Labor) <http://www.state.gov/g/drl/rls/ irf/2005/51580.htm>.

Bútora, M., Bútorová, Z. and Gyárfásová, O. (1994), 'From Velvet Revolution to Velvet Divorce? Reflections on Slovakia's Independence', in J.M. Kovács (ed.), *Transition to Capitalism? The Communist Legacy in Eastern Europe* (New Brunswick, NJ: Transaction), pp. 229–58.

Bútorová, Z. and Bútora, M. (1995), 'Political Parties, Value Orientations and Slovakia's Road to Independence', in G. Wightman (ed.), *Party Formation in East-Central Europe: Post-Communist Politics in Czechoslovakia, Hungary, Poland and Bulgaria* (Brookfield, VT: Edward Elgar), pp. 107–33.

Bútorová, Z., Gyárfásová, O. and Velsic, M. (2005), 'Public Opinion', in G. Meseznikov and M. Kollar (eds), *Slovakia 2004: A Global Report on the State of Society* (Bratislava: Institute for Public Affairs), pp. 251–78.

Carley, M. (2005), 'Pay Developments – 2005', *EIROnline Document TN0606101U* (Dublin: European Foundation for the Improvement of Living and Working Conditions) <http://www.eurofound.europa.eu/eiro/2006/06/update/tn0606101u.htm>.

Casale, G., Kubinkova, M. and Rychly, L. (2001), 'Social Dialogue: The Czech Success Story', *InFocus Programme on Strengthening Social Dialogue, Working Paper 4* (Geneva: International Labour Organization) <http://www.ilo.org/public/english/dialogue/ifpdial/downloads/papers/czech.pdf>.

Castle-Kanerova, M. (1997), 'Social Security and Social Insurance in the Czech Republic', in J. Clasen (ed.), *Social Insurance in Europe* (Bristol: The Policy Press), pp. 223–39.

Chayes, A. and Handler Chayes, A. (1993), 'On Compliance', *International Organization* 47:2, 175–205.

Ciavarini Azzi, G. (ed.) (1985), *L'application du droit communautaire par les états membres* (Maastricht: European Institute of Public Administration).

—— (1988), 'What is this New Research into the Implementation of Community Legislation Bringing Us?', in J. Ziller (ed.), *Making European Policies Work: The Implementation of Community Legislation in the Member States*, vol. 1: *Comparative Syntheses* (London: Sage), pp. 190–201.

Council of the European Union (2004a), *The 2004 Update of the Broad Economic Policy Guidelines* (Luxembourg: Office for Official Publications of the European Communities) <http://ue.eu.int/uedocs/cms_data/librairie/PDF/EN%20REVISED%20CONSOLIDATED%20TEXT.pdf>.

—— (2004b), Press Release, 2594th Council Meeting, Economic and Financial Affairs, Brussels, 5 July 2004 <http://www.consilium.europa.eu/ueDocs/cms_Data/docs/pressData/en/ecofin/81394.pdf>, accessed 2 November 2005.

—— (2006), Press Release, Extraordinary Council Meeting, Employment, Social Policy, Health and Consumer Affairs, Brussels, 7 November 2006 <http://www.consilium.europa.eu/ueDocs/cms_Data/docs/pressData/en/lsa/91539.pdf>, accessed 9 March 2007.

Cowles, M.G., Caporaso, J. and Risse, T. (eds) (2001), *Transforming Europe: Europeanization and Domestic Change* (Ithaca, NY: Cornell University Press).

Csepeli, G. (2000), 'Transition Blues: The Roots of Pessimism', *The Hungarian Quarterly* 41:158, 64–72 <http://www.hungarianquarterly.com/no158/064.html>.

Cumaraswamy, D.P. (2001), *Civil and Political Rights, Including the Question of Independence of the Judiciary, Administration of Justice, Impunity*, report of the special rapporteur on the independence of judges and lawyers (Geneva: United Nations, Economic and Social Council, Commission on Human Rights) <http://www.unhchr.ch/Huridocda/Huridoca.nsf/0/a79f3cc87e9 cca5bc1256a1100325f2a?Opendocument>.

Czíria, L. (2002), 'The Organisation of the Social Partners', *EIROnline Document SK0208102F* (Dublin: European Foundation for the Improvement of Living and Working Conditions) <http://www.eurofound.europa.eu/eiro/2002/08/feature/sk0208102f.htm>.

de la Porte, C. and Pochet, P. (eds) (2002), *Building Social Europe through the Open Method of Co-Ordination* (Brussels: European Interuniversity Press).

de Sadeleer, N., Roller, G. and Dross, M. (2005), *Access to Justice in Environmental Matters and the Role of NGOs* (Groningen: European Law Publishing).

Debreceniova, J. and Ocenasova, Z. (2005), *Equal Opportunities for Women and Men – Monitoring Law and Practice in Slovakia* (Brussels: Open Society Institute) <http://www.soros.org/initiatives/women/articles_publications/publications/equal_20050502/eowmslovakia_2005.pdf>.

Deegan-Krause, K. (2004), 'Slovakia', in S. Berglund, J. Ekman and F. Aarebrot (eds), *The Handbook of Political Change in Eastern Europe* (Cheltenham: Edward Elgar), pp. 255–88.

Deimann, S. and Dyssli, B. (1995), *Environmental Rights: Law, Litigation and Access to Justice* (London: Cameron May).

Dimitrakopoulos, D. (2001), 'The Transposition of EU Law: "Post-decisional Politics" and Institutional Economy', *European Law Journal* 7:4, 442–58.

Dimitrova, A. and Steunenberg, B. (2000), 'The Search for Convergence of National Policies in the European Union: An Impossible Quest?' *European Union Politics* 1:2, 201–26.

Douglas, M. (2001), 'Culture as Explanation: Cultural Concerns', in N.J. Smelser and P.B. Baltes (eds), *International Encyclopedia of the Social and Behavioral Sciences*, vol. 5 (Amsterdam: Elsevier), pp. 3147–51.

Downs, G.W., Rocke, D.M. and Barsoom, P.N. (1996), 'Is the Good News about Compliance also Good News about Cooperation?', *International Organization* 50:3, 379–406.

Duina, F.G. (1997), 'Explaining Legal Implementation in the European Union', *International Journal of the Sociology of Law* 25:2, 155–79.

—— (1999), *Harmonizing Europe: Nation-States within the Common Market* (Albany, NY: State University of New York Press).

Duina, F.G. and Blithe, F. (1999), 'Nation-States and Common Markets: The Institutional Conditions for Acceptance', *Review of International Political Economy* 6:4, 494–530.

Ebbesson, J. (2002), *Access to Justice in Environmental Matters in the EU* (The Hague: Kluwer Law International).

Ellerman, D. (1998), 'Voucher Privatization with Investment Funds: An Institutional Analysis', *World Bank Working Paper No. 1924* (Washington, DC: The World Bank).

Ellis, E. (1998), *EC Sex Equality Law* (Oxford: Clarendon Press).

Elmore, R.F. (1982), 'Backward Mapping: Implementation Research and Policy Decisions', in W. Williams (ed.), *Studying Implementation: Methodological and Administrative Issues* (Chatham: Chatham House Publishers), pp. 18–35.

Employment Office (2004), *The Hungarian Labour Market 2004* (Budapest: National Employment Foundation).

Equinet (2006), *Strategic Enforcement, Powers and Competences of Equality Bodies* (Brussels: Equinet, the European Network of Equality Bodies).

Esping-Andersen, G. (1990), *The Three Worlds of Welfare Capitalism* (Cambridge: Polity Press).

EU Network of Independent Experts on Fundamental Rights (2005), *Opinion No 4–2005: The Right to Conscientious Objection and the Conclusion by EU Member States of Concordats with the Holy See* (Brussels: EU Network of Independent Experts on Fundamental Rights) <http://ec.europa.eu/justice_home/cfr_cdf/doc/avis/2005_4_en.pdf>.

European Commission (1997), *Agenda 2000: Opinion on Slovenia's Application for Membership of the European Union* (Brussels: European Commission) <http://ec.europa.eu/enlargement/archives/pdf/dwn/opinions/slovenia/sn-op_en.pdf>.

—— (1998), *Regular Report from the Commission on Hungary's Progress Towards Accession* (Brussels: European Commission) <http://ec.europa.eu/enlargement/archives/pdf/key_documents/1998/hungary_en.pdf>.

—— (2001), *European Governance. A White Paper*, COM(2001) 428 final (Brussels: European Commission) <http://eur.lex.europa.eu/LexUriServ/site/en/com/2001/com2001_0428en01.pdf>.

—— (2002a), *2002 Regular Report on Slovakia's Progress Towards Accession*, SEC(2002) 1410 (Brussels: Commission of the European Communities).

—— (2002b), *Regular Report on Slovenia's Preparation for EU Accession* (Brussels: European Commission) <http://ec.europa.eu/enlargement/archives/pdf/key_documents/2002/sl_en.pdf>.

—— (2002c), *Regular Report on the Czech Republic's Progress Towards Accession* (Brussels: European Commission) <http://ec.europa.eu/enlargement/archives/pdf/key_documents/2002/cz_en.pdf>.

—— (2003a), *Comprehensive Monitoring Report on Hungary's Preparation for Membership* (Brussels: European Commission) <http://ec.europa.eu/enlargement/archives/pdf/key_documents/2003/cmr_hu_final_en.pdf>.

—— (2003b), *Comprehensive Monitoring Report on the Czech Republic's Preparations for Membership* (Brussels: European Commission) <http://ec.europa.eu/enlargement/archives/pdf/key_documents/2003/cmr_cz_final_en.pdf>.

—— (2003c), *Equality, Diversity and Enlargement: Report on Measures to Combat Discrimination in Acceding and Candidate Countries* (Brussels: European Commission) <http://ec.europa.eu/employment_social/fundamental_rights/pdf/arc/stud/eden_en.pdf>.

—— (2003d), *Report from the Commission on the Implementation of Council Directive 96/34/EC of 3rd June 1996 on the Framework Agreement on Parental*

Leave Concluded by UNICE, CEEP and the ETUC, COM(2003) 358 final (Brussels: European Commission) <http://ec.europa.eu/employment_social/equ_opp/documents/com2003358_en.pdf>.

—— (2004a), *Candidate Countries Eurobarometer 2004.1 – National Report, Hungary* (Brussels: European Commission) <http://ec.europa.eu/public_opinion/archives/eb/eb61/exec_hu.pdf>.

—— (2004b), Enlargement Archives: Relations with Slovenia <http://ec.europa.eu/enlargement/archives/enlargement_process/past_enlargements/eu10/slovenia_en.htm>, accessed 20 October 2006.

—— (2004c), *Green Paper: Equality and Non-discrimination in an Enlarged European Union*, COM/2004/0379 final (Brussels: European Commission) <http://ec.europa.eu/employment_social/publications/2004/ke6004078_en.pdf>.

—— (2004d), Senior Labour Inspectors Committee (SLIC) <http://ec.europa.eu/employment_social/health_safety/slic_en.htm>, accessed 2 April 2007.

—— (2004e), *The Situation of Roma in an Enlarged European Union* (Brussels: European Commission) <http://ec.europa.eu/employment_social/publications/2005/ke6204389_en.pdf>.

—— (2005a), *Developing Anti-Discrimination Law in Europe: The 25 EU Member States Compared* (Brussels: European Commission) <http://www.migpolgroup.com/multiattachments/3077/DocumentName/legal_comparative1_en.pdf>.

—— (2005b), *Standard Eurobarometer 64/Autumn 2005: Public Opinion in the European Union* (Brussels: European Commission) <http://ec.europa.eu/public_opinion/archives/eb/eb64/eb64_first_en.pdf>.

—— (2006a), *Bulletin Legal Issues in Gender Equality, No. 1* (Brussels: European Commission) <http://ec.europa.eu/employment_social/gender_equality/docs/2006/bulletin06_1_en.pdf>.

—— (2006b), *Bulletin Legal Issues in Gender Equality, No. 2* (Brussels: European Commission) <http://ec.europa.eu/employment_social/gender_equality/docs/2006/bulletin06_2_en.pdf>.

—— (2006c), *Croatia 2006 Progress Report*, COM(2006) 649 final, SEC(2006) 1385 (Brussels: European Commission) <http://ec.europa.eu/enlargement/pdf/key_documents/2006/nov/hr_sec_1385_en.pdf>.

—— (2006d), Database on Women and Men in Decision-making <http://ec.europa.eu/employment_social/women_men_stats/out/measures_out418_en.htm>, accessed 10 October 2006.

—— (2006e), *Economic Forecasts: Spring 2006*, No 2/2006 (Brussels: European Commission) <http://ec.europa.eu/economy_finance/publications/publication7941_en.pdf>.

—— (2006f), *The Former Yugoslav Republic of Macedonia 2006 Progress Report*, COM(2006) 649 final, SEC(2006) 1387 (Brussels: European Commission) <http://ec.europa.eu/enlargement/pdf/key_documents/2006/nov/fyrom_sec_1387_en.pdf>.

—— (2006g), *Industrial Relations in Europe* (Luxembourg: Office for Official Publications of the European Communities).

—— (2006h), *Key Findings of the May 2006 Monitoring Reports on Bulgaria and Romania*, MEMO 06/201 (Brussels: Commission of the European Communities).

—— (2006i), *Public Finances in EMU 2006*, SEC(2006) 751 (Brussels: European Commission) <http://ec.europa.eu/economy_finance/publications/european_economy/2006/ee306_en.pdf>.

European Commission against Racism and Intolerance (2004), *Third Report on Hungary* (Strasbourg: Council of Europe) <http://www.coe.int/t/e/human_rights/ecri/1–ecri/2–country-by-country_approach/hungary/third_report_Hungary.pdf>.

European Council (1997), *Presidency Conclusions, European Council Meeting in Luxembourg on 12 and 13 December 1997* (Luxembourg: European Council) <http://www.consilium.europa.eu/ueDocs/cms_Data/docs/pressData/en/ec/032a0008.htm>.

European Forum for Democracy and Solidarity (2005), Slovakia Update <http://www.europeanforum.net/country/slovakia_update>, accessed 9 May 2005.

European Foundation for the Improvement of Living and Working Conditions (2003), *Social Dialogue and EMU in the Acceding Countries* (Dublin: European Foundation for the Improvement of Living and Working Conditions) <http://www.eurofound.eu.int/pubdocs/2003/88/en/1/ef0388en.pdf>.

European Judicial Network in Civil and Commercial Matters (2006), Jurisdiction of the Courts: Slovenia <http://ec.europa.eu/civiljustice/jurisdiction_courts/jurisdiction_courts_sln_en.htm>, accessed 4 May 2006.

European Network of Legal Experts in the Non-discrimination Field (2005a), *European Anti-Discrimination Law Review, No. 1* (Brussels: European Commission) <http://www.stop-discrimination.info/mc_scripts/doclib/files/lawrev1_en.pdf>.

—— (2005b), *European Anti-Discrimination Law Review, No. 2* (Brussels: European Commission) <http://www.stop-discrimination.info/mc_scripts/doclib/files/05lawrev2_en.pdf>.

—— (2006), *European Anti-Discrimination Law Review, No. 3* (Brussels: European Commission).

Eurostat (2007), 'Population and Social Conditions' <http://epp.eurostat.ec.europa.eu/portal/page?_pageid=0,1136184,0_45572598&_dad=portal&_schema=PORTAL>, accessed 2 April 2007.

Falkner, G. (2003), 'The EU's Social Dimenision', in M. Cini (ed.), *European Union Politics* (Oxford: Oxford University Press), pp. 264–77.

Falkner, G., Causse, E. and Wiedermann, C. (2006), 'Post-Accession Compliance in Central and Eastern Europe: Transposition and Application after the Age of Carrots and Sticks', conference paper, *epsNet Plenary Conference*, 16–17 June 2006, Budapest <http://www.epsnet.org/Publications/2006Proceedings/pps/falkner.pdf>.

Falkner, G., Hartlapp, M., Leiber, S. and Treib, O. (2002), 'Transforming Social Policy in Europe? The EC's Parental Leave Directive and Misfit in the 15 Member States', *MPIfG Working Paper 02/11* (Cologne: Max Planck Institute for the Study of Societies) <http://www.mpi-fg-koeln.mpg.de/pu/workpap/wp02–11/wp02–11.html>.

—— (2004), 'Non-Compliance with EU Directives in the Member States: Opposition Through the Backdoor?', *West European Politics* 27:3, 452–73.

Falkner, G., Hartlapp, M. and Treib, O. (2007), 'Worlds of Compliance: Why Leading Approaches to European Union Implementation are Only "Sometimes-true Theories"', *European Journal of Political Research* 46:3, 395–416.

Falkner, G. and Treib, O. (2008), 'Three Worlds of Compliance or Four? The EU15 Compared to New Member States', *Journal of Common Market Studies* 46:2, 293–313.

Falkner, G., Treib, O., Hartlapp, M. and Leiber, S. (2005), *Complying with Europe: EU Harmonisation and Soft Law in the Member States* (Cambridge: Cambridge University Press).

Featherstone, K. and Radaelli, C.M. (eds) (2003), *The Politics of Europeanization* (Oxford: Oxford University Press).

Ferge, Z. (2003), 'The Actors in Hungarian Pension Reform', in J.M. Kovács (ed.), *Small Transformations: The Politics of Welfare Reform-East and West* (Münster: Lit Verlag), pp. 131–55.

Ferge, Z. and Juhász, G. (2004), 'Accession and Social Policy: The Case of Hungary', *Journal of European Social Policy* 14:3, 233–51.

Fialová, Z. (2005), 'Human Rights', in G. Meseznikov and M. Kollar (eds), *Slovakia 2004: A Global Report on the State of Society* (Bratislava: Institute for Public Affairs), pp. 149–66.

Fila, L. (2002), 'MPs Drop Anti-discrimination Bill', *Slovak Spectator*, 8 July 2002 <http://www.spectator.sk/articles/view/9763>.

—— (2004), 'Slovaks, Please Behave', *Slovak Spectator*, 23 February 2004 <http://www.spectator.sk/articles/view/15158>.

Filipic, U. (1998), 'Soziale Sicherung in Tschechien', in E. Tálos (ed.), *Soziale Sicherung im Wandel, Österreich und seine Nachbarstaaten – Ein Vergleich* (Wien: Böhlau), pp. 365–437.

Fink Hafner, D. (2000), 'The Case of Slovenia', in H. Riegler (ed.), *Transformation Processes in the Yugoslav Successor States between Marginalisation and European Integration* (Baden-Baden: Nomos), pp. 11–43.

Fink Hafner, D. and Lajh, D. (2003), *Managing Europe from Home: The Europeanisation of the Slovenian Core Executive* (Ljubljana: Faculty of Social Sciences).

Fodor, G.T. and Neumann, L. (2004), 'New Working Time Regulations for Healthcare Workers', *EIROnline Document HU0401104F* (Dublin: European Foundation for the Improvement of Living and Working Conditions) <http://www.eurofound.europa.eu/eiro/2004/01/feature/hu0401104f.htm>.

Freedom House (2004), *Nations in Transit: Slovakia* (Washington, DC: Freedom House) <http://www.freedomhouse.org/template.cfm?page=47&nit=343&year=2004>.

Frege, C. and Tóth, A. (1999), 'Institutions Matter: Union Solidarity in Hungary and East Germany', *British Journal of Industrial Relations* 37:1, 117–40.

From, J. and Stava, P. (1993), 'Implementation of Community Law: The Last Stronghold of National Control?', in K.A. Eliassen (ed.), *Making Policy in Europe: The Europeification of National Policy-Making* (London: Sage), pp. 55–67.

Gaál, P. (2004), *Health Care Systems in Transition: Hungary* (Copenhagen: World Health Organisation Regional Office for Europe) <http://www.euro.who.int/Document/E84926.pdf>.

Gál, R.I., Mogyorósy, Z., Szende, Á. and Szivós, P. (2003), *Study on the Social Protection Systems in the 13 Applicant Countries: Hungary Country Study* (Brussels: European Commission) <http://ec.europa.eu/employment_social/spsi/docs/social_protection/hungary_final.pdf>.

Galgóczi, B. (2001), 'Twelve Years of Privatisation in Hungary – Drawing up a Balance Sheet', *South East Europe Review* 01s/2001, 45–54.

Gaube, A. (2004), 'Promoting Accountability', *Transitions Online*, 6 December 2004 <http://www.csees.net/?page=country_analyses&country_id=7&ca_id=1474>.

Giuliani, M. (2003), 'Europeanization in Comparative Perspective: Institutional Fit and Domestic Adaptation', in C.M. Radaelli (ed.), *The Politics of Europeanization* (Oxford: Oxford University Press), pp. 134–55.

Goetschy, J. (1994), 'A Further Comment on Wolfgang Streeck's "European Social Policy after Maastricht"', *Economic and Industrial Democracy* 15:3, 477–85.

Goetz, K.H. (2005), 'The New Member States and the EU: Responding to Europe', in S. Bulmer and C. Lequesne (eds), *The Member States of the European Union* (New York: Oxford University Press), pp. 254–80.

Goetz, K.H. and Hix, S. (eds) (2001), *Europeanised Politics? European Integration and National Political Systems* (London: Frank Cass).

Government of the Czech Republic (2005), *National Lisbon Programme 2005 – 2008, National Reform Programme of the Czech Republic* (Prague: Government of the Czech Republic) <http://wtd.vlada.cz/files/eu/national_reform_programme_en.pdf>.

Government of the Republic of Slovenia (2005), 'Former Governments' <http://www.vlada.si/index.php?lng=eng&vie=cnt&gr1=prdVld&gr2=prjVld>, accessed 17 May 2005.

Government Office for European Affairs (1999), 'Republic of Slovenia's National Programme for the Adoption of the Acquis' <http://www.svez.gov.si/index.php?id=1351&L=1>, accessed 24 May 2006.

Government Public Relations and Media Office (2000), 'Slovenia Gets its Sixth Government' <http://www.uvi.si/eng/slovenia/background-information/elections2000–government>, accessed 17 May 2005.

Hagan, J. and Radeova, D. (1998), 'Both Too Much and Too Little: From Elite to Street Crime in the Transformation of the Czech Republic', *Crime, Law and Social Change* 28:3–4, 195–211.

Hála, J. and Kroupa, A. (2005), 'Factors Constraining Social Dialogue and Social Partners' Influence Examined', *EIROnline Document CZ0412102F* (Dublin: European Foundation for the Improvement of Living and Working Conditions) <http://www.eurofound.europa.eu/eiro/2004/12/feature/cz0412102f.htm>.

Hála, J., Kroupa, A., Mansfeldová, Z., Kux, J., Vasková, R. and Pleskot, I. (2002), *Development of Social Dialogue in the Czech Republic* (Prague: Research Institute for Labour and Social Affairs) <http://www.vupsv.cz/ Kroupa_Hala_Soc_dialog-eng.pdf>.

Halmai, G. (2005a), *Report on the Situation of Fundamental Rights in Hungary in 2004* (Brussels: European Commission) <http://cridho.cpdr. ucl.ac.be/documents/Download.Rep/Reports2004/nacionales/CFR-CDF. repHUNGARY.2004.pdf>.

—— (2005b), *Report on the Situation of Fundamental Rights in Hungary in 2005* (Brussels: European Commission) <http://cridho.cpdr.ucl.ac.be/documents/ Download.Rep/Reports2005/NationalReport/CFRHungary2005.pdf>.

Harris, E. (2004), 'Europeanization of Slovakia', *Comparative European Politics* 2:2, 185–211.

Hartlapp, M. (2005a), *Die Kontrolle der nationalen Rechtsdurchsetzung durch die europäische Kommission* (Frankfurt/M.: Campus).

—— (2005b), 'Two Variations on a Theme: Different Logics of Implementation Management in the EU and the ILO', *European Integration Online Papers* 9:7 <http://eiop.or.at/eiop/texte/2005–007a.htm>.

—— (2007), 'On Enforcement, Management and Persuasion: Different Logics of Implementation Policy in the EU and the ILO', *Journal of Common Market Studies* 45:3, 653–74.

Hartlapp, M. and Falkner, G. (2008), 'Problems of Operationalisation and Data in EU Compliance Research', *Discussion Paper SP I 2008–104* (Berlin: Social Science Research Center Berlin) <http://skylla.wz-berlin.de/pdf/2008/i08–104. pdf>.

Havelkova, B. (2005), *Equal Opportunities for Women and Men – Monitoring Law and Practice in the Czech Republic* (Brussels: Open Society Institute) <http://www.soros.org/initiatives/women/articles_publications/publications/ equal_20050502/eowmczech_2005.pdf>.

Haverland, M. (2000), 'National Adaptation to European Integration: The Importance of Institutional Veto Points', *Journal of Public Policy* 20:1, 83–103.

Henderson, K. (2004), 'Developments in the Applicant States', *Journal of Common Market Studies* 42:s1, 153–67.

Héritier, A. (2001), 'Differential Europe: National Administrative Responses to Community Policy', in T. Risse (ed.), *Transforming Europe: Europeanization and Domestic Change* (Ithaca, NY: Cornell University Press), pp. 44–59.

Héritier, A., Kerwer, D., Knill, C., Lehmkuhl, D., Teutsch, M. and Douillet, A.-C. (eds) (2001), *Differential Europe: The European Union Impact on National Policymaking* (Lanham, MD: Rowman and Littlefield).

Héritier, A. and Knill, C. (2001), 'Differential Responses to European Policies: A Comparison', in A.-C. Douillet (ed.), *Differential Europe: The European Union Impact on National Policymaking* (Lanham, MD: Rowman and Littlefield), pp. 257–321.

Héthy, L. (1999), 'Under Pressure: Workers and Trade Unions in Hungary During the Period of Transformation 1989–1998' (Budapest: International Labour

Organization) <http://www.ilo.org/public/english/region/eurpro/budapest/download/hethy.pdf>.

—— (2001), 'Social Dialogue and the Expanding World: The Decade of Tripartism in Hungary and in Central and Eastern Europe 1988–99' (Brussels: European Trade Union Institute).

Hjern, B. and Porter, D.O. (1981), 'Implementation Structures: A New Unit of Administrative Analysis', *Organization Studies* 2:3, 211–27.

Hlavacka, S., Wágner, R. and Riesberg, A. (2004), *Health Care Systems in Transition: Slovakia* (Copenhagen: World Health Organisation Regional Office for Europe) <http://www.euro.who.int/Document/E85396.pdf>.

Höferl, A. (2004), *Privatisierung und Liberalisierung öffentlicher Dienstleistungen in der EU – neue Mitgliedsstaaten: Slowakei* (Vienna: Österreichische Gesellschaft für Politikberatung und Politikentwicklung) <http://www.politikberatung.or.at/typo3/fileadmin/02_Studien/1_Liberalisierung/Slowakischerepublik.pdf>.

Hoós, J. (2002), 'Impact of Globalisation on Social Security Systems in Hungary', conference paper, *The Tenth Annual NISPAcee Conference on Delivering Public Services in CEE Countries*, 25–27 April 2002, Cracow, Poland <http://www.nispa.sk/news/papers/wg3/Hoos.rtf>.

Human Rights Ombudsman (2004), *Annual Report 2004*, 10 (Ljubljana: Human Rights Ombudsman).

Hungarian Central Statistical Office (2006), Population census 2001 <http://www.nepszamlalas2001.hu/eng>, accessed 28 April 2006.

Hungarian Ministry of Employment and Labour (2004), *Equal Opportunities for All: Background paper for Employment Week 2004* (Budapest: Hungarian Ministry of Employment and Labour) <http://www.szmm.gov.hu/download.php?ctag=download&docID=10985>.

Hungarian Office of the National Council of Justice (2006), 'The Judicial System in Hungary' <http://www.birosag.hu/engine.aspx?page=birosag_english_03_judicial>, accessed 2 May 2006.

Illner, M. (1998), 'The Changing Quality of Life in a Post-Communist Country: The Case of Czech Republic', *Social Indicators Research* 43:1–2, 141–70.

Inotai, A. and Stanovnik, P. (2004), 'EU Membership: Rationale, Costs, and Benefits', in M. Mrak, M. Rojec and C. Silva-Jáuregui (eds), *Slovenia: From Yugoslavia to the European Union* (Washington, DC: The World Bank), pp. 353–66.

International Helsinki Federation (2006), *Slovakia Country Report* (Vienna: International Helsinki Federation for Human Rights) <http://www.ihf-hr.org/viewbinary/viewdocument.php?download=1&doc_id=6794>.

International Labour Organisation (2002), *Comments of the International Labour Office on the Labour Code of the Slovak Republic, 2001* (Geneva: International Labour Organization).

Jaichand, V., Sembacher, A. and Starl, K. (2006), *Challenges to Access to Justice in Austria, Hungary, Slovakia and Slovenia* (Wien: Neuer Wissenschaftlicher Verlag).

Javornik, J. (2004), 'Equal Opportunities Policy', *Slovenian Economic Mirror* 1/2004.

Javornik, J. and Skledar, S. (2004), 'Gender Equality Legislation Examined', *EIROnline Document SI0407102F* (Dublin: European Foundation for the Improvement of Living and Working Conditions) <http://www.eurofound. europa.eu/eiro/2004/07/feature/si0407102f.htm>.

Jójart, P., Siposová, M. and Dauciková, A. (2002), *Report on Discrimination of Lesbians, Gay Men and Bisexuals in Slovakia* (Bratislava: Q Archive/ Documentation and Information Centre).

Juhasz, L. (2004), 'Equal Rights Fight Quiets', *Slovak Spectator*, 26 January 2004 <http://www.spectator.sk/articles/view/14885//>.

Jurinova, M. (2004), 'Poll: 85 Percent of Slovaks Favour Anti-discrimination Bill', *Slovak Spectator*, 8 October 2004 <http://www.spectator.sk/articles/ view/17486>.

Jurinová, M. (2005), 'Court Delays Cost Millions', *Slovak Spectator*, 16 May 2005 <http://www.spectator.sk/articles/view/19753>.

Kádár, A. and Farkas, L. (2005), *Report on Measures to Combat Discrimination: Directives 2000/43/EC and 2000/78/EC: Country Report Hungary* (Brussels: European Commission) <http://www.europa.eu.int/comm/employment_social/ fundamental_rights/pdf/legnet/hurep05_en.pdf>.

Kádár, A., Farkas, L. and Pardavi, M. (2001), *Legal Analysis of National and European Anti-discrimination Legislation: A Comparison of the EU Racial Equality Directive and Protocol N.12 with Anti-discrimination Legislation in Hungary* (Budapest: Hungarian Helsinki Committee).

Kádár, A., Pardavi, M. and Zádori, Z. (2003), *Access to Justice Country Report: Hungary* (Budapest: Public Interest Law Initiative) <http://www.pili.org/en/ dmdocuments/CR_Hungary.pdf>.

Kadavá, C. (2005), 'Discrimination against Women with Children in the Czech Republic', *EIROnline Document CZ0504101N* (Dublin: European Foundation for the Improvement of Living and Working Conditions) <http://www. eurofound.europa.eu/eiro/2005/04/inbrief/cz0504101n.htm>.

Kanjuo Mrcela, A. (2004), 'Thematic Feature – Individual Labour/Employment Disputes and the Courts', *EIROnline Document SI0403204T* (Dublin: European Foundation for the Improvement of Living and Working Conditions) <http:// www.eurofound.europa.eu/eiro/2004/03/tfeature/si0403204t.htm>.

Kenner, J. (2004), 'Re-evaluating the Concept of Working Time: An Analysis of Recent Case Law', *Industrial Relations Journal* 35:6, 588–602.

Kéri, L. and Ádám, L. (1995), 'The First Three Years of the Multi-party System in Hungary', in G. Wightman (ed.), *Party Formation in East-Central Europe: Post-Communist Politics in Czechoslovakia, Hungary, Poland and Bulgaria*, Studies of Communism in Transition (Brookfield, VT: Edward Elgar), pp. 134–53.

Kling, J. (2003), 'Regional Policy and Regional Development', in G. Meseznikov, M. Kollar and T. Nicholson (eds), *Slovakia 2002: A Global Report on the State of Society* (Bratislava: Institute for Public Affairs), pp. 463–80.

Knill, C. and Lenschow, A. (1998), 'Coping with Europe: The Impact of British and German Administrations on the Implementation of EU Environmental Policy', *Journal of European Public Policy* 5:4, 595–614.

—— (2000a), 'Do New Brooms Really Sweep Cleaner? Implementation of New Instruments in EU Environmental Policy', in A. Lenschow (ed.), *Implementing EU Environmental Policy: New Directions and Old Problems* (Manchester: Manchester University Press), pp. 251–82.

—— (eds) (2000b), *Implementing EU Environmental Policy: New Directions and Old Problems* (Manchester: Manchester University Press).

—— (2001), 'Adjusting to EU Environmental Policy: Change and Persistence of Domestic Administrations', in T. Risse (ed.), *Transforming Europe: Europeanization and Domestic Change* (Ithaca, NY: Cornell University Press), pp. 116–36.

Köllô, J. and Nacsa, B. (2005), 'Flexibility and Security in the Labour Market: Hungary's Experience', *Flexibility paper 2004/2* (Budapest: International Labour Organization).

Konèar, P. (1999), *Workers' Protection: The Case of Slovenia* (Geneva: International Labour Organization) <http://www.ilo.org/public/english/dialogue/ifpdial/downloads/wpnr/slovenia.pdf>.

Kontler, L. (2002), *A History of Hungary: Millennium in Central Europe* (Houndmills: Palgrave Macmillan).

Kornai, J. (2005), 'The Great Transformation of Central and Eastern Europe: Success and Disappointment', conference paper, *World Congress of the International Economic Association*, 29 August, 2005, Marrakech, Morocco.

Körösényi, A. (1999), *Government and Politics in Hungary* (Budapest: Central European University Press).

—— (2002), 'Das politische System Ungarns', in W. Ismayr (ed.), *Die politischen Systeme Osteuropas* (Opladen: Leske und Budrich), pp. 310–53.

Kostelecký, T. (1995), 'Changing Party Allegiances in a Changing Party System: the 1990 and 1992 Parliamentary Elections in the Czech Republic', in G. Wightman (ed.), *Party Formation in East-Central Europe: Post-Communist Politics in Czechoslovakia, Hungary, Poland and Bulgaria* (Brookfield, VT: Edward Elgar), pp. 79–106.

Kotnik, A. (2003), 'A Woman Politician', *Slovenia Times*, 8 September 2003.

Krislov, S., Ehlermann, C.-D. and Weiler, J. (1986), 'The Political Organs and the Decision-making Process in the United States and the European Community', in J. Weiler (ed.), *Integration Through Law: Europe and the American Federal Experience*, vol. 1 (Berlin: Walter De Gruyter), pp. 3–110.

Kristan, I. (1999), 'Die Rechtsstellung der Minderheiten in Slowenien', in G. Brunner and B. Meissner (eds), *Das Recht der nationalen Minderheiten in Osteuropa* (Berlin: Arno Spitz).

Krizsán, A. and Pap, E. (2005), *Equal Opportunities for Women and Men – Monitoring Law and Practice in Hungary* (Brussels: Open Society Institute) <http://www.soros.org/initiatives/women/articles_publications/publications/equal_20050502/eowmhungary.pdf>.

Kroupa, A., Vasková, R. and Hála, J. (2004), 'Public Views of Trade Unions Analysed', *EIROnline Document CZ0411105F* (Dublin: European Foundation for the Improvement of Living and Working Conditions) <http://www. eurofound.europa.eu/eiro/2004/11/feature/cz0411105f.htm>.

Küffer, C. (2001), About the Bibliography Transdisciplinarity <http://www. transdisciplinarity.ch/bibliographie/Transdis_e.html>, accessed 16 January 2006.

Kühn, Z. (2005), 'The Application of European Law in the New Member States: Several (Early) Predictions', *German Law Journal* 6:3, 563–82.

Lampinen, R. and Uusikylä, P. (1998), 'Implementation Deficit: Why Member States Do Not Comply with EU Directives?' *Scandinavian Political Studies* 21:3, 231–51.

Lazarova, D. (2005), 'Prime Minister Paroubek and President Klaus at Loggerheads over EU Constitution' <http://www.radio.cz/en/article/66964>, accessed 2 April 2007.

Leiber, S. (2005), *Europäische Sozialpolitik und nationale Sozialpartnerschaft* (Frankfurt/M.: Campus).

—— (2007), 'Transposition of EU Social Policy in Poland: Are there Different "Worlds of Compliance" in East and West?' *Journal of European Social Policy* 17:4, 349–60.

Leibfried, S. and Pierson, P. (eds) (1995), *European Social Policy: Between Fragmentation and Integration* (Washington, DC: The Brookings Institution).

Lichtenstein, J. (2001), 'Hungarian Jurisdiction in Transition Challenge and Reform', *Justice in the World Online Edition, 8th edition* <http://www. justiceintheworld-foundation.org/n08/op_hjt_jl_e.shtml>.

Linden, R.H. (2002), 'Conclusion: International Organizations and East Europe – Bringing Parallel Tracks Together', in R.H. Linden (ed.), *Norms and Nannies. The Impact of International Organizations on the Central and East European States* (Lanham, MD: Rowman and Littlefield), pp. 369–82.

Linden, R.H. and Pohlman, L.M. (2003), 'Now You See It, Now You Don't? Anti-EU Politics in Central and Southeast Europe', *European Integration* 25:4, 311–34.

Linos, K. (2007), 'How can International Organizations Shape National Welfare States? Evidence from Compliance with European Union Directives', *Comparative Political Studies* 40:5, 547–70.

Lipsky, M. (1980), *Street-level Bureaucracy: The Dilemmas of Individuals in the Public Service* (New York: Sage).

Lomnici, Z. (2005), 'Der nationaler Richter, als Richter des Rechtes der Europäischen Gemeinschaft', conference paper, *Institute for European Integration Research, EU-Symposium: National Judges as Judges of EC law*, 21–23 April 2005, Vienna, Austria.

Lukšic, I. (2001), *The Political System of the Republic of Slovenia* (Ljubljana: Znanstveno).

Malová, D. and Rybár, M. (2005), 'Organized Interests', in G. Meseznikov and M. Kollar (eds), *Slovakia 2004: A Global Report on the State of Society* (Bratislava: Institute for Public Affairs), pp. 231–49.

Manning, N. (2004), 'Diversity and Change in Pre-accession Central and Eastern Europe Since 1989', *Journal of European Social Policy* 14:3, 211–32.

Mansfeldová, Z. (2004), 'The Czech Republic', in S. Berglund, J. Ekman and F. Aarebrot (eds), *The Handbook of Political Change in Eastern Europe* (Cheltenham: Edward Elgar), pp. 223–53.

Masselot, A. (2004), 'The New Equal Treatment Directive: Plus ça Change ...', *Feminist Legal Studies* 12:1, 93–104.

Mastenbroek, E. (2003), 'Surviving the Deadline: The Transposition of EU Directives in the Netherlands', *European Union Politics* 4:4, 371–95.

Mastenbroek, E. and van Keulen, M. (2006), 'Beyond the Goodness of Fit: A Preference-based Account of Europeanization', in R. Holzhacker and M. Haverland (eds), *European Research Reloaded: Cooperation and Integration among Europeanized States* (Dordrecht: Springer), pp. 19–42.

Mazmanian, D.A. and Sabatier, P.A. (1983), *Implementation and Public Policy* (Glenview, IL: Scott).

Mbaye, H.A.D. (2001), 'Why National States Comply with Supranational Law: Explaining Implementation Infringements in the European Union 1972–1993', *European Union Politics* 2:3, 259–81.

McGlynn, C. (2000), 'Ideologies of Motherhood in European Community Sex Equality Law', *European Law Journal* 6:1, 29–44.

Mencinger, J. (2004), 'Transition to a National and a Market Economy: A Gradualist Approach', in M. Mrak, M. Rojec and C. Silva-Jáuregui (eds), *Slovenia: From Yugoslavia to the European Union* (Washington, DC: The World Bank), pp. 67–82.

Mencinger, J.E. (2001), 'Why Is Transition in Slovenia Often Considered a Success Story', *Journal des Economistes et des Etudes Humaines* 11:1, 159–72.

Merton, R.K. and Kendall, P.L. (1946), 'The Focused Interview', *American Journal of Sociology* 51:6, 541–57.

Meseznikov, G. (2005), 'Domestic Politics and the Party System', in G. Meseznikov and M. Kollar (eds), *Slovakia 2004: A Global Report on the State of Society* (Bratislava: Institute for Public Affairs), pp. 23–100.

Ministry of Labour and Social Affairs of the Czech Republic (2005), *Report on the Fulfilment of Government's Priorities and Procedures in the Promotion of Equality for Men and Women* (Prague: Ministry of Labour and Social Affairs).

Ministry of Labour Social Affairs and Family of the Slovak Republic (1999), *The Implementation of the Beijing Action Platform: The National Report of the Slovak Republic* (Bratislava: Ministry of Labour Social Affairs and Family of the Slovak Republic).

Morgan, D.L. (1997), *Focus Groups as Qualitative Research* (London: Sage).

Mormont, M. (2004), *Monographs on the Situation of Social Partners in the Acceding and Candidate Countries: Intersectoral Level* (Louvain: Institute des Sciences du Travail) <http://www.trav.ucl.ac.be/recherche/relations%20industrielles/rapports%202003/rapport%20intersectoriel%20peco.pdf>.

Mrak, M., Rojec, M. and Silva-Jáuregui, C. (2004), 'Overview: Slovenia's Threefold Transition', in M. Mrak, M. Rojec and C. Silva-Jáuregui (eds),

Slovenia: From Yugoslavia to the European Union (Washington, DC: The World Bank), pp. xix–lvi.

Mucha, J., Rakovsky, J., Krepelka, F., Passer, J., Rakovsky, J., Krepelka, F. and Passer, J. (2005), '1 Jahr EU Mitgliedschaft: Erste Bilanz aus der Sicht der tschechischen Höchstgerichte', *EIF Working Paper No. 17* (Wien: Institut für Europäische Integrationsforschung) <http://www.eif.oeaw.ac.at/downloads/workingpapers/wp18.pdf>.

Nellis, J. (1999), 'Time to Rethink Privatization in Transition Economies?', *Discussion Paper No. 38* (Washington, DC: The World Bank).

Neumann, L. (2004), 'The Impacts of European Labour Standards on an Accession Country: The Case of the Hungarian Transposition of the "Transfer of Undertakings" and "Working Time" Directives of the EU', conference paper, *Industrial relations in Europe conference: 'Governance Issues in Shifting Industrial and Employment Relations'*, 26–28 August 2004, Utrecht.

Novak, J. (2001), 'The Role of Labour Court Judges in the Implementation of Social Policies: Questionnaire for Slovenia', conference paper, *International Labour Organization, Ninth Meeting of European Labour Court Judges*, 3–4 December 2001, Geneva.

—— (2004), 'Do We Need Labour Courts? Questionnaire for Slovenia', conference paper, *International Labour Organization, Twelfth Meeting of European Labour Court Judges*, 8–9 September 2004, Budapest <http://www.ilo.org/public/english/dialogue/ifpdial/downloads/lc_05/slovenia_1.pdf>.

Oblath, G. and Richter, S. (2002), 'Macroeconomic and Sectoral Aspects of Hungary's International Competitiveness and Trade Performance on EU-markets: Competitive Positions and Sectoral Growth of the Hungarian Economy', conference paper, *Hungary and EU Eastern Enlargement*, 6 June 2002, Vienna, Institute for Advanced Studies.

Office for Equal Opportunities (2004), *UN Questionnaire to Governments on Implementation of the Beijing Platform for Action (1995) and the Outcome of the Twenty-Third Special Session of the General Assembly (2000)* (Ljubljana: Governmental Office for Equal Opportunities).

Open Society Institute (2001), *Monitoring the EU Accession Process: Judicial Independence* (Budapest: EU Accession Monitoring Program) <http://www.eumap.org/topics/judicial/reports/judicial01>.

—— (2002a), *Equal Opportunities for Women and Men in the Czech Republic* (Prague: Open Society Institute).

—— (2002b), *Monitoring the EU Accession Process: Judicial Capacity* (Budapest: EU Accession Monitoring Program) <http://www.eumap.org/topics/judicial/reports/judicial02>.

Organization for Economic Cooperation and Development (2006), Country Statistical Profile 2006: Hungary <http://stats.oecd.org/WBOS/ViewHTML.aspx?QueryName=184&QueryType=View&Lang=en>, accessed 19 May 2006.

Örkény, A. and Csepeli, G. (1994), 'Social Change, Political Beliefs, and Everyday Expectation in Hungarian Society: A Comparitive View', in J.M. Kovács (ed.),

Transition to Capitalism? The Communist Legacy in Eastern Europe (New Brunswick, NJ: Transaction), pp. 259–74.

Orosz, É., Klára, F. and Czibere, K. (1999), 'The Social Security System in Hungary', in M. Brusis (ed.), *Central and Eastern Europe on the Way into the European Union: Welfare State Reforms in the Czech Republik, Hungary, Poland and Slovakia* (Munich: Center for Applied Policy Research), pp. 21–40.

Österreichische Gesellschaft für Europapolitik (2006), *EU-Erweiterung – Demokratie – Vertrauen in Institutionen – persönliche Sicherheit: Das Meinungsklima in Österreich, Ungarn, Slowenien und Südosteuropa* (Wien: Österreichische Gesellschaft für Europapolitik) <http://cms.euro-info.net/received/_3628_Studie1.pdf>.

Paoli, P. and Parent-Thirion, A. (2003), *Working Conditions in the Acceding and Candidate Countries* (Luxembourg: Office for Official Publications of the European Communities) <http://eurofound.europa.eu/publications/htmlfiles/ef0306.htm>.

Parekh, B. (2000), *Rethinking Multiculturalism: Cultural Diversity and Political Theory* (Cambridge, MA: Harvard University Press).

Pavlic Možina, S. (2005), *Facts about Slovenia* (Ljubljana: Government of the Republic of Slovenia Public Relations and Media Office) <http://www.ukom.gov.si/eng/slovenia/publications/facts-book>.

Pavlík, P. (2004), *Shadow Report on Equal Treatment and Equal Opportunities for Women and Men* (Prague: Gender Studies o.p.s.) <http://www.feminismus.cz/download/shadow_report/_Report_PDF.pdf>.

Phillips, R., Jefferey, H., Laslo, A. and Hulme, D. (2006), 'Usurping Social Policy: Neoliberalism an Economic Governance in Hungary', *Journal of Social Policy* 35:4, 585–606.

Pisarova, M. (2001a), 'Gay Community Proposes Life Partnerships', *Slovak Spectator*, 22 October 2001 <http://www.spectator.sk/articles/view/2766>.

—— (2001b), 'Homosexuals Denied Labour Code Umbrella', *Slovak Spectator*, 16 July 2001 <http://www.spectator.sk/articles/view/853>.

—— (2003a), 'Anti-discrimination Law on Agenda Again', *Slovak Spectator*, 22 September 2003 <http://www.spectator.sk/articles/view/13885>.

—— (2003b), 'KDH: Gays Should not be Teachers', *Slovak Spectator*, 7 April 2003 <http://www.spectator.sk/articles/view/12366>.

—— (2003c), 'MPs Fudge Gay Issue', *Slovak Spectator*, 2 June 2003 <http://www.spectator.sk/articles/view/12915>.

—— (2004a), 'KDH Fears for Family', *Slovak Spectator*, 1 March 2004 <http://www.spectator.sk/articles/view/15224>.

—— (2004b), 'KDH Wants Law Protecting "Traditional Family"', *Slovak Spectator*, 19 February 2004 <http://www.spectator.sk/articles/view/15147>.

Pollert, A. (2003), 'Women, Work and Equal Opportunities in Post-Communist Transition', *Work, Employment and Society* 17:2, 331–57.

Potrata, M. (2005), 'Women between Silence and Scream', in S. Lokar (ed.), *From Quota to Parity* (Ljubljana: CEE Network for Gender Issues), pp. 19–34.

Potucek, M. (1999), 'Havel versus Klaus: Public Policy Making in the Czech Republic', *Journal of Comparative Policy Analysis* 1:1, 163–76.

—— (2004), 'Accession and Social Policy: The Case of the Czech Republic', *Journal of European Social Policy* 14:3, 253–66.

Powell, R.A. and Single, H.M. (1996), 'Focus Groups', *International Journal of Quality in Health Care* 8:5, 499–504.

Pressman, J.L. and Wildavsky, A. (1973), *Implementation: How Great Expectations in Washington Are Dashed in Oakland: Or, Why it's Amazing that Federal Programs Work at all this Being a Saga of the Economic Development Administration as Told by Two Sympathetic Observers Who Seek to Build Morals on a Foundation of Ruined Hopes* (Berkeley, CA: University of California Press).

Pridham, G. (1995), 'Political Parties and Their Strategies in the Transition from Authoritarian Rule: the Comparative Perspective', in G. Wightman (ed.), *Party Formation in East-Central Europe: Post-Communist Politics in Czechoslovakia, Hungary, Poland and Bulgaria* (Brookfield, VT: Edward Elgar), pp. 1–28.

Procházka, I., Janík, D. and Hromada, J. (2003), *Discrimination of Lesbians, Gay Men and Bisexuals in the CR* (Prague: Gay Initiative in the CR).

Prunk, J. (1994), *A Brief History of Slovenia* (Ljubljana: Založba Mihelac).

Puchala, D.J. (1972), 'Of Blind Men, Elephants and International Integration', *Journal of Common Market Studies* 10:3, 267–84.

Putnová, A. (2003), 'Czech Women's Entrepreneurship', *Electronic Journal of Business Ethics and Organization Studies* 8:1 <http://ejbo.jyu.fi/articles/0801_5.html>.

Reynolds, M.J. (2001), 'Gay Leaders Take Case to MPs', *Slovak Spectator*, 19 March 2001 <http://www.spectator.sk/articles/view/306>.

Rhodes, M. (1995), 'A Regulatory Conundrum: Industrial Relations and the Social Dimension', in S. Leibfried and P. Pierson (eds), *European Social Policy. Between Fragmentation and Integration* (Washington, DC: The Brookings Institution), pp. 78–122.

Richardson, J.J. (1996), 'Eroding EU Policies: Implementation Gaps, Cheating and Re-Steering', in J.J. Richardson (ed.), *European Union: Power and Policy-Making* (London: Routledge), pp. 278–94.

Risse, T., Cowles, M.G. and Caporaso, J. (2001), 'Europeanization and Domestic Change: Introduction', in T. Risse (ed.), *Transforming Europe: Europeanization and Domestic Change* (Ithaca, NY: Cornell University Press), pp. 1–20.

Röpke, O. (2005), 'Zur Revision der EU-Arbeitszeitrichtlinie', *Das Recht der Arbeit* 5/2005, 460–66.

Ross, G. (1994), 'On Half-Full Glasses, Europe and the Left: Comments on Wolfgang Streeck's "European Social Policy after Maastricht"', *Economic and Industrial Democracy* 15:3, 486–96.

—— (1995), 'Assessing the Delors Era and Social Policy', in S. Leibfried and P. Pierson (eds), *European Social Policy: Between Fragmentation and Integration* (Washington, DC: The Brookings Institution), pp. 357–88.

Sándor, B. (2001), *Report on the Discrimination of Lesbians, Gay Men and Bisexuals in Hungary* (Budapest: Hátter Society for Gays and Lesbians in Hungary/Labrisz Lesbian Association) <http://www.policy.hu/sandor/report.html>.

Schanda, B. (1999), 'Freedom of Religion and Minority Religions in Hungary', *Social Justice Research* 12:4, 297–313.

Schimmelfennig, F., Engert, S. and Heiko, K. (2005), 'The Impact of EU Political Conditionality', in F. Schimmelfennig and U. Sedelmeier (eds), *The Europeanization of Central and Eastern Europe* (Ithaca, NY: Cornell University Press), pp. 29–50.

Schimmelfennig, F. and Sedelmeier, U. (2004), 'Governance by Conditionality: EU Rule Transfer to the Candidate Countries of Central and Eastern Europe', *Journal of European Public Policy* 11:4, 661–79.

—— (2005a), 'Conclusions: The Impact of the EU on the Accession Countries', in F. Schimmelfennig and U. Sedelmeier (eds), *The Europeanization of Central and Eastern Europe* (Ithaca, NY: Cornell University Press), pp. 210–28.

—— (2005b), 'Introduction: Conceptualizing the Europeanization of Central and Eastern Europe', in F. Schimmelfennig and U. Sedelmeier (eds), *The Europeanization of Central and Eastern Europe* (Ithaca, NY: Cornell University Press), pp. 1–28.

Schmidt, A., Zschiesche, M. and Rosenbaum, M. (2004), *Die naturschutzrechtliche Verbandsklage in Deutschland: Praxis und Perspektiven* (Berlin: Springer).

Schmidt, V.A. (2002a), 'Europeanization and the Mechanics of Economic Policy Adjustment', *Journal of European Public Policy* 9:6, 894–912.

—— (2002b), *The Futures of European Capitalism* (Oxford: Oxford University Press).

Schwarze, J., Becker, U. and Pollack, C. (1993), *The 1992 Challenge at National Level: A Community-Wide Joint Research Project on the Realization and Implementation by National Governments and Business of the Internal Market Programme: Reports and Conference Proceedings 1991/92* (Baden-Baden: Nomos).

Schwarze, J., Govaere, I., Helin, F. and van den Bossche, P. (1990), *The 1992 Challenge at National Level: A Community-wide Joint Research Project on the Realization and Implementation by National Governments and Business of the Internal Market Programme: Reports and Conference Proceedings 1989* (Baden-Baden: Nomos).

Shaw, J. (ed.) (2000), *Social Law and Policy in an Evolving European Union* (Oxford: Hart).

Sicáková-Beblavá, E. (2005), 'Transparency and Corruption', in G. Meseznikov and M. Kollar (eds), *Slovakia 2004: A Global Report on the State of Society* (Bratislava: Institute for Public Affairs), pp. 681–98.

Siedentopf, H. and Ziller, J. (eds) (1988), *Making European Policies Work: The Implementation of Community Legislation in the Member States*, 2 vols (London: Sage).

Silva-Jáuregui, C. (2004), 'Macroeconomic Stabilization and Sustainable Growth', in M. Mrak, M. Rojec and C. Silva-Jáuregui (eds), *Slovenia: From Yugoslavia to the European Union* (Washington, DC: The World Bank), pp. 115–31.

Sissenich, B. (2005), 'The Transfer of EU Social Policy to Poland and Hungary', in F. Schimmelfennig and U. Sedelmeier (eds), *The Europeanization of Central and Eastern Europe* (Ithaca, NY: Cornell University Press), pp. 157–77.

Skledar, S. (2002), 'New Labour Relations Law Passed', *EIROnline Document SI0206101N* (Dublin: European Foundation for the Improvement of Living and Working Conditions) <http://www.eurofound.europa.eu/eiro/2002/06/inbrief/si0206101n.htm>.

—— (2003), 'Collective bargaining Legislation Examined', *EIROnline Document SI0212101F* (Dublin: European Foundation for the Improvement of Living and Working Conditions) <http://www.eurofound.europa.eu/eiro/2002/12/feature/si0212101f.htm>.

SKUC-LL (2001), *Sexual Orientation Discrimination in Slovenia* (Ljubljana: SKUC-LL) <http://www.ljudmila.org/siqrd/sods.html>.

Slovak Spectator (2002a), 'EP Wants Anti-discrimination Law', *Slovak Spectator*, 28 October 2002 <http://www.spectator.sk/articles/view/10822>.

—— (2002b), 'Sexual Orientation not a Legal Matter', *Slovak Spectator*, 24 June 2002 <http://www.spectator.sk/articles/view/9600>.

—— (2003a), 'Anti-discrimination Draft Still a Problem', *Slovak Spectator*, 3 November 2003 <http://www.spectator.sk/articles/view/14278>.

—— (2003b), 'Call for Anti-discrimination Law', *Slovak Spectator*, 15 December 2003 <http://www.spectator.sk/articles/view/14651>.

—— (2003c), 'Extreme Voices in Moderate Parties Risk Alienating the Electorate', *Slovak Spectator*, 7 April 2003 <http://www.spectator.sk/articles/view/12386>.

Slovenian Labour Inspectorate (2005), *Competences, Organisation and Activities of the Labour Inspectorate*, Annual Report 2005 (Ljubljana: Ministry of Labour, Family and Social Affairs) <http://www.id.gov.si/fileadmin/id.gov.si/pageuploads/Splosno/english/Annual_report_2005.pdf>.

—— (2006), Home page <http://www.id.gov.si/index.php?id=2592&L=1>, accessed 24 May 2006.

Stanojevic, M. (2005), 'Slovenia: Rigidity or "Negotiated" Flexibility?', in D.C. Vaughan-Whitehead (ed.), *Working and Employment Conditions in New EU Member States: Convergence or Diversity?* (Geneva: International Labour Organization), pp. 339–81.

Stanovnik, T. (2004), 'Social Sector Developments', in M. Mrak, M. Rojec and C. Silva-Jáuregui (eds), *Slovenia: From Yugoslavia to the European Union* (Washington, DC: The World Bank), pp. 315–33.

Statistical Office of the Republic of Slovenia (2002), Population Census 2002 <http://www.stat.si/popis2002/en>, accessed 22 September 2006.

—— (2005), Home page <http://www.stat.si/eng/stat_povezave.asp>, accessed 31 May 2005.

Steunenberg, B. (2006), 'Turning Swift Policy-making into Deadlock and Delay: National Policy Coordination and the Transposition of EU Directives', *European Union Politics* 7:3, 293–319.

Streeck, W. (1994), 'European Social Policy after Maastricht: The "Social Dialogue" and "Subsidiarity"', *Economic and Industrial Democracy* 15:1, 151–77.

—— (1995), 'From Market Making to State Building? Reflections on the Political Economy of European Social Policy', in S. Leibfried and P. Pierson (eds),

European Social Policy: Between Fragmentation and Integration (Washington, DC: The Brookings Institution), pp. 389–431.

Sum, N.-L. and Jessop, B. (2003), 'On Pre- and Post-Disciplinary Perspectives in (Cultural) Political Economy', *Économies et Sociétés (Hors série)* 39, 993–1015 <http://eprints.lancs.ac.uk/229/>.

Sverdrup, U. (2004), 'Compliance and Conflict Management in the European Union: Nordic Exceptionalism', *Scandinavian Political Studies* 27:1.

Swidler, A. (2001), 'Cultural Expression and Action', in N.J. Smelser and P.B. Baltes (eds), *International Encyclopedia of the Social and Behavioral Sciences*, vol. 5 (Amsterdam: Elsevier), pp. 3063–69.

Szabó, S. (2003), *Gender Assessment of the Impact of EU Accession on the Status of Women in the Labour Market in CEE. National Study: Hungary* (Bupadest: Social Innovation Foundation) <http://karat.org/documents/Gender.pdf>.

Szikra, D. (2002), 'The Origins of the Hungarian Welfare State in a Comparative Perspective', *Periodica Polytechnica: Social and Management Sciences* 10:1, 143–49.

Szoboszlai, G. (1992), 'Constitutional Transformation in Hungary', in G. Szoboszlai (ed.), *Flying Blind: Emerging Democracies in East-Central Europe* (Budapest: Hungarian Political Science Association), pp. 315–29.

Szomolányi, S. (2004), 'Slovakia: From a Difficult Case of Transition to a Consolidated Central European Democracy', in T. Hayashi (ed.), *Democracy and Market Economics in Central and Eastern Europe: Are New Institutions Being Consolidated?* (Hokkaido: Slavic Research Center, Hokkaido University), pp. 149–88 <http://src-h.slav.hokudai.ac.jp/sympo/03september/2003september-contents.html>.

Taggart, P. and Szczerbiak, A. (2002), 'The Party Politics of Euroscepticism in EU Member and Candidate States', *SEI Working Paper No. 51* (Sussex: Sussex European Institute) <http://www.sussex.ac.uk/sei/documents/wp51.pdf>.

Takács, J. (2005), 'How to Put Equality into Practice? Anti-discrimination and Equal Treatment Policymaking and LGBT People' (Budapest: Central European University) <http://pdc.ceu.hu/archive/00002516/01/takacs.pdf>.

Tallberg, J. (2002), 'Paths to Compliance: Enforcement, Management, and the European Union', *International Organization* 56:3, 609–43.

Taschowsky, P. (2004), 'EU-Enlargement and the Social Dimension of the European Union: The Cases of Poland and Hungary', *European Studies Hannover Working Paper No. 6* (Hannover: University of Hannover, Political Science Department) <http://www.gps.uni-hannover.de/europe/working papers/taschowsky.pdf>.

Thomson, R. (2007), 'Time to Comply: National Responses to Six EU Labour Market Directives Revisited,' *West European Politics* 30:5, 987–1008.

Toft, C. (2003a), 'KDH Rejects Anti-discrimination Law', *Slovak Spectator*, 27 March 2003 <http://www.spectator.sk/articles/view/12284>.

—— (2003b), 'KDH: Homosexuals Should not be Teachers', *Slovak Spectator*, 31 March 2003 <http://www.spectator.sk/articles/view/12343>.

Tóka, G. (2004), 'Hungary', in S. Berglund, J. Ekman and F. Aarebrot (eds), *The Handbook of Political Change in Eastern Europe* (Cheltenham: Edward Elgar), pp. 289–335.

Tóth, A., Nacsa, B. and Neumann, L. (2004), 'Thematic Feature – Individual Labour/Employment Disputes and the Courts', *EIROnline Document HU0403101T* (Dublin: European Foundation for the Improvement of Living and Working Conditions) <http://www.eurofound.europa.eu/eiro/2004/03/ tfeature/hu0403101t.htm>.

Tóth, A. and Neumann, L. (2003), 'Labour Dispute Settlement in Four Central and Eastern European Countries', *EIROnline Document TN0301101S* (Dublin: European Foundation for the Improvement of Living and Working Conditions) <http://www.eurofound.europa.eu/eiro/2003/01/study/tn0301101s.htm>.

—— (2005), 'Reorganisation of European Level Representation of Hungarian Employers', *EIROnline Document HU0506102N* (Dublin: European Foundation for the Improvement of Living and Working Conditions) <http:// www.eurofound.europa.eu/eiro/2005/06/inbrief/hu0506102n.htm>.

Transparency International (2005), *Global Corruption Report 2005* (Berlin: Transparency International) <http://www.transparency.org/publications/gcr/ download_gcr/download_gcr_2005>.

Tratar, M.K., Hot, M., Ladiha, M., Ogradi, M., Pelicon, G. and Cvetek, J. (2005), *Report on Measures to Combat Discrimination: Directives 2000/43/EC and 2000/78/EC: Country Report Slovenia* (Brussels: European Commission) <http://ec.europa.eu/employment_social/fundamental_rights/pdf/legnet/ slrep05_en.pdf>.

Treib, O. (2003), 'Die Umsetzung von EU-Richtlinien im Zeichen der Parteipolitik: Eine akteurzentrierte Antwort auf die Misfit-These', *Politische Vierteljahresschrift* 44:4, 506–28.

—— (2004), *Die Bedeutung der nationalen Parteipolitik für die Umsetzung europäischer Sozialrichtlinien* (Frankfurt/M.: Campus).

—— (2006), 'Implementing and Complying with EU Governance Outputs', *Living Reviews in European Governance* 1:1 <http://www.livingreviews.org/ lreg-2006-1>.

Tröster, P. (2000), 'Das System sozialer Sicherheit in Tschechien', in T. Tomandl and W. Mazal (eds), *Soziale Sicherheit in Mitteleuropa – Ein Systemvergleich zwischen Kroatien, Österreich, Polen, Slowakei, Slowenien, Tschechien und Ungarn* (Wien: Orac), pp. 205–40.

Tscherteu, A. (2002), 'Die Entwicklung des tschechischen Arbeitsmarktes', *Der Donauraum* 42:1–2, 61–73.

Tünde, H. (2003), 'European Equality Law in Labour Court Proceedings: Questionnaire for Hungary', conference paper, *International Labour Organization, Eleventh Meeting of European Labour Court Judges*, 24 October 2003, Florence.

US Department of State (2006), *Czech Republic, International Religious Freedom Report 2006* (Washington, DC: US Department of State,) <http://www.state. gov/g/drl/rls/irf/2006/71376.htm>.

UNICEF (1999), *Women in Transition: The MONEE Project – CEE/CIS/Baltics Regional Monitoring Report, No. 6* (Florence: United Nations Children's Fund, International Child Development Centre) <http://www.unicef-irc.org/cgi-bin/unicef/Lunga.sql?ProductID=36>.

UNIFEM (2006), *The Story Behind the Numbers: Women and Employment in Central and Eastern Europe and the Western Commonwealth of Independent States* (Bratislava: United Nations Development Funds for Women) <http://www.unifem.org/attachments/products/StoryBehindTheNumbers_eng.pdf>.

Vajda, R. (2006), *The Perception of Mobbing and Related Services in Hungary: Report for Daphne Project Mobbing II* (Budapest: Mona Foundation Hungary) <http://www.surrey.ac.uk/politics/cse/Report_MONA.pdf>.

Van Meter, D.S. and Van Horn, C.E. (1975), 'The Policy Implementation Process: A Conceptual Framework', *Administration and Society* 6:4, 445–88.

Versluis, E. (2003), *Enforcement and Compliance of European Directives in Four Member States* (Delft: Eburon).

—— (2004), 'Explaining Variations in Implementation of EU Directives', *European Integration Online Papers* 8:19 < http://eiop.or.at/eiop/texte/2004–019a.htm>.

Vidovic, H. (2002), 'Labour Market Trends in Central and Eastern European Countries', in B. Funck and L. Pizzati (eds), *Labour, Employment, and Social Policies in the EU Enlargement Process: Changing Perspectives and Policy Options* (Washington, DC: The World Bank), pp. 27–46.

Vodièka, K. (2002), 'Das politische System Tschechiens', in W. Ismayr (ed.), *Die politischen Systeme Osteuropas* (Opladen: Leske und Budrich), pp. 239–72.

Vodopivec, M. (2004), 'Labor Market Developments in the 1990s', in C. Silva-Jáuregui (ed.), *Slovenia: From Yugoslavia to the European Union* (Washington, DC: The World Bank), pp. 292–314.

Weiler, A. (2006), 'Deadlock in Progress on Revision of Working Time Directive', *EIROnline Document EU0612019I* (Dublin: European Foundation for the Improvement of Living and Working Conditions) <http://www.eurofound.europa.eu/eiro/2006/12/articles/eu0612019i.html>.

Weiss, P. (2006), 'Slowakei: Reformeifer auf dem Weg in die EU', in R. Hrbek (ed.), *Die zehn neuen EU-Mitgliedsstaaten: Spezifika und Profile* (Berlin: Berliner Wissenschaftsverlag), pp. 71–84.

Wierink, M. (2006), 'Les relations professionnelles dans les pays d'Europe centrale et orientale au tournant de l'entrée dans l'Union européenne', *Document d'études No. 110* (Paris: Ministère de l'emploi, de la cohésion sociale et du logement).

Wightman, G. (1995), 'The Development of the Party System and the Break-up of Czechoslovakia', in G. Wightman (ed.), *Party Formation in East-Central Europe: Post-Communist Politics in Czechoslovakia, Hungary, Poland and Bulgaria*, Studies of Communism in Transition (Brookfield, VT: Edward Elgar), pp. 59–78.

World Bank (1999), *Czech Republic: Toward EU Accession – Main Report* (Washington, DC: The World Bank).

World Bank, Foundation SPACE, INEKO and Open Society Institute (2002), *Poverty and Welfare of Roma in the Slovak Republic* (Washington, DC: The World Bank) <http://siteresources.worldbank.org/EXTROMA/Resources/povertyinslovak.pdf>.

Zeitlin, J. and Pochet, P. (eds) (2005), *The Open Method of Coordination in Action: The European Employment and Social Inclusion Strategies* (Brussels: European Interuniversity Press).

Zürn, M. and Joerges, C. (eds) (2004), *Law and Governance in Postnational Europe: Compliance beyond the Nation-State* (Cambridge: Cambridge University Press).

Index

Printed in Great Britain
by Amazon

68367974R00129